A Complete Collection Of Scottish Proverbs Explained And Made Intelligible To The English Reader

A

COMPLETE COLLECTION

OF

SCOTTISH PROVERBS

EXPLAINED

AND MADE INTELLIGIBLE

TO THE

𝕰𝖓𝖌𝖑𝖎𝖘𝖍 𝕽𝖊𝖆𝖉𝖊𝖗.

—◆—

BY JAMES KELLY, M. A.

—◆—

The genius, wit, and spirit of a nation, are discovered
by their *Proverbs.*—Bacon.

LONDON :

PRINTED FOR RODWELL & MARTIN, BOND STREET.

1818.

TO

HIS GRACE

JAMES,

Duke of Hamilton, &c. First Peer of the Kingdom of
Scotland, and to the most Noble and
Right Honourable the

NOBILITY,

THE RIGHT WORSHIPFUL THE

GENTRY,

AND MY BELOVED COUNTRYMEN THE

COMMONALTY,

OF THAT ANCIENT AND NOBLE KINGDOM,

THIS COLLECTION OF

THEIR

𝔓roberbs

Is with all Duty and Humility dedicated by their

GRACES, LORDSHIPS, AND HONOURS

Affectionate Countryman

And most humble Servant,

JA. KELLY.

a 2

THE INTRODUCTION.

I SUPPOSE it to be a thing common to all nations, and languages, to deliver their minds, as occasion offers, in proverbs: which are short, dogmatical, concise sentences, accommodated to the principal concerns of life ; commonly used, and commonly known ; and, for the most part, conceived in figurative expressions, where one thing is said, and another thing understood and applied.

Among others, the Scots are wonderfully given to this way of speaking : and, as the consequence of that, abound with proverbs, many of whom are very expressive, quick, and home to the purpose. And indeed this humour prevails universally over the whole nation, especially among the better sort of the commonalty, none of whom will discourse you any considerable time, but he will confirm every assertion and observation with a Scottish proverb.

To that nation I owe my birth and education ; and to that manner of speaking I was used from my infancy, and that to such a degree, that I became, in some measure, remarkable for it.

Once, upon a very trifling occasion, I would try, for experiment, how many Scottish proverbs I could readily remember : and, in a very short time, I wrote down above one thousand two hundred, as they offered in discourse, or occurred to my memory. I then began to think that a longer time would certainly produce a greater number ; and so resolved to divert myself that way for some time. I do not know that there was ever any collection of this sort, save one, and that was made above one hundred and twenty years ago, by one Mr. David Fergusson, minister of Dumfermlin, who died in the year 1598. I had made a considerable progress in this Collection before I could possibly meet with that book : and when I did, I found that they only amounted to nine hundred forty-five, of which I had already anticipated the most and best. The rest were either obsolete, that I did not understand, or insignificant by words, and silly comparisons that were not worth the transcribing.

When I first began to think of publishing this my Collection, I proposed to myself four things :

I. To write down none but those which I knew to be native, genuine Scottish proverbs ; but, as I proceeded, I found it impossible strictly to distinguish the Scottish from the English. For both nations speak the same language, have constant intercourse the one with the other, and, no doubt borrow their proverbs the one from the other. Not only so, but I found, upon further inquiry, that many of these proverbs, which I believed to be genuine Scottish proverbs, were not only English, but French, Italian, Spanish, Latin, and Greek proverbs ; for the sense and sentiments of mankind, as to the main concerns of life, are much the same, and their observations about them, being often repeated, became proverbs, which though differing in words, express the same thoughts. Let a man read over Phocilides, Theognis, and other fragments of the Greek Gnomists, he shall find many of these proverbs almost literally expressed ; so hard a thing it is to know what proverbs are proper to any one nation : so that I found myself obliged to set down all those for Scottish proverbs that are used in Scotland, and by Scottish men, though many are common to the English ; and not a few, perhaps, originally of that nation.

II. I resolved to collect none but those which had been the result of prudent observation, or carried in them some moral instruction, or, at least, were odd and comical in the expression ; for I did not think trifling by-words, silly phrases, or insignificant comparisons worth my while : and, in pursuance of this resolution, I have left out more than I have taken in. As,

First, All superstitious observations of times, persons, places, or other things which the vulgar call *sonsie* or *unsonsie.* As,

> It is no sonsie to meet a bare foot in the morning.
> The first snail going with you, and the first lamb meeting you, bodes a good year.

For these are apt to fill men's minds with panick apprehensions, and debauches their sense of, and dependance upon Almighty God.

Secondly, I have omitted all proverbial imprecations with which the Scots abound. As,

> Dee'l ding a divat off your weime with a slaughter spade.
> Dee'l pish in your arse, and make twa-penny tape of it.
> Dee'l raise you, and set you down with a rattle.

For these are abominable, and wholly inconsistent with the Christian profession; yet I have retained some proverbial ill wishes, because they are comically expressed, and commonly used without malice.

Thirdly, I have left out all those which are openly obscene; and these are very many, pat, and expressive. But since it does not become a man of manners to use them, it does not become a man of my age and profession to write them.

Fourthly, I have left out all insignificant comparisons, which are only forms and phrases, but can make no man the wiser, or better for using or knowing them. As,

> As bare as the birk at Yule even.
> As wanton as a wet hare.
> As busy as a bee in a tar barrel.

Fifthly, I have left out all trifling by-words, and proverbial phrases, I mean such as are equally silly and useless. As,

> Good day to you all and deal't among you.
> Go fiddle my dog a dance.
> Eat your fill and leave your leavings.

And, indeed, to have written down all the Scottish proverbial phrases, had been to have transcribed a great share of the language used in that country.

Sixthly, I have rejected all those proverbs that seem to make too homely with the Almighty Being, for they are apt to wear off that awful sense that every good man ought to have of the Divine Majesty.

III. My third resolution was to explain those of them whose sense and meaning was not so obvious; either by shewing the original from whence they arose, the occasion on which they are spoken, the objects to which they are apply'd, or their meaning is given in a short paraphrase. This was wanting in the first Collection, and therefore the meaning of some of them is not now so easily understood.

IV. My fourth resolution was to make these proverbs plain and intelligible to the English: and, in order to this, I have written the English words in the margin that correspond to the Scottish in the proverb: and I have spelled the Scottish words that differ from the English only in accent and pronunciation as the English do; except where the rhyme and decorum of the proverb necessarily require it to be otherways: so instead of writing *stain, bean, mair, sair,* I have written *stone, bone, more, sore,* for so the Scots write these words on other occasions, and have done so ever since the year 1613. I know my countrymen will quarrel with me for this, as spoiling a great deal of the briskness and vigour of the phrase; but I am not without apprehensions, that if I had spelled them as they pronounce them, they themselves would have found some difficulty in reading of them, whereas here they will find none. I have now and then interspersed some English proverbs, and Latin sentences, agreeable to the sense of the preceding proverb, but without any great industry or design, for the most part, as they occurred to my memory as I was writing.

It is not possible that so large a Collection should deserve any other character than that which Martial gives to his epigrams, viz. part good, part bad, and part indifferent. Yet I believe I may venture to say, that there will be found among these as great a number of good, significant, and useful proverbs, as in any collection of that nature yet extant: not excepting the Greek and Latin of Erasmus, or Mr. Ray's English. For though the first has collected three chiliads and a half; yet, if you take from among those, trifling comparisons, and insignificant phrases, the useful and instructive proverbs will be far from making one chiliad. The design of that great person being not so much to collect instructive proverbs, as to explain the allusive and proverbial phrases in the Greek, and Latin authors, that were then coming in use upon the revival of learning. The ingenious Mr. Ray was odds of ten years in collecting the English Proverbs, had the use of all the former collections, and the assistance of his friends and acquaintance in the several parts of England; yet his whole Collection amounts only to two thousand seven hundred sixty-five. And of these he rejects six hundred fifty-five, which, so far as he knew, were not in use in England, but by former collectors borrowed from other languages; and he writes two hundred five in *italick* character, as not being sure that they are English; and he has only nine hundred eighty-one sentences, the rest being phrases, similes, and local proverbs, of the manners and remarkable things in the several shires of England; whereas there are here above three thousand, all entire sentences, all of them in present common use among the Scots, over and above the interspersed English and Latin, which will outdo even Erasmus himself: and, though this number may seem very great to belong to one nation, yet I doubt not but there are many hundreds more which either I have not heard, or has not occurred to me.

I am not unsensible that a great many of these proverbs are variously pronounced in the different parts of that nation, and even in one and the same place, as they are spoken on different occasions, and apply'd to various objects. I have wrote them down here either as I have heard them oftenest, or as I think they will do best.

It was my misfortune not to have met with Mr. Ray before this Collection was arrived to too great a height to be unravelled, otherways I had certainly imitated him in his rational alphabetical method; but I have endeavoured to supply that defect by an Index, not of the initial words, which (as he well observes) are variable without the least diminution to the sense of the proverb, but of the principal word in it, so that a man remembring the principal word of any proverb it is but looking for that word in the Index, and that will point to him the letter and number where it is to be found. If there be more principal words than one, I have either taken them all, or that word that seems to be the hinge upon which the proverb turns.

If there be any other objection against this my performance, I have one apology for all, and that is, that I made this Collection without any regard either to honour or profit, but only to give myself a harmless, innocent, scholar-like divertisement in my declining years; yet if what I have done be any way grateful either to the English, whom I honour and esteem, or to the Scots, whom I love and affect, I shall be well pleased.

———Quibus hæc sint qualiacunque
Arridere velim; doliturus si placeant spe
Deterius nostra.

SCOTTISH PROVERBS

COLLECTED, EXPLAINED, AND MADE INTELLIGIBLE TO
THE ENGLISH.

A [a] Yell sow was never good to [b] grices.

Spoken to those, who having no children of their own, deal harshly by other peoples.

2. A [c] bony bride is soon [d] busked.

3. A short horse is soon [e] whisked.

These two proverbs are often repeated together for the rhyme's sake: the first signifies, that what is of itself beautiful, needs but little adorning: and the other, that a little task is soon ended; and answers to the English, A thin meadow is soon mow'd.

4. After word comes [f] weird; [g] fair fall them that call me madam.

A facetious answer to them who call you by a higher title than your present station deserves; as calling a young clergyman doctor, or a young merchant alderman, as if you would say, all in good time.

Lat.—Non raro parva sunt magnarum rerum indicia.

5. All overs is vice, but over the water.

This shews the folly of all extremes, translated from the Latin, Omne nimium vertitur in vitium.

Eng.—There is a difference between staring and stark mad.

Lat.—Dum vitant humum nubes & mania captant.

6. A head full of hair, a [h] kirkle full of hips, and a briest full of papes, are three sure marks of a [i] daw.

These physiognomical proverbs have little truth or certainty in them, and miss as oft as they hit.

7. A wilful man wanted never woe.

Because he often miscarries in his attempts, by sticking too close to his own opinion.

Eng.—Will will have wilt, though it wo win.

---

[a] Barren [b] pigs; the Scots spell it gryses. [c] Pretty.
[d] Dress'd. [e] Curried. [f] Good fortune. [g] Well may they be.
[h] Petticoat. [i] Slut.

B

8. A wilful man should be very wise.

Because he will not take the assistance of other mens wisdom.

9. A poor man gets a poor marriage, and that's no
   meet for him.

Spoken when people of mean condition are meanly treated.
The literal sense is well expressed by Juvenal ;

Quis gener hic placuit censu minor, atque puellæ Sarc-
cinulis impar.

10. A [k] sooth bourd is no [l] bourd.

Spoken when people reflect too satyrically upon the real
vices, follies, and miscarriages of their neighbours.

Eng.—The truest jest sounds worst in guilty ears.

11. All new things [m] sturts ; quoth the good wife,
    when she [n] gae'd ly to the [o] hireman.

People are generally much affected with novelties.

Lat.—Est natura hominum novitatis avida.

12. A hungry man sees meat far.

Necessity sharpens industry and invention.

13. A pound of care will not pay an ounce of debt.

Care here is taken for trouble, vexation and concern, by which
no business will be effected, but rather by patience and industry.

Eng.—Sorrow quits no scores.

14. A begun turn is half ended ; quoth the good
    wife, when she stuck the [p] grape in the [q] midding.

Eng.—Well begun half ended.

Answerable to the Latin.

Dimidium facti qui bene cæpit habet.

15. Ay, as you thrive your feet falls from you.

Spoken when people meet with unexpected interruptions in
their business. The English say,

The further you go, the further behind.

16. All is not gold that glisters, nor maidens that
    wear their hair.

It was the fashion some years ago for virgins to go bare
headed ; the proverb means, that every thing is not so good
as it appears.

Lat.—Fronti nulla fides.

Item.—Non omne quod splendet aurum est.

17. All corn is not shorn by [r] kempers.

Things may be done well enough by men of ordinary
strength, power, or skill, though not excelling in any of

---

[k] True. [l] Jest. [m] Affects. [n] Went to bed. [o] Servantman.
[p] Dungfork. [q] Dunghill. [r] Great reapers that strive for the
mastery.

these; and it is offer'd in excuse for a man who may be useful in his art or profession, though there are many better.

Eng.—The greatest strokes make not the finest music.

18. All the winning is in the first buying.

For if you buy dear at first, you can hardly propose to gain by retailing.

19. As good a merchant tines as wins by a time.

For a good merchant may meet with misfortunes.

20. As broken a ship has come to land.

A thing has been in as great danger, and escaped : or, as unlikely a thing has come to pass.

21. A nod of an honest man is enough.

Because an honest man will make good all his promises, though they were only given in signs.

22. A good * grieve is better than an ill worker.

Because he will oversee the work with discretion, and keep the labourers to their work.

23. A dumb man never got land.

24. Spare to speak, and spare to speed.

These two signify, that unless a man make interest, and importune, he will not readily come to profit, honour, or advancement.

Eng.—A close mouth catcheth no flies.

25. An ass may spear mo questions than a doctor can answer.

Apply'd to them that ask impertinent questions.

Eng.—A fool may ask more questions in an hour, than a wise man can answer in seven years.

Lat.—Plus rogabit asinus, quam respondeat Aristoteles.

26. All cracks may not be ' trowed.

An encouragement not to fear when ice, or any thing else we stand upon cracks. The jest is in the double signification of the word *crack*, which sometimes signifies the noise of a thing in breaking, and sometimes a merry story.

27. A man of many trades begs his bread on Sunday.

It is observ'd, that a man of many trades seldom thrives so well, as he that sticks closely to one. The English have a proverb near akin to this, viz.

The better the tradesman, the worse the husband.

28. A wie house has a wide throat.

Spoken to deter people from marriage, because a family, though never so small, will require something to support it.

---

* Overseer.　　' Believ'd.

29. As good never a bit, as never the better.

Unless you make a thing the better for you, you had as good let it alone.

30. A man is a lion in his own cause.

No man so zealous for, or assiduous in, a man's business, as himself.

Lat.—Proque suâ causâ quisque disertus erit.

31. A borrow'd loan should come laughing home.

What a man borrows he should return with thankfulness, rather better than worse.

32. A wight man never wanted a weapon.

A man of sense, and good presence of mind, will never want means to carry on his business, but will make a tool of the first thing that comes to his hands.

33. All that you'll get will be a ᵘ kist, and a ᵛ sheet after all.

Spoken to them that are too eager on the world, intimating that they can take nothing to the grave, save a coffin, and a windingsheet.

Lat.—Haud ullas portabis opes Acherontis ad undas,
    Nudus ad infernas, stulte, vehere, rates.

34. A gentle horse should be ʷ sindle spur'd.

A man of a free spirit should not be too much importun'd.

Lat.—Non opus admisso fodere calcar eqao.

35. An ill cow may have a good calf.

Bad people may have good children, and good, bad.

Natura a parentibus, gratia a Deo.

36. As soon goes the lambskin to the market as the old sheeps. The English say,

Of young die many,
Of old men 'scape not any.

Lat.—Mista senum ac juvenum densantur funera, nullum
    Sæva caput proserpina fugit.

37. A ounce of mother wit is worth a pound of clergy.

The English have two special proverbs to this purpose.

The greatest clerks are not always the wisest men.

A handful of good life is better than a bushel of learning.

I have observed that a man of mean parts, and slow understanding, though he may have a memory to make him a sort of a scholar, makes the vilest figure in the world.

Lat.—Merus scholasticus, merus asinus.

38. A good pawn never sham'd its master.

ᵘ A coffin. ᵛ A windingsheet. ʷ Seldom.

It is no shame for a man to borrow on a good pawn; though I think it would be more for his honour, to be trusted without one.

39. A ^x fidging mare should be well girded.

A cunning tricky fellow should not be trusted without great caution.

40. A cock is ^y crouse on his own ^z midding.

A man is stout when he is at home, and has his friends and relations about him.

Lat.—Gallus, in suo sterquilinio, plurimum potest.

41. As one flits, another sits, and that makes the ^a mealings dear.

The reason why farms give a good price, is, because when one man gives them up, another is ready to take them; but apply'd only, when one sits down in the seat that another rose out of.

42. A penny more buys the whistle.

Spoken when one gets a bargain for a little more than was offer'd for it; or at cards, when a card is taken by a card just bigger by one.

43. A good tongue is a good weapon.

Because it will give no provocation, and so supersede all use of any other weapon.

Eng.—He that would live in peace and rest,
Must hear, and see, and say the best.

44. All your geese are swans.

Spoken to those who are highly conceited of what is their own.

45. A dry summer never made a dear peck.

I do not know any observation of weather, or seasons, that holds so true as this in these nations; for though the straw in such years be short, yet the grain is good and hearty. I remember no remarkable dry summers but three, 1676, 1690, 1713, and all of them very plentiful.

Eng.—Drought never bred dearth.

46. A' that is said should not be seal'd,

Spoken when people tell us that such a thing is said, which we are not willing to have believed.

Eng.—They say so, is half a lie.

Lat.—Credere fallaci, gravis est dementia famæ.

47. All that is said in the kitchen, should not be heard in the ^b hall.

---

^x Skittish.　^y Stout, courageous.　^z Dunghil.　^a Farms.
^b Parlour.　　　　　　B 3

Every thing that a man may say of his neighbour, perhaps with no ill intention, should not be whisper'd to him, for he may take that ill, that was not ill design'd; and indeed such usage can do him little service, and may do him much harm.

48. A guilty conscience self accuses.

A man that has done ill, by his slight, fear, or diffidence, shews his guilt.

Lat.—Se judice nemo nocens absolvitur.

49. All cats are alike grey in the night.

Eng.—Joan's as good as my lady, in the dark.

Lat.—Sublatá lucerná, nihil interest inter mulieres. *Item.*
　　　Nocte latent mendæ, vitioque ignoscitur omni,
　　　Horaque formosam quamlibet ista facit.

50. A hungry louse bites sore.

Spoken when needy people are importunate in their craving or exacting.

51. A word to a wise man.

Spoken when you give a man a small hint of a thing, intimating that, if he has sense, he'll understand you.

Eng.—Send a wise man of an errand, and say nothing to him.

Lat.—Verbum sapienti sat est.

52. A tinklar was never a town-taker,
　　　A taylor was never a hardy man,
　　　Nor yet a webster [c] leal of his trade,
　　　Nor ever was since the world began.

A rhyme upon the vagrant life of the first, the sedentary unactive life of the second, and the thievish disposition of the third: but this rule admits large exceptions.

53. A man of five, may be a fool of fifteen.

A pregnant, pert, witty child, may prove but a heavy worthless man, of which I have known many instances.

Lat.—Odi puerulos præcoci sapientia.

54. All ills are good untry'd.

Spoken to dissuade people from dangerous exploits, of whose consequence they have no experience.

Lat.—Dulce bellum inexpertis.

55. A hen that lays without, has need of a white nest-egg.

A man given to extravagant amours in his single life, has need to marry a handsome wife to keep him at home.

56. A [d] silverless man goes fast through the market.

Because he does not stay to cheapen or buy.

---

[c] Honest.　　　　　[d] A man that has no money.

57. A halfpenny cat may look at a king.

An answer to them that ask you, why you look at them, or what you look at.

58. A scal'd head is ᵉ eith to bleed.

A thing that was but tender before, will easily be put out of order: The English is much the same.

A scal'd head is soon broken.

59. A ᶠ full man, and a hungry horse, make good speed home.

The drunken man, not being able to sit straight upon his horse, sticks the spurs in his sides: and the hungry horse would be gladly at the manger.

60. A going foot is ay getting, if it were but a thorn.

A man of industry will certainly get a living: though this proverb is often applied to those who went abroad, and got a mischief, when they might have staid safely at home.

61. An ill ᵍ willy cow should have short horns.

It were a pity that a man of ill nature should have much authority; for he'll be sure to abuse it.

Eng.—A curst cur should be short ty'd.

Lat.—Dat Deus immiti cornua curta bovi.

62. All the keys of the world hings not at your belt.

Spoken to those who refuse us their help, support, or assistance; intimating, that others may afford what they deny us.

63. All is not ʰ bint that's in peril.

Signifying, that our affairs may come to a better effect, than is now expected.

Eng.—It is not lost that comes at last.

64. A green wound is half game.

Because it commonly smarts more afterwards.

65. All things have an end, and a pudding has two.

Spoken sullenly; signifying that the power of those who now oppose us, will soon come to an end.

66. A friend in court is worth a penny in the purse.

A purse-seems to be the only friend at court, for, without that, there is nothing there but neglect, and empty promises. But perhaps this proverb came in use before the fashion of buying commissions, and placing of money.

67. A friend's dinner is soon ⁱ dight.

Because a friend will be content with any thing.

Lat.—Vilis amicorum annona est.

ᵉ Easy. ᶠ Drunk. ᵍ Ill natured. ʰ Lost.
ⁱ Made ready.

68. As sore crys the bairn that is [k] dung at night, as
    he that was dung in the morning.

He that is now in prosperity, when I am in adversity, may
find as severe a change of fortune afterwards.

Eng.—Better the last smile than the first laughter.

69. An ill [l] shearer never got a good [m] hook.

Spoken to those who complain of the tool that they are
working with, alledging that they may rather blame their own
unskilfulness.

Eng.—A bad workman quarrels with his tools.

Lat.—Proba est materia, si probam adhibeas artificem.

70. As the old cock crows, the young cock [n] learn.

Eng.—When old age is evil, youth can learn no good.

Lat.————Ne crimina nostra sequantur.
      A nobis geniti.

71. All is fish that comes in the net.

Spoken of them that make gain of every thing.

72. A handful of trade is worth a handful of gold.

A handful of gold is soon spent, whereas a trade will be a
continual support.

73. A [o] tarrowing bairn was never fat.

That is, a person always complaining of, and unsatisfied
with his condition, cannot be happy.

74. All things helps, quoth the wren, when she pish'd
    in the sea.

Spoken when we make a little addition to a great heap.

Eng.—Something has some savour.

Lat.—Ex granis fit acervus.

75. As mickle water goes by the miller when he sleeps.

Spoken to those who make their excuse for not doing what
you desired them, because they are otherwise employ'd, and
cannot neglect their master's business; intimating, that at
another time they will loiter much longer.   They say also,

76. Mickle water goes by the miller when he sleeps.

But this has a quite different signification, viz. That a man
may have a great deal of his goods spoil'd, wasted, or purloin'd,
that he knows nothing of; which Horace well expresses:

    Exigna est domus ubi non & multa supersunt,
    Et dominum fallunt, & prosunt furibus.

77. A morning-sleep is worth a fold full of sheep, to a
    [u] huderon, duderon daw.

---

    [k] Beaten.   [l] Reaper.   [m] Sickle.   [n] Learns.
    [o] Complaining of their food.   [u] A dirty, lazy drab.

A reflection upon lazy, sleepy drabs, who prefer nothing to soaking in their bed in the morning, and willingly consents to that of Erasmus,

Nunquam dulcior somnus, quam post exortum solem.

78. A safe conscience makes a sound sleep.

And doubtless a bad conscience will have the contrary effect.

——Quos diri conscia facti
Mens habet attonitos, & surdo verbere cædit.

79. All Stewarts are not 'sub to the king.

Mens pretences to great things are not always well grounded; spoken when people boast of some great man of their name.

80. An ill fish gets an ill bait.

Spoken when bad people fall into misfortunes. Translated literally from the Latin.

Malus piscis malus hamus.
Item.—Malis mala proveniunt.

81. As ill a guesser has gotten a drink.

A senseless, but common saying, when one guesses aright.

82. A falling master makes a standing servant.

Men fall behind in the world by negligence and carelessness in looking after their concerns, which knavish servants will be sure to take their advantage of: it is no new thing to see a receiver buy his master's estate.

83. A pretty man I "ma'n say, take a peat and sit down.

An ironical expression to a mean boy, who would gladly be esteem'd.

Eng.—You're a man among the geese when the gander is away.

84. As you love me look in my dish.

That is, if you pretend kindness to me, shew it by your deeds.

85. A new besom sweeps clean.

Spoken of new servants, who are commonly very diligent; and new officers who are commonly very severe.

86. A receipter is worse than a thief.

True! for if there were none to receive stol'n goods, thieves would be discouraged.

Eng.—As good eat the devil, as the broth he is boil'd in.

87. A man that would thrive, must ask his wife's leave.

If a man have an extravagant wife, he cannot thrive, unless his funds were inexhaustible.

Lat.—Prodiga non sentit pereuntem fœmina censum.

' Akin.   " Must.

88. A man will see his friend in need, that will not see his head bleed.

A man will see his relation struggle with poverty and want, that will not suffer his head to be broken, or his life to be in danger, without interposing his interest in his behalf.

89. As you make your bed, so you lye down.

According to your conditions you have your bargain.

Eng.—He that makes his bed ill, lies there.

90. A spoonful of skitter will ˣ spill a potful of ʸskink.

An ill mixture will spoil a good composition. As dead flies make the ointment of the apothecary send forth a stinking savour; so does a little folly him that is in reputation for wisdom. Eccles. x. 1.

Eng.—One ill weed will spoil a potful of pottage.

91. Among you be't, priest's bairns, for 'am but a priest's ᶻoye.

Spoken when we see people contending, in whose contests we have little concern.

Eng.—Fight dog, fight bear, dee'l part.

92. A good fellow never lost, but at an ill fellow's hand.

Because none but an ill fellow would let him lose.

93. A good fellow is a costly name.

Because it requires a great deal to procure it, and more to uphold it; spoken when people urge us to spend, that we may be reckoned good fellows.

94. As good holds the stirrup, as he that ᵃloups on.

That is, the servant may be as good a man as the master sometimes; but often spoken when our friend holds our stirrup, when we mount our horse.

95. A penny-weight of love is worth a pound-weight of law.

A dissuasive from law suits among neighbours; used also when we value a man more for his good humour than his skill in the laws; and so the English say,

A good lawyer, a bad neighbour.

96. A wise man carries his cloak in fair weather, and a fool wants his in rain.

An encouragement to care, caution, and foresight, and especially not to leave your cloak, be the weather never so encouraging.

97. A winter's night, a woman's mind, and a laird's purposes change oft.

ˣ Spoil. ʸ Strong broth. ᶻ Grandchild. ᵃ Gets a horse back.

98. A woman's mind is like the wind in a winter's night.

Both these to the same purpose, viz. To signify the fickleness and inconstancy of women, in which, I must say, they are very much rival'd by the men.

Lat.—Varium & mutabile semper fœmina.

99. A man can no sooner let down his [b] breeks, but you are ready to kiss his arse.

A satyrical, spiteful reflection on them who are ready to offer for these bargains, which we, in hopes to get them cheaper, give up; be it farm, house, or any such thing.

100. A Scotch mist will wet an Englishman to the skin.

I never knew the meaning of this very common proverb; unless it be, that a Scottish man will bear more foul weather than an English.

101. As fine as fippence, you'll give a groat [c] raking.

A jest upon a girl who is finely drest, whereas she us'd to be dirty.

102. A man cannot sell his [d] tinsel.

Spoken when a man has refused a good rate for a commodity, and afterwards lost it.

103. A reproof is no poison.

No indeed! but a wholesome medicine, which whosoever refuseth, is brutish.

104. A dog's life, mickle hunger, mickle ease.

Apply'd to careless, lazy lubbers, who will not work, and therefore have many a hungry meal.

105. A sore sigh from a heal heart.

A ridicule upon hypocritical pretenders to sorrow.

106. As day break, butter break.

Spoken when a person, or thing, that was wanting, comes opportunely.

107. A hasty meeting, a hasty parting.

An observation upon marriage suddenly contracted, as if it were ominous, and portended a sudden separation.

108. As the wind blows seek your [e] heel.

A politick proverb! advising us to make our interest as the times change. This proverb some act very dextrously, and others cannot get acted.

---

[b] Breeches.   [c] Readily, or (as they say of rabbetskins) running.   [d] Loss.   [e] Shelter.

Eng.—Pull down your hat on the wind side.

Lat.—Is sapiens, qui se ad causas accommodat omnes.

109. A ᶠwad is a fool's argument.

Spoken when, after hot disputing, we offer to lay a wager
that we are in the right.

> I have heard antient sagers
> Say, Fools, for arguments lay wagers.   *Hud.*

110. All are good lasses, but where comes the ill
     wives from?

No body can blame young women for putting the best
side outmost, and concealing their bad humours till they get
husbands: and yet many a good lass is made an ill wife by
froward, graceless, ill-natur'd husbands.

111. All was ᵍtint that fell by.

Spoken when correction is given to them who deserve it
well; as if no blows were amiss, but those which did not hit.

Lat.—Leniter ex merito quicquid patiare ferendum est.

112. An ill ʰplea should be well pled.

113. Make the best of a bad cause.

Both to the same purpose; and the one explains the other.

Lat.—Addit & invalidæ robur facundia causæ.

114. A skittering cow in the ⁱloan would have many
     ᵏmarrows.

Spoken when ill people pretend that others are as bad as
themselves.

115. A bread house ˡskail'd never.

Bread is the staff of life, and while people have that, they
need not give over housekeeping: spoken when we have
bread, and perhaps want something finer.

116. A bonny sport to fare well and pay nothing for't.

Diogenes is said to have thought that the best wine which
cost him nothing; but it is oft us'd as an exclamation.

Eng.—The wholesomest meat is at another man's cost.

117. A man of words, and not of deeds,
     Is like a garden full of weeds.

That is, both at a distance seem something, but, when
narrowly inspected, are nothing.

118. Another would play a ᵐspring, e're you tune
     your pipes.

ᶠ Wager.   ᵍ Lost.   ʰ Lawsuit.   ⁱ Milking-place.
ᵏ Companions.   ˡ Gave up housekeeping.   ᵐ Tune.

That is, some would do a great deal of work, while you are preparing for it.

Eng.—Your long musing mars your memory.

119. A bastard may be as good as a bowstock by a time.

Bastard kail are a sort of cabbage that never close; those that close we call bowstocks; the meaning is, that a bastard may prove as worthy a person, sometimes, as the full begotten.

120. An empty hand no lure for a hawk.

If you would have any thing done for you, you must give something, for people will not serve you for nothing.

Pro nihilo, as well as de nihilo, nihil fit.

Lat.—Da si vis accipere.

121. All is not at hand that helps.

True! for assistance and support may come from whence we cannot foresee.

122. A [o] toom purse, makes a [p] bleat merchant.

A man will have little confidence to buy, when he wants money to pay for it.

123. As long runs the fox as he foot has.

Spoken when a man has done his utmost, and can do no more. This does not answer the English.

Every fox must pay his skin to the slayer.

For this signifies that the crafty are at last taken. Thieves most commonly come to the gallows at last.

124. A sturdy beggar should have a stout [q] naysayer.

Spoken when we give a flat denial to any importunate solicitor, signifying that his importunity deserves such usage.

125. An [r] olight mother makes a [s] sweir daughter.

Because she does the work herself, and does not set her daughter about it, whereby she contracts a habit of laziness.

Lat.—Blanda patrum segnes facit indulgentia natos.

126. A proud heart in a poor briest has mickle [t] dolour to [u] dree.

Because their pride will not give them leave to condescend to mean and low shifts to supply their wants.

127. A black shoe makes a [v] blythe heart.

When a man's shoe is blackened and bedawb'd with industry, it will procure him such a supply as will make him chearful.

128. A blythe heart makes a bloomy visage.

---

[o] Empty. [p] Bashful. [q] Denyer. [r] Nimble. [s] Lazy. [t] Sorrow. [u] Suffer. [v] Glad.

A man's inward chearfulness is often shewed by his counte-
nance. And on the contrary,

Tristitia corrugat vultum.

129. An old mason will make a good barrow-man.

Spoken by those who are giving us advice in those things
in which they have been conversant when young; intimating,
that they must needs know what belongs to them.

130. An unhappy man's cart is ᵂ eith to ˣ tumble.

Spoken of an unfortunate man, when misfortunes follow him.

131. An old dog bites sore.

Spoken to discourage one from provoking a man of advanc'd years; for though he is not able to tugg, or wrestle,
yet he will give a desperate blow.

132. A travelled man has leave to lie.

Travellers are often supposed to lie, either because some
of them do so, or because they tell us things which we never
saw, which makes us suspect them.

Eng.—Old men and travellers lie by authority.

133. As good ʸ ha'd as draw.

Better keep what I have, than give it out of my hand, and
have difficulty to get it again.

Eng.—Brag is a good dog, but hold fast is a better.

134. An ill won penny will cast down a pound.

Because cheating and overreaching ruins a man's credit,
and so mars his interest; to which add a secret curse of God,
who casts away the substance of the wicked.

135. An ill cook should have a good cleaver.

He that is not dextrous at his work, should have good tools.

136. At open doors dogs come ᶻ benn.

And so will thieves and impertinent persons; an argument
to keep the doors shut at night.

137. A word before is worth two behind.

A word spoken in season, how good is it, saith Solomon.

138. All fellows, jock and the laird.

Spoken when unworthy persons intrude themselves into the
company of their betters.

Eng.—Hail fellow well met.

Item.—All fellows at football.

139. All the speed is in the spurs.

Spoken when a man rides a lazy horse, or when a man
must ride hard or lose his business.

ᵂ Easy.   ˣ Overturn.   ʸ Hold.
ᶻ Into the inward part of the house.

140. As mickle up with, as mickle down with.

Spoken when a man has got a quick advancement, and as sudden depression.

Eng.—The highest tree, the greatest fall.

Lat.—Ut lapsu graviore rnant, tolluntur in altum.

141. As the carle riches, he wratches.

Many men are found to grow the more niggardly as their wealth encrease, which has given occasion to many proverbs.

Eng.—The more you heap, the worse you cheap.

Lat.—Crescit amor nummi quantum ipsa pecunia crescit.

Item.— Creverunt opes, & opum furiosa cupido,

Et quum possideas plurima, plura cupis.

142. An old sack craves mickle clouting.

Spoken when an old utensil goes often out of order, and wants repairing.

143. An old sack is ay ª skailing.

Spoken of old men who cannot keep their water long.

144. A fair fire makes a ᵇ room ᶜ slett.

Because it makes people sit at a distance.

145. A man may ᵈ speer the gate to Rome.

Spoken to those, who being bid to go an errand, excuse themselves, because they know not the way.

146. A man has no more goods than he gets good of.

What a man enjoys of his substance is really his, the rest he has only the keeping of.

Eng.—The gown is her's that wears it : and the world his that enjoys it.

Lat.—Nullus argenti color est—Nisi temperato splendeat usn.

147. A fool may give a wise man counsel by a time.

An apology of those who offer their advice to them, who may be supposed to excel them in parts and sense.

Lat.—Sæpe etiam olitor verba opportuna loquutus.

148. A ᵉ bleat cat makes a proud mouse.

When parents and masters are too mild and easy, it makes their children and servants too saucy and impertinent.

149. A man is well or wo as he thinks himself so.

A contented mind will sweeten every condition, and a repining heart will produce the contrary effects.

150. A ᶠ shor'd tree stands long.

ª Losing what is put in it.   ᵇ Large.   ᶜ Fireside.   ᵈ Ask.
ᵉ Bashful.   ᶠ Threatened.

c 2

Spoken when people threaten us, who we believe dare not execute their threatenings.

Eng.—Threatened folks live long.

151. A man may spit in his hand and do full ill.

When a man is about to give a blow he will spit in his hand, that he may hold the cudgel the faster : meaning that a man may make good offers to act stoutly, whose heart may yet misgive him after all.

152. A horse with four feet may ᶠ snapper, by a time.

An excuse for those who inadvertently misplace their words.

153. All things ʰ wytes that no well fares.

A man that miscarries in his business will lay the blame on any thing, rather than take it to himself.

Lat.—Omnes, quibus res sunt minus secundæ, magis sunt suspiciosi.

154. All things thrive at thrice.

An encouragement to those who have miscarried in their attempts, once, and again, to try the third time. They will say the third's a charm, or there are three things of all things.

155. A brain must ⁱ creep ere it gang.

An excuse for them who do not so well at first, as it is hoped they will do afterwards.

Eng.—No man is a crafts master the first day.

Item.—You must spoil before you spin.

156. As long as you serve the tod ᵏ you must bear up his tail.

When you have engaged in any man's service you must not think yourself too good for any thing he employs you in.

Lat.—Ut homo est, ita morem geras.

157. A man may woo where his will, but wed where his wife is.

Spoken of a man who having courted many mistresses, has at last married to his disadvantage. Taken from the strict destiny believed to be in marriage.

158. A ˡ mein pot never ᵐ play'd even.

Projects and properties in which many have a share (by the backwardness of some, and the ill nature of others) seldom come to a good account.

Eng.—There is falshood in fellowship.

159. A foul foot makes a full ⁿ weime.

ᶠ Stumble. ʰ Blames. ⁱ Go. ᵏ Fox. ˡ In which many have a share. ᵐ Boyl'd. ⁿ Belly.

Industry will be sure of a maintenance. A man that carefully goes about his business will have foul feet.

160. A full belly makes a stiff back.

Good keeping will make a man fit for labour. There is a return to this but it is smutty.

161. A hearty hand to give a hungry [o] meltith.

An ironical ridicule upon a niggardly dispenser.

162. A [p] yule feast may be quit at [q] Pasch.

A good office, done at one time, may be requit at another.

163. A tulying dog comes halting home.

A man given to quarrels will often come off with maims and hurts.

Eng.—Brabling dogs have sore ears.

164. A houndless hunter, and a gunless gunner see ay game enough.

Spoken to those who tell what a fine shot they could have had; but that they wanted a gun.

165. A Scottish man is wise behind the hand.

Without doubt the warm temper of that nation makes them easily receive the first impression; especially if gilded over by men of eloquence, cunning, and artifice; and seem to offer a present profit. Witness their giving up the king of Newcastle, and consenting to the terms of the union. Hence a great foreigner gives them this character, Scoti, quicquid volunt valde volunt.

Lat.—Sero sapiunt phryges.

A shiting sow is ay doing.

A satyrical reproof to those who pretend that they have been busy, when they have done but little work.

167. An old [r] tout in a new horn.

Spoken when we hear, (perhaps in other words) what we have heard before.

68. An inch of a nag is worth a span of an [s] aver.

A little man, if smart and stout, is much preferable to an unwieldy lubber, though much bigger.

The English have many proverbs to this purpose. As,

Eng.—A piece of a kid's worth two of a cat.

Item.—A leg of a lark is worth the whole body of a kite.

Lat.—Inest sua gratia parvis.

169. A good word is as soon said as an ill.

---

[o] Meal of meat. [p] Christmas. [q] Easter. [r] Blast. [s] Work-horse.

Spoken to dissuade men from passionate words, which may mar their business ; whereas mild words may do better.

Eng.—Good words cost nothing.

170. A drunken wife will get the drunken penny, but a drudge will get a *t* dark.

They that are free and liberal will have to spend, when the saving and penurious will get hard labour. They have another proverb of a drunken woman, intimating that she may be easily debauched, but I shall not trouble the reader with it. It answers the Latin ;

Quid enim Venus ebria curat, &c.

171. An even hand to cast a louse in the fire.

A ridicule upon them that pretend to hit a mark well, or carry a dish evenly,

172. A new pair of *u* breeks will soon draw down an old doublet.

Spoken when an old man marries a young woman who will prove o'er strong meat for his weak stomach : They will say also, He'll play her a supple trick.

173. A fool of a *v* nurrish makes a wise child.

An excuse for nurses nonsensical baubling to their children.

Eng.—The nurses tongues are privileged to talk.

174. A hungry man is an angry man.

Eng.—Hungry bellies have no ears.

Lat.—Ubi de pastu agitur non attenditur rectæ rationi.

175. A *w* findsily bairn gars his *x* dady be hang'd.

It is hard to make this good sense ; but it is spoken to children when they say that they found a thing which we suspect they pick'd.

176. A green yule makes a fat church-yard.

This, and a great many proverbial observations, upon the seasons of the year, are groundless, superstitious, and vain.

177. As *y* fain as fool of a fair day.

Spoken to our children when they ask leave to go to a fair, as if fools only were fond of going thither.

178. A *z* wie mouse will creep under a mickle corn-stack.

An apology for a little woman's marriage to a big man.

179. A good goose, but she has an ill *a* gansel.

Spoken when one has done a good turn, and by their after behaviour spoil the grace of it.

---

t Day's-work.   *u* Breeches.   *v* Nurse.   *w* Apt to be finding.
x Father.   Papa.   *y* Glad.   *z* Little.   *a* Gabble.

180. A hardy man to draw a sword to a ʰ haggish.

An ironical ridicule upon a braggadochio.

181. An ill lesson is ᵃ erth to learn.

Lat.—Pravi docilis Romana juventus.

182. A good wife and health is a man's best wealth.

Add but a good conscience, and a competent estate, and the composition is compleat.

183. A wie house well fill'd, a wie bit land well till'd, and a wie wife well will'd, will make a happy man.

The two first is for the sake of the last, but apply'd to any thing good in kind, though little in quantity.

184. A willing mind makes a light foot.

Eng.—Nothing impossible to a willing mind.

185. A proud heart and a poor purse are ill met.

A true proverb! and the worst is, they meet often.

186. As ᵇ sub as sive and riddle that grew both in one wood.

Spoken to them who groundlessly pretend kindred to great persons.

187. A bit ᶜ butt, and bit ᵈ bend, make a ᵉ moy maiden at the bore end.

A jocose reflection upon young maids when they eat almost nothing at dinner; intimating that if they had not eaten a little in the pantry or kitchen, they would eat better at the table.

188. At ᶠ fasten e'en night the maiden was ᵍ fow.

She said she would fast all ʰ Lentron through.

Spoken when people in plenty commend temperance.

Somnum plebis laudant saturi altilibus.

189. A ⁱ tugherless dame sits long at ᵏ hame.

A maid without a portion will be long unmarried.

Lat.—Veniunt a dote sagittæ.

190. A maiden with many woors often chuses the worst.

Often true literally, but apply'd to those, who having many things in their proffer, chuse the worst.

191. Ale sellers should not be tale tellers.

Public house-keepers should not blaze abroad what their

ᵇ A pudding made in the great gut of a sheep. ᵃ Easy.
ᵇ Akin. ᶜ In the upper part of the house. ᵈ In the lower part. ᵉ Modest. ᶠ Shrove-Tuesday. ᵍ Fall. ʰ Lent time.
ⁱ Without a portion. ᵏ Home.

guests may say, or do, in their houses, for that, when discovered, will make them lose their customers.

192. All ills are good a[l] frist.

The longer a mischief is a coming, the better; apply'd to those who either threaten, or promise something hereafter; the one we fear not, and the other we value not.

193. All is yours from the door down.

A jest upon those who pretend that such and such things in the house is theirs. As if you would say all the household goods without the doors are yours.

194. A bow o'er bent will weaken.

Eng.—All work and no play makes Jack a dull boy.

Lat.—Otia corpus alant, animus quoque pascitur illis.

Immodicus, contra, carpit utrumque labor.

Item.—Quod caret alternâ requie durabile non est.

195. A kiss, and a drink of water is a [m] werch [n]disjune.

An answer of a girl when she is asked a kiss.

196. A [o] crooning cow, a crowing hen, and a whistling maid boded never luck to a house.

The two first are reckoned ominous, but the reflection is on the third, in whom whistling is unbecoming.

197. A silly man will be sleely dealt with.

Intimating that cunning rogues will be apt to impose upon and make a property of a simple man.

Eng.—He that makes himself a sheep, shall be eaten by the wolf.

Lat.—Veterem ferendo injuriam invitus novam.

Item.—Post folia cadunt & arbores.

198. All things angers you, and the cat breaks your heart.

Spoken to those who are troubled for little or nothing.

199. A good tale is no the worse to be twice told.

An apology for those that say grace twice, unawares.

200. All the clothes on your back was once in clues.

A senseless rhyme to them that ask you what news.

201. A belly-full is a belly-full if it were but of [p] bear [q] coff.

If a man gets his satisfaction, though but of coarse meat, he has no reason to complain.

---

[l] A trust. [m] Insipid. [n] Refreshment. [o] Bellowing like a bull. [p] Barley. [q] Chaff.

202. A sheaf of a ʳ stook is enough.

An answer to those who propose to match twice into the same family : and hits the patter if the first match was not very fortunate.

203. As ˢ wight as a webster's westcoat, that every morning takes a thief by the neck.

The Scots have but an ill opinion of weavers honesty. Apply'd to those who brag of their stoutness.

204. As the websters stealing through the world.

Stealing in this proverb has a double signification, for sometimes it signifies to go quietly, unperceived : thus a man is said to steal away, to steal out of the room, that is to go off softly and unperceiv'd.

205. A mare's shoe, and a horse shoe are both alike.

The same that the English say, but not so good—
What's sauce for a goose is sauce for a gander.

206. A man may bind a sack, before it be full.

A man may be satisfied with what he has got, though short of what he desired, or expected.

207. A ᵗ thraward question should a thraward answer.

Spoken to him that asks an impertinent, unreasonable, or ensnaring question, that cannot easily or safely be answered.

208. A man may lose his own for lack of craving.

Lat.—Optima nomina, non appellando, fiunt mala.

209. An old knave is no bairn.

A reflection upon cunning old companions, who are throughly versed in cheating and deceit.

Eng.—An old fox need learn no tricks.

210. An inch of a miss is as good as a spaw.

Spoken when a thing was near the effecting, and yet did not hit.

211. A short grace is meet for hungry folk.

Eng.—Sharp stomachs make short devotions.

212. As merry as the maltman.

213. As well as the wife that brew'd it.

Both these signify that a man was drunk ; for the maltman drinks with his customers, and the publick house-keeper is supposed to take a share of what is going.

214. A slothful hand makes a sober fortune.

The reverse of what Solomon says, The hand of the diligent maketh rich.

ʳ An artificial heap of twelve sheaves.   ˢ Stout.   ᵗ Perverse.

215. A ᵘ vaunter and a lyar are near akin.

They are much the same ; for when a man once takes a hu-mour of boasting of what he has done or seen, he will not stop at the most palpable lies.

216. A great ᵛ ruser was never a good rider.

A man that boasts much, seldom performs well ; this is ap-ply'd commonly to those who boast of their performances in a way not proper to be spoken.

Lat.—In pace leones, in prælio cervi.

217. A scabbed horse is good enough for a scal'd squire.

Mean things become mean people.

Lat.—Parvum parva decent.

218. A man's mind is a ᵂ mirk ˣ mirrour.

Hard to pry into a man's thoughts, or know his designs.

219. As sore feights wrens as cranes.

Little people (if rightly match'd) will fight as bitterly and eagerly as those who are stronger or bigger.

220. A good year will not make him, and an ill year will not break him.

Spoken of slothful, idle, lazy fellows, who live from hand to mouth ; and are equally poor all years.

Eng.—A beggar will never be a bankrupt.

221. A man was once hanged for leaving his drink.

It took its rise from the villain that assassinated the Prince of Orange. Spoken when men proffer to go away be-fore their drink be out.

222. All the truth should not be told.

Because it may be ill-natured, uncharitable, or unseason-able.

223. All I got by him I may put in my eye, and see nothing the worse for it.

Intimating that I got nothing by him.

224. As the sow fills the draff sowres.

When peoples stomachs begin to fill, their meat insensibly loses its relish ; whereas on the contrary,

Hunger is good sauce.

225. A nag with a weime, and a mare with nane.

226. A mare with a horse's belly, and a horse with a mare's.

ᵘ Boaster.   ᵛ Praiser, boaster, commender of himself.
ᵂ Dark.   ˣ Looking-glass.

The nonsensical jargon of conceited jockeys is without ground or reason.

227. A black man is a jewel in a fair woman's eye.

Only a piece of flattery to a man who has not the advantage of a fair complexion.

228. A man may love the kirk well enough, and not ride on the y riggen of it.

A man may love a thing, or person, very well, and yet not shew too much fondness.

229. A z tale-teller is worse than a thief.

The one steals my goods, but the other my good name, and sometimes my peace and quiet; but it is often used as a facetious answer of children when their companions bid them tell a tale.

230. A a cumbersome cur is hated in company.

Spoken to an impertinent fellow, when he begins to be quarrelsome and breed disturbance.

231. Almost a mare's as great as a mountain.

Spoken when people tell us that they have almost done such a thing; shewing the uncertain signification of that word.

Eng.—Almost was never hanged.

Item.—Almost and very nigh save many a lye.

232. A man may love a b haggish that wo'd not have the bag c bladed in his teeth.

A man may say, or do, a thing in his airs, and humour, who would not be told of it again.

233. An ill wife, and a new lighted candle, are the better to have their heads held down.

But both must be done with care, caution, and discretion, otherwise you may put the candle out, and make the wife worse. They will say also, if a man complain of his wife's stubbornness, make a new lighted candle of her.

234. A leasure, as lairds dies.

Eng.—Softly and fair, as lawyers go to heaven.

235. A long gathered damm is soon run out.

Spoken to old batchelors, when they are new married.

236. As long as a dog would be bound with a blood pudding.

That is a short while, for he would soon eat his binding.

---

y The top of the roof. z A tale-bearer. a Troublesome, ill-natured. b A pudding made in the great gut of a sheep. Thrown cross his chaps.

237. A lass is a lad's leavings.

A senseless return of a girl, to them that call her lass, and not by her name.

238. A sorrowful heart is ay dry.

Spoken when widows or widowers drink liberally, alledging it was to quench their sorrow.

> Money we want and cannot borrow;
> Yet drink we must to [d] slocken sorrow.

Says the ingenious author of Linton lines.

239. As you are stout be merciful.

Spoken in a taunting manner to them that threaten us, whom we are not afraid of.

Lat.—Satis est protrâsse Leoni.

240. A man may be kind and give little of his geer.

Viz. By civil salutations, kindly expressions, speak me well behind ones back, &c.

241. All your debtors convey you to the [e] widdy.

Spoken facetiously, when a man craves what you have no mind to pay, nor he to exact.

242. A given game was never won.

Spoken when one desires us to give up our game as desperate.

243. A hungry man's meat is long a making ready.

Or at least seems so, because of his impatience.

244. A fair maiden [f] togherless will get more sweethearts than husbands.

Her beauty will get her sweethearts; but they say a togherless dame sits long at home.

245. As long lasts the hole as the [g] heal leather.

Spoken to them that quarrel with a hole in your coat or shoe: often apply'd otherways.

246. A short nebbed sparrow might have picked dirt at his arse.

Signifying that such an one was in a terrible fright. Or, as they say, Dirt flay'd.

247. A taking man will never want,
Let the world be never so scant.

A reproof to boys, or children when they take their meat, before it be given them.

248. A kindly [h] aver was never a good nag.

Those who are naturally of a low, mean mind, will make but a sorry figure in a higher station.

---

[d] Quench.   [e] Gallows.   [f] Without a portion.   [g] Whole.
[h] Work-horse.

Eng.—A carrion kite will never make a good hawk.

Item.—Jack will never be a gentleman.

Lat.—Qui semel scurra nunquam paterfamilias.

249. A ᵃ fow heart lied never.

A man in his cups will tell his mind.

Lat.—In vino veritas.

250. A fool when he has spoken has done all.

That is, has made a full discovery of his weakness, which his silence would have conceal'd.

251. A good yeoman makes a good woman.

As if a good husband would make a good wife; but I never saw this effected; many a good woman have I known to have reclaimed a bad man, but never a good man to have reclaimed a bad woman: either they must have more enticing charms, or more perverse humours.

252. A beltless bairn cannot lie.

I have not heard this used, but it is in the old Scotch Collection: I suppose it means a child before it be so old as to wear belted truese, will not have the cunning to invent a lie.

253. A hired horse ᵇ tired never.

Because the rider will so ply the spurs that he must go on. The English have a saying much like this.

Never spare a livery, a hackney, nor a whore; for you will get no thanks for it.

254. A full sack will take a clout on the side.

A man may make a shift to eat a little after he has din'd: I have heard it otherways apply'd.

255. All cracks, all bears.

Spoken against bullies who keep a great hectoring and blustering: yet, when put to it, tamely pocket an affront.

256. A bawdy father makes a begging ᶜ bairn-time.

Because he will squander, what should support and provide for them, among his whores.

Eng.—Whoring and bawdry end in beggary.

257. As mickle thanks as if you (I) did.

Spoken when we excuse ourselves from receiving what is proffered, or when we slight it.

258. All you run you win.

Taken from playing at bowls; apply'd to endeavours about a project that seems not feasible, where what you can make is clear gain.

ᵃ Full, drunk.　　ᵇ Jaded.　　ᶜ Posterity.

D

259. A dog will not [d] yowl, if you strike him with a
bone.

People will bear easily some rough usage, nay even blows,
if they see their advantage in it.

260. An apple is better given than eaten by a time.

A man may get more favour by giving a thing, than using it.

261. Any thing is better than the [e] yell kail.

An apology for having little, or bad, flesh meat.

262. A bonny [f] grice makes an ugly old sow.

Spoken facetiously to him that tells what a fine child he was.
Eng.—Fair in the cradle, and foul in the saddle.

263. After you is good manners.

Spoken when our betters offer to serve us first.

264. A man cannot bear all his kin on his back.

Spoken when we are upbraided with some bad kinsman.

265. A [g] crooked man should sow beans, and a [h] woad
man pease.

The one agrees to be thick sown, and the other thin.

266. All gou'd, or all dirt.

Spoken to them who are excessive both in their fondness
and aversion.

Eng.—All honey, or all turd.

267. As long as the bird sings before candle-mass so
long she greets after.

Intimating that a good January betokens a bad spring.

268. An ill turn is soon done.

Lat.—Compendiaria res improbitas.
Item.—Nullus enim magni sceleris labor.

269. A seven years maiden is ay at the slight.

An answer to a maiden who says she will not marry these
seven years, upon supposition that a fair offer would soon
make her break that resolution.

270. A long tongue has a short hand.

They who are lavish in their promises, are often short in
their performance.

271. A peck of March dust and a shower in May,
Makes the corn green, and the fields gay.

Eng.—A peck of March dust, is worth a king's ransom.

---

[d] Howl.   [e] Yell is properly what gives no milk, here it
signifies boil'd without meat, or having no butter.   [f] Pig.
       [g] Lame.   [h] Mad.

272. A shower in July when the corn begins to fill,
Is worth a plough of oxen, and all belongs therefill.

These observations upon weather and seasons are very silly.

273. A horn spoon holds no poison.

They who cannot procure better spoons are not worth poisoning.

Lat.—Nulla aconita bibuntur fictilibus.

274. An honest man is soon bound ; and you cannot bind a knave.

Because he will have tricks and fetches, that will soon elude all your securities.

Lat.————Adde mille catenas
Effugiet tamen scelerntus hæc vincula proteus.

275. An egg is a mouthful of meat and a townful of shame.

That is if it be stol'n, intimating that a little thing pick'd will procure a great disgrace.

276. A house with a [i] reek, and a wife with a [k] reerd, will soon make a man run to the door.

No man will willingly bear with a smoky house or a scolding wife, but escape them as soon as he can.

277. A [l] fow heart is ay kind.

Spoken when a man in his cups shews impertinent fondness.

278. A turn well done is twice done.

Because done to purpose ; for when it is slightly done it will soon require to be done anew.

279. A greedy eye had never a full [m] weime.

That is, such are never satisfied.

280. After a sort, as Costlet serv'd the king.

One Captain Costlet boasting much of his loyalty, was asked how he serv'd the king, when he was a captain in Cromwell's army; answered, After a sort. Spoken when a thing is done slightly.

281. Arse give me leave.

Spoken to lazy people who are loth to rise, as if they should first ask leave of their weighty backside.

282. At yale and pasch, and high times.

That is, such a thing must be done, worn, or expended only upon extraordinary occasions.

283. A dog in a deer's den.

---

[i] Smoke.   A scolding noise.   [l] Drunk.   [m] Belly.

Spoken when a widow, or a widower, marries a person inferior to their former match.

284. As long as you stand you do not stay.

It is enough to make it appear that you did not stay, if you
can say you never sate down; an argument to make our
friend, who is in haste, to stand and chat awhile.

285. Abundance of law breaks no law.

An argument rather to do more than the law requires, rather than leave any thing undone that it does.

Eng.—Take heed is good read.

Item.—Take good heed will surely speed.

Lat.—Abundantia juris non nocet.

**286. A leakie house and a scolding wife are two bad
companions.**

I remember Solomon compares oftener than once.

287. A duck cannot dable ay in [n] yee hole.

An argument for variety, often ill applied.

**288. A nice wife, and a back door, will soon make a
rich man poor.**

The wife will spend, and the servants purloyn.

289. A man of straw is worth a woman of gold.

It seems that the men contrived these proverbs, they run so
much in their favours.

290. A black hen lays a white egg.

And so may a black woman have a fair child.

291. Alike every day makes a clout on Sunday.

A reprimand to them who wear their best suit every day,
which will soon make them improper to be worn on Sunday.

**292. As good be hang'd for an old sheep as a young
lamb.**

This proverb seems to have an ill aspect; but it is for the
most part used at a game at tables, when I venture high in order to recover my game which otherwise would be lost, and
exactly answers to the English, Over shoes, over boots.

**293. As true as Biglam's cat crew, and the cock
rocked the cradle.**

Spoken when we hear one call that true that we know to be
a lye.

294. A friend in need is a friend indeed.

Lat. —Amicus certus in re incerta cernitur.

**295. An error in the first concoction cannot be recti-
fied in the second.**

---

[n] One.

When a thing is wrong in its primitive design, and contrivance, it is hardly after with any care to be amended.

296. A good shape in the [b] sheer's mouth.

Taken from taylors cutting of cloaths, spoken when we are going about some new project or design.

297. All is good that God sends.

An answer to them that think what they have given us, or what we have gotten not good enough.

298. A sleer would ay have a follower.

Spoken when young girls flee from young men, as if it were on purpose that they should follow them, as Virgil says,

Malo me Galatea petit, lasciva puella,
Et fugit ad salices, & se cupit ante vederi.

299. All things [c] sturts you, no wonder you be old like.

Spoken disdainfully to them who make a bustle about the things that they have little to do with.

300. A hard beginning is a good beginning.

Spoken to hearten those who meet with difficulties at their first setting out.

301. A great cry and little wool quoth the deel when he clip'd the swine.

Spoken of great pretences and small performances.

Eng.—Noise about nothing.

Item.—Much bruit, and little fruit.

Lat.—Parturiunt montes nascetur ridiculus mus.

302. A good face needs no band, and an ill one deserves none.

What is of itself handsome needs no adorning, and ornament is thrown away upon what is naturally ugly.

303. A wonder lasts but nine days in a town.

People will make a great deal of noise about any new emergent, and it will be the talk of every body for a few days, and then quite forgotten.

304. A ragged colt may prove a good horse.

And so may an untoward slovenly boy prove a decent and useful man.

305. A misty morning may prove a good day.

Things may prove a little confused and backward in the beginning, which with care and industry may come to good effect.

Eng.—Cloudy mornings may turn to clear evenings.

---

[b] Scissors.   [c] Troubles.

Item.—After clouds clear weather.
Lat.—Post nubila Phœbus.
Item.—Flebile principium melior fortuna sequatur.
306. After meat mustard.
Spoken when a thing is brought in after the proper time.
Lat.—Post bellum auxilium.
307. As long lives the merry man as the sad, and a
night longer.
A chearful temper is no enemy to health and long life,
but rather a friend
308. All is well that ends well.
Spoken with diffidence, that what is now in hand will no
end well.
Lat.—Finis coronat opus.
309. A man is not so soon heal'd as hurt.
Misfortunes come suddenly, but their remedies by more
slow degrees.
Eng.—One may sooner fall than rise.
Lat.—Labitur exiguo quod partum est tempore longo.
310. A groaning wife and a grunting horse never
feal'd their master.
It is observ'd that tender and sickly wives commonly live
long, and a horse that grunts under a man proves often very
durable.
311. A tumbling stone never gathers [1] fog.
From the Latin, Saxum volutum non obducitur musco. A
man that often removes seldom grows rich.
312. Any thing for a quiet life.
That is, we will take any thing rather than make a bustle.
313. All comparisons are odious.
Because they can hardly be made without some disparagement to one of the parties.
314. A spur in the head is worth two in the heel.
A man when drunk rides hard ; because not being able to
sit straight, his heels stick in his horse's side.
315. A word to a wise man.
Lat.—Verbum sapienti sat est.
316. A man cannot wive and thrive in a year.
For courting, marriage, and their appurtenance, occasions
an expence that one year cannot retrieve.
317. As the fool thinks the bell clinks.

---

[1] Moss.

Lat.—Quod valde volumus facile credimus.

318. A toom pantry makes a thriftless good wife.

A poor woman cannot make great industry, when she wants materials to work with.

Eng.—Bare walls make a giddy housewife.

Lat.—Haud facile emergunt quorum virtutibus obstat Res angusti domi.

319. A secret fo gives a sudden blow.

Because unseen and unprovided against.

Lat.—Magis nocent insidiæ quæ latent.

320. A good beginning makes a good ending.

Eng.—Good to begin well, better to end well.

321. A gifted horse should not be look'd in the mouth.

I have seen a munckish rhyme to this purpose.

Si quis det mannos ne quære in dentibus annos.

322. A dear ship stays long in the harbour.

Apply'd often to nice maids.

323. A liar should have a good memory.

Lest he tell the same lye different ways.

Lat.—Oportat mendacem esse memorem.

324. An ill life makes an ill end.

Lat.—Qualis vita finis ita

325. A muffed cat was never a good hunter.

Spoken to them that set about work with their gloves on.

326. An ill servant never proved a good master.

Lat.—Male imperat qui parere nescit.

327. A light purse makes a heavy heart.

328. A man has no worse friends than those he brings with him.

For if they disparage him they are believed, as being supposed to know him. Spoken also when they whom we thought to have been our friends, in such a case, were against our interest.

Eng.—You are good to help a lame dog o'er a stile.

329. A whore, in a fine dress, is like a dirty house with a clean door.

A whore may be handsome outwardly; but vile and ugly in the inside. As Oldham well describes her,

Within a gawdy case, a nesty soul,
Like turd of quality in gild close-stool.

330. After dinner sit a while:
After supper walk a mile.

The first I approve of, the other is ridiculous.

331. A wet May and a windy, makes a full barn yerd and a ^c findy.

Like the rest of the proverbs about season and weather.

332. A horse broken and a wife to break.

I do not know what reason there may be for the choice. The breaking of a horse may break a man's neck ; true! but may not the breaking of a wife break his heart? one thing I am sure of, that a skittish, furious young horse may be much sooner, and with greater ease, made tractable, and useful, than a foolish, froward, saucy wife, made good, virtuous, and peaceable.

332. A house made and a wife to make.

That is even as she proves, for some women are so perverse and foolish, that you may build Versailes before you can make them good.

333. All the months in the year causes a fair Februar.

334. A young saint may prove an old devil.

It were a thousand pities he should ; this is a devilish proverb, and often as devilishly apply'd.

335. As the market goes wares must sell.

336. April showers make May flowers.

337. As the day lengthens the cold strengthens.

It is often found that February and March are much more cold and piercing than December or January.

338. An ounce of good fortune is worth a pound of fore-cast.

Lat.—Gutta fortuna præ dolio sapientiæ.

339. After a delay comes a let.

When people put off a business for some time, they afterward quite forget it.

340. An eating horse never ^d funnied.

Intimating that people will not catch cold while they are eating.

341. After cheese come nothing.

As being always the last dish.

342. A cram'd belly makes a crazy corps.

Eng.—A man may dig his grave with his teeth.

Item.—Much meat, much maladies.

Lat.—Plures necat gula quam gladius.

343. An ill bush is better than no ^e beri.

---

^c Solid, full, substantial.   ^d Founder'd.   ^e Shelter.

344. A toom purse makes a [f]thrawn face.

345. A [g]bald moon quoth [h]Benny Gask, another pint quoth [h]Lesley.

Spoken when people encourage themselves to stay a little longer in the ale-house, because they have moon-light.

346. A man gets little thanks for losing his own.

If a man do not exact those perquisites that he has a title to, people will think them not due.

347. A laughing fac'd lad makes a [i]lither servant.

It is supposed such are too full of roguery to be diligent.

348. An inch breaks no squares.

A little difference ought not to occasion any contests among good neighbours.

349. An ill tongue may do much.

Spoken when people name the thing that would disappoint you; often said at game in merriment.

350. As long as I live I'll fart at my own fire-side.

That is, I will not give up my house and estate to my son.

351. All's i'the dirt.

Spoken when they whom we have taken pains to please take pet, because disappointed in some small matter.

Eng.—All the fat is in the fire.

352. A full purse never wanted a friend.

An empty one seldom finds one.

353. A wife knows enough, who know the good man's [k]breeks from [l]weilycoat.

This is an old proverb, and a good one, if rightly understood: that is, she is a good wife who knows the true measure of the husband's authority, and her obedience.

354. After company welcome [m]thrump'ry.

Spoken by them who are not well pleas'd that you took not notice of them as soon as other company. Or when people come to visit us that we care not for.

355. A [n]denk maiden makes a dirty wife.

It is very often found that women who go very neat and dress finely when they are maidens, turn very sluttish and careless of their dress when they are married.

356· Any thing for you about an honest man's house but a day's work.

---

[f]Wrinkles.　Bright.　[h]The titles of two Scottish lairds. [i]Careless, faint, lazy.　[k]Breeches.　[l]Petticoat.　[m]Trash, refuse.　[n]Neat, nice, finely dress'd.

357. A careless parting, between the old mare and
the broken carr.

Spoken when a husband or wife dies who did not love one
another; as if the surviving party was not sorry for the loss.
They will say, on such occasions,

358. It is not a death but ° lousance.

That is, rather a recovery of freedom from bondage.

359. As false as Waghorn, and he was nineteen-times
falser than the dee'l.

360. A tale never loses in the telling.

The fame or report of a matter of fact, good or ill, commonly receives an addition as it goes from hand to hand.

Lat.—Qui de magnis majora loquuntur.

Item.—Mobilitate viget, viresque acquirit eundo, viz. fama.

361. A ᵖ prin a day is a groat a year.

Spoken when we lift a pin: though at 96 a penny the cal-
culation is somewhat short.

B.

1. BETTER be ᑫ sansie, ʳ as soon up.

That is, better good fortune, than great industry.

2. Better late thrive, as never do well.

Lat.—Præstat sero sapere, quam nunquam.

Item.—Nunquam sera est, ad bonos mores, via.

3. Better hold by a hair, as draw by a tedder.

Better have a thing in present possession, than have never
so good a title to it.

4. Burn'd bairn fire dreads.

He that has been in danger from any thing, or in any place,
will be more cautious how he engages with any of these afterwards.

Eng.—A scalded cat fears cold water.

Lat.—Piscator ictus sapit.

Et mea cymba semel, vastâ percussa procellâ
Illum, quo læsa est, horret adire locum.

5. Better half egg, as toom ˢ doup.

Eng.—Half a loaf is better than no bread.

Item.—Better one eye, than quite blind.

Lat.—Princeps luscus inter cæcos.

° A freedom from bondage.   ᵖ A pin.   ᑫ Lucky, happy.
ʳ As in Scotch in comparison answers to than in English.
ˢ Bottom.

6. Better hold with the hound, as run with the hare.

Better be able to grapple with a difficulty, than to have a probability to escape it.

7. Better finger off as ay wagging.

Better put an end to a troublesome business, than to be always vex'd with it.

Eng.—Better pass a danger once, than be always in fear.

8. 'Bourd not with " Bawty, lest he bite you.

Do not jest too familiarly with your superiors, lest you provoke them to make you a surlish return.

Eng.—Good to be familiar, but not too bold.

9. Bite not my ˣ bannock.

That is, do not intrude upon my interest or property, which no man will willingly part with.

Eng.—Two wives in a house, two cats with a mouse, two dogs with a bone, will never agree in one.

Lat.—Esurienti leoni prædam ne exculpas.

10. Better give the slight than get it.

Spoken by a maid, when she is courted by one whom she believes not to be in earnest. In that case she will say, I care as little for you, as you do for me, better give the slight as get it: that is, better I refuse you now, than you reject me afterwards.

11. Better wait on the cooks as the ᵃ leaches.

Better have patience till your meat be ready, than, by eating it raw, or ill dress'd, to throw yourself into diseases.

12. Better the head of the yeomanry, as the arse of the gentry.

Better be the highest in a low degree, than the lowest in a higher.

13. Be a friend to thyself, and others will befriend thee.

Mens friends commonly bear a proportion to their circumstances in the world. And therefore if we be such friends to ourselves, as to make our circumstances easy, and plentiful, we will not want friends. Whereas,

Infelicium nulli sunt cognati, nec amici.

14. Better never begun, as never ended.

A project begun, and not ended, will occasion expence, and expose to ridicule.

15. Better a dee'l as a ᵇ daw.

ᵗ Jest.　ᵘ A dog's name.　ˣ A cake bak'd in the ashes or before the fire.　ᵃ Physicians.　ᵇ Slut.

A stirring active woman, though somewhat ill-natur'd and turbulent, is preferable to a lazy dirty drab, though quiet and peaceable.

Eng.—Better a shrew than a sheep.

16. Between two stools, arses fall down.

Commonly he that depends upon two contrary parties, will be disappointed by both.

Lat.—Duos lepores sequutus, neutrum assequutus.

17. Be thou well, be thou wo, thou shall not be ay so.

Mens circumstances, and conditions, will not be always the same; but will altar, sometimes for the better, and sometimes for the worse.

Lat.—Non si male nunc, & olim sic erit.

18. Between the dee'l, and the deep sea.

That is, between two difficulties equally dangerous.

Eng.—Go back and fall, go forward and mar all.

Lat.—A fronte præcipitium, a tergo lupi.

19. Blue and better blue.

That is, there may be difference between things of the same kind, and persons of the same station.

Lat.—Servus servum præstat, & dominus dominum.

20. Better eat grey bread in your youth, than in your age.

Better be in low circumstances in our younger years, when we have strength and vigour to bear them, than in our decrepid age. For as they say Eild and poortha is a sore burthen upon one back.

Eng.—If youth knew what age will crave,
     It would both get and save.

21. Better hold at the brim, than hold at the bottom.

Better live sparingly while we have something, than spend lavishly, and afterwards want.

Lat.—Sera est in fundo parsimonia.

22. Better hand loose, than on an ill teddering.

Better at liberty, than an ill service. Better a batchelor, than married to an ill wife.

23. Bread and cheese is fair to see, but man kee thou thine honesty. Said the landlady.

24. Bread and cheese is good to eat, when men can get no other meat. Said the guest.

The one implies the excellency of modesty, in the midst of plenty. The other, the necessity of eating, when a man is hungry.

25. Better buy than borrow.

True! for he that goes a borrowing goes a sorrowing. But this will not hold when a man wants money, for in that case, he must either borrow, or want.

26. Better the ill ken'd, than the ill unken'd.

27. Better ᶜ rue sit, than rue flit.

Both these spoken to them that long to change their masters, servants, houses, farms and the like. Signifying that we know the inconveniences of our present condition, but not the consequences of a change.

28. Better short and sweet, than long and lax.

Apply'd to discourses, speeches, sermons, and the like, where a perspicuous brevity is better than a tedious length.

Lat.—Sermonis prolixit as odiosa.

Item.—Quicquid præcipias esto brevis.

29. Better marry o'er the ᵈ midding, than o'er the ᵉ moor.

Better marry a neighbour's child, whose humours and circumstances you know, than a stranger.

Eng.—Like blood, like good, like age,
  Make the happiest marriage.

Lat.—Si qua voles apte nubere, nube pari.

30. Better play for nought, than work for nought.

For the one hath some pleasure, but the other, neither pleasure nor profit.

31. ᶠ Bigging, and bairns marrying are great wasters.

What expence building of houses, and marrying of children requires, is best known by experience.

32. Better a clout, than the hole out.

Spoken to them who find fault with a patch about you.

33. Better a mouse in the pot than no flesh.

Better something than nothing at all; for, as they say, Something has some savour.

34. Better an old maid than a young whore.

An answer of an old maid, to a young woman who calls her so, as if she was the one, and she the other.

35. Better a ᵍ wic fire to warm us, than a mickle fire to burn us.

An ordinary fortune is safest, and exposes us to less danger, which has occasioned many proverbs.

ᶜ Repent. ᵈ Dunghill. ᵉ Heath. ᶠ Building.
ᵍ Little.

E

Eng.—Little sticks kindle a fire, but great ones put it out.

Item.—Better ride an ass that carries me, than a horse that throws me.

Lat.—Medio tutissimus ibis.

Item.—Raro venit in coenaculo miles.

36. Break my head, and draw on my ʰ hoo.

Eng.—Burn me first, and then blow me.

Item.—Break my head, and bring me a plaister.

Item.—He covers me with his wings, and beats me with his bill.

37. Buy a thief from the gallows, and he'll help to hang your self.

I knew a very worthy clergyman in Scotland, who, by his interest and importunity, saved a villain from the gallows: and twelve years after, he was the first that rabbled him, and the sorest upon him.

Eng.—Put a snake in your bosom, and it will sting when it is warm.

38. Better hold out than put out.

39. Better keep the devil at the door, than turn him out of the house.

Both these signify, that it is better to keep out a bad inmate, because you will not so easily get rid of him, if he be once entertain'd ; though I have heard the last apply'd in a literal sense, better to resist the temptations of the evil one, than to master them when they are comply'd with.

40. Better bairns greet as bearded men.

Better you make your children cry with seasonable correction, than they make you cry by their after miscarriage.

Eng.—Birchen twigs break no ribs.

41. Bairns mother brust never.

Because she will keep meat out of her own mouth, and put it into theirs.

42. Bring the head of the sow to the tail of the ˡgrice.

ᵢ That is, balance your loss with your gain.

Eng.—Set the hare's head to the goose giblets.

43. ᵏ Boden geer stink ay.

Eng.—Proffered service stinks.

Lat.—Merx ultronea putet.

Item.—Par odio importuna benevolentia.

ʰ Night-cap.   ˡ Pig.   ᵏ Forc'd upon you.

44. Bid me to the roast, and beat me with the spit.

Spoken when we are invited to our cost.

45. Beg from beggars and you'll never be rich.

Spoken when we ask that from one which they sought from another.

46. Better be the happy man, than the happy man's son.

Spoken when a prosperous man's son is faln into want.

47. Better be off the world as out of the fashion.

A proverb used by, and often to, vain girls, and empty beaus.

48. Be still taking and tarrowing.

Take what you can get, though not all that is due.

49. Better guide well, as work sore.

And indeed good management will very much excuse hard labour.

Lat.—Maxima supplex parsimonia.

50. Better a shameless eating than a shameless leaving.

51. Better belly brust as good meat spill.

Both these spoken facetiously, to urge your friend to eat.

52. Bode good, and get it.

53. Bode a robe, and wear it ; bode a sack, and bear it.

Speak heartily, and expect good, and it will fall out accordingly.

54. Between ten and thirteen, bow the [1] waind while it is green.

Give your children correction, while they are young, or there is a hazard that they will outgrow it.

Eng.—Best bend while it is a twig.

Item.—The trick the colt gets at his first backing.

Will while he continueth never be lacking.

Lat.—Udum & molle latum es; nuno nuno properandus & aori

Fingendus sine fine rotâ.

55. Better learn from your neighbour's skathe, than your own.

Lat.—Felix quem faciunt aliena pericula cautum.

56. Better a dog fawn on you, as bark at you.

It is good to have the good will even of the meanest.

57. [m] Bourd not with my eye, nor with my honour.

Both these are too tender points to be jested with : and the honour often more nice than the eye.

---

[1] Twig.　[m] Jest.

58. Better long little, than soon nothing.

A persuasive to saving, and good husbandry.

59. Better ⁿ saught with little ° aught, than care with many a cow.

Solomon says, Better a little and quietness therewith, than a house full of sacrifices with strife.

60. Bear wealth, for poverty will bear itself.

Wealth is subject to a great many more tentations than poverty.

Lat.—Haud facile est æquâ commoda mente pati.   ʼ

61. Beggars ᵖ dow ۹ bide no wealth.

Spoken to those who having risen from a mean estate to a wealthy, turn proud and insolent.

Lat.—Luxuriant animi rebus plerumque secundis.

62. Better good sale than good ale.

That is, great fame may do better than great feats.

Lat.—Fama bellum geritur.

63. Blow the wind ne'er so fast, it will ʳ lown at the last.

Let the present disturbances be never so great, they will at gᵗʰ settlo.

Eng.—After a storm comes a calm.

64. Better old debts than old sores.

The debts may come in, and the sores will ake. Spoken when we receive a debt that we did not expect.

65. Better well beloved than ill won geen.

It is better to procure the love of many, by dealing justly and honestly, than by cheating, knavery, and oppression to procure the hatred and detestation of mankind.

66. Better say here it is, than here it was.

Better be at some pains to secure a thing that is in danger of being lost, or going astray, than to lament the loss of it when it is gone.

67. Better plays the full weime than the new coat.

A child will be more chearful upon being well fed than new cloath'd.

Eng.—Hunger pinches more than cold.

Lat.—Famem pellere satius est quam purpurâ nidus.

68. Better happy at court than good service.

ⁿ Easy quiet.   ° Good in possession.   ᵖ Are able to
۹ Bear.   ʳ Turn calm.

Courtiers are often raised by some lucky turn of good fortune, rather than by good service, or great qualifications.

69. Better two skathes, than one sorrow.

Losses may be repaired, but sorrow will break the heart, and ruin the constitution.

70. Better sit still than rise and get a fall.

Better continue in a low condition than be promoted, and afterwards disgrac'd.

71. Better leave than * lack.

In carrying on of a project, better to abound in material tools, and other necessaries, than be in the least deficient.

72. Better unborn than untaught.

An hyperbolical expression of our esteem of learning.

73. Black will take no other hue.

Intimating the difficulty of reclaiming perverse people.
Can the Ethiopian change his colour.
Lat.—Lanarum nigræ nullum colorem bibunt.

74. Better be alone, than in ill company.

Ill company is tedious and vexatious, whereas a good man is nonquam minus solus quam eum solus.

75. Better a ᵗ thigging mother than a riding father.

76. Better the mother with the poke than the father with the sack.

Both these signify that the mother, though in a low condition, will be more kindly to, and more careful of, orphans, than the father can be, though in a better. And in case of a second marriage, children will have a far better life under a step-father than a step-mother.

77. Bannocks is better than no bread.

Better a coarse thing than nothing at all.

78. Birth is much, but breeding is more.

Great birth without good breeding makes but a vile figure.
Lat.—Dedecorant bene nata culpæ.

79. Better a laying hen than a lying crown.

Better a small thing, by which you get daily advantage, than a more considerable thing lying useless.

80. Better fed than nurtur'd.

Spoken to children of wealthy parents, who are commonly saucy, insolent, and ill-natured.

81. Better fill'd than ᵘ prick'd.

---

* Want.　　ᵗ Thigging is somewhat less than begging.
ᵘ Skivered.

E 3

Taken from blood puddings, apply'd jocosely to them who have often evacuations.

82. Better wear shoon than sheets.

Sick men wear sheets and sound men shoes, an excuse of, or for, boys who wear many shoes.

83. Better an empty house than an ill tenant.

An excuse for breaking wind backward unseasonably.

84. By chance a cripple may ᵛ grip a hare.

Spoken when an improbable thing is proposed, by saying, By chance it may do.

85. Be going the gate's before you.

A coldrife farewel.

86. Better rough and ʷ sonsie, than bare and ˣ donsie.

Better a plentiful condition, though not so neat and nice, than too much cleanliness, with penury.

87. Better give than take by a time.

It may fall out that giving of a gift, may do more service than taking a reward.

88. Be what you seem, and seem what you are.

The best way! for hypocrisy is soon discovered and afterward abominated. For,

Lat.—Nemo diu egit hypocritam.

Item.—Cura esse quod audis.

89. Beauty ʸ but bounty availeth nothing.

Solomon compares a fair woman, without discretion, to a jewel in a swine's snout.

Eng.—Handsome is that handsome doth.

90. Because is woman's reason.

An answer to them, who, being asked why they did such a thing, say, Because, and no more.

91. Bastard brood is ay proud.

Spoken to bastards when they behave themselves saucily.

92. Begin with needles and ᶻ prines, and leave off with horse and horn'd ᵃ nout.

Intimating that they, who begin with pilfering and picking will not stop there, but proceed to greater crimes.

Eng.—He that will steal an egg will steal an ox.

93. Better my bairns seek of me, than I of them.

An excuse of parents, for not giving their children too great a portion.

ᵛ Catch.   ʷ Lucky.   ˣ Poor, mean, despicable.
ʸ Without.   ᶻ Pins.   ᵃ Cattel.

94. Before I [h] ween'd, but now I wat.

Spoken upon the full discovery of some malefice, which before we only suspected.

95. Bitter pills may have blessed effects.

Present afflictions may tend to our future good.

96. Buchannan's Almanack, long foul, long fair.

When weather continues long of one sort, it commonly continues as long of the contrary, when it changes.

97. Black arse quoth the pot to the caldron.

Spoken when others upbraid us with those faults that they are guilty of themselves; this is expressed in many proverbs.

Lat.—Loripedem rectus derideat, ethiopen albus.

98. Better spar'd than ill spent.

Spoken against luxury and riot, intimating that the money that they squander in ruining soul, body, and estate, were better for more worthy occasions.

99. [i] Belaive is two hours and a half.

An answer to them who, being bid to do a thing, say, Belaive, that is, by and by.

Eng.—Two anons, and by and by, is an hour and a half.

100. But beginning yet, as the wife did that run [k] wood.

A woman being mad and raging furiously stopped a little; some said, She has done now; but she answered, I am but beginning yet. It is since an answer to them who ask us if we have done.

101. Before an ill wife be a good; if she was all turn'd to the tongue.

Used when we promise to do a thing soon, tho' the promise need not oblige us to haste, for it will be a considerable time before a woman reform an ill tongue. They say also,

102. Before the dee'l go blind, and he's not gone blear'd yet.

Eng.—Before the cat lick her ear.

103. Black's my apron, and am ay washing't.

A senseless exclamation at hearing of a misfortune that we are not much concern'd about. 1 suppose it came from people saying, upon hearing of a real and concerning misfortune, Black's my heart.

104. Be long sick, that you may be soon heal.

Spoken to women in childbed, whom too early stirring may throw into some distemper.

---

[h] Suspected.   [i] Within a little.   [k] Went mad.

105. Be quick, for you'll never be cleanly.

A phrase desiring girls to go nimbly on in their business.

106. Better find iron, than [1] tine silver.

A truism upon finding a piece of iron.

107. Better a [m] togber in her than with her.

Better marry a well-bred, good-natur'd, virtuous woman, who is active and expert about business, than an idle, lazy, humoursome drab, with a much greater portion. Probatum est.

108. Better no ring than a ring of a rush.

I have not heard this us'd, it is in the old collection. I cannot see where the preference lies between nothing and a thing of no value, unless it be that nothing has no shew or pretence, whereas the other has an empty appearance.

109. Borrow as I did.

A facetious answer to a man who asks his loan before I have done with it.

110. Bridale feud is soon forgotten.

Those who are angry with you because you came not to their wedding, when invited, will soon be appeased. Apply'd when we are told that such an one is angry that you do not come to see him, and eat with him.

111. Better o'er't than on't.

An answer to him that says that he will give you O're the head, that is, break your head for you, as if O're imply'd a distance, and On fix'd the blow.

112. Between you and the long day be it.

An appeal to the day of judgment.

113. Better a good fame than a good face.

Better a deserv'd reputation, than a fam'd beauty.

Eng.—Grace will last, savour will blast.

114. Beds are best, quoth the good man to the guest.

A cant inviting to bed.

115. Better master one than fight with ten.

It is no honour to undertake an impracticable attempt, and perish in the undertaking.

Eng.—He that bravely ventures, bravely breaks his neck.

116. Better unkind, than o'er troublesome.

117. Better my friend think me [n] framet than [o] fashious.

The two signify the same thing, viz. that he that sees his friend too seldom, errs on the right side.

---

[1] Lose.   [m] Portion.   [n] Strange.   [o] Troublesome.

Lat.—Malim in hanc peccare partem, ut desiderer, quam ut obtundam.

118. Busy folks are ay medling.

Spoken against pragmatic officious fellows.

119. Boot who better has.

He that has the best bargain, give the boot.

120. Better be merry with something, as sad with nothing.

121. But [p] bonny [p] o't like Boles good mother.

Spoken when we think a thing little.

122. Better be John Tomson's man, than Ring and Dinn's, or John Knox's.

John Thomson's man is he that is complaisant to his wife's humours, Ring and Dinn's is he whom his wife scolds, John Knox's is he whom his wife beats.

123. Bare words make no bargain.

A preface to the demanding of earnest.

124. Burn a candle at both ends, and it will not last long.

Spoken when both the husband and the wife are spenders.

125. Bread and milk is bairns meat; I wish they had sorrow that loves't.

A sort of a riddle, not meaning the bread and milk, but sorrow, spoken to children when they ask such victuals.

126. [q] Baken bread and brown ale will not bide long.

127. Bare shoulders make burn'd shins.

When a boy is ill cloath'd he will sit so near the fire that his legs will burn.

128. Better be idle than ill occupied.

Eng.—The brain that sows not corn plants thistles.

129. [r] Bowked brides should have bor'd maidens.

They who are with child before they are married should be attended by whores.

130. Better you laugh than I [s] greet.

A careless return to those who laugh at us, or at what we say or do.

131. Better bow than break.

Better give way to a present torrent, than by obstinately withstanding or opposing it, ruin ourselves.

132. Better skathe sav'd, than mends made.

---

[p] Pretty, little. [q] Bak'd. [r] Bulky, big-bellied. [s] Cry.

Keep your cattel from trespassing on my grain, for though you make up my loss, that will be your loss, and nothing of my advantage.

133. Better the end of a feast than the beginning of a fray.

You may get scraps at the one, and blows at the other.

134. Before you make a friend eat a peck of salt with him.

That you may be the better apprised of his humours.

135. Better be envied than pitied.

Happiness provokes the one, and calamity the other.

136. Blind men should not judge of colours.

Men should not give their opinions in those things in which they cannot be supposed to have skill.

Lat.—Quid cæco cum coloribus.

137. Better a bit in the morning than fast all day.

Sometimes they say, than on the bare shins with a beetle.

138. Butter is gold in the morning, silver at noon, and lead at night.

A common saying, of whose truth or reason I know nothing.

139. Better an old man's darling, than a young man's wonderling, say the Scots, warling, say the English.

I know not what either wonderling or warling signifieth, but it is used as an argument to induce a young girl to marry an old man, to the doing of which no arguments should prevail.

140. Be it better, be it worse, be rul'd by him that has the purse.

The vast influence that money has on the minds of mortals, has given occasion to this, and many other proverbs.

141. Beggars breed and rich men feed.

Poor peoples children find a support in the service of the rich and great.

142. Birds of a feather will flock together.

Spoken when people of a humour, temper, or trade, consort together.

Lat.—Similes cum similibus facilis congregantur.

143. Better kiss a knave than be troubled with him.

Spoken upon any occasion, when we do a thing to be freed from teazing and importunity.

144. Better * ken'd than car'd for.

---

* Known.

Spoken to those who, in vindication of themselves, say that they are well ken'd, meaning that many know them to be good and honest, as if they were known to be the contrary.

145. Better cry [t] fy salt, than [u] phy stink.

An apology for having our meat too much powdered, because otherwise it would stink.

146. Be it so, is no banning.

Spoken when we unwillingly give our consent to a thing.

147. Boyl stones in butter and you may sup the broth.

Good ingredients will make very coarse meat savoury.

148. Breeding wives are ay [v] beddie.

A reason why we let such taste what is in our hands.

149. [w] Birk will burn, if it was [x] burn [x] drawn.

[y] Saugh will sob if it was sommer sawn.

Signifying that birch will burn readily; but that willows will not, but yield water.

150. Bonnet aside, how sell you your malt?

Only a jest upon them whose bonnet, cravat, or other parts of their dress, we see sit crooked.

151. Beauty draws more than oxen.

This is an English proverb, the Scottish one that answers it is smutty.

C.

1. CLAW me, and I'll [a] claw thee.

Spoken when we see two mutually obliging one another for their interest.

Lat.—Manum manus fricat.

Item.—Se invicem scabunt muli.

2. Counsel is no command.

That is, I advise you so; but you may do as you please.

3. Cats and [b] carlins sit i'the [c] sun.

But fair maidens sit within.

Spoken to decoy our children to sit within, that they be not sun-burn'd.

4. Come day, go day, God send Sunday.

Spoken to lazy unconscionable servants, who only mind to serve out their time, and get their wages.

---

[t] We say fy when a thing displeases us. [u] Phy when it is filthy, vile, distasteful. [v] Covetous of some silly things. [w] Birch. [x] Drawn through the river. [y] Willows, osier. [a] Scratch. [b] Old women. [c] In Scotch pronounced sin.

5. Cannot has no craft.

An answer to those who, being bid do a thing, say they cannot.

6. Come uncall'd, sit unserv'd.

They have no reason to expect good usage, who go to a feast uncall'd.

7. Changes of works is lightening of hearts.

8. Change of dee'ls is lightsome.

Variety is always pleasing, whereas one continual talk is tedious.

Lat.—Est quoque cunctarum novitas gratissima rerum.

9. ^d Carles and cart ^e avers win all.

And carles and cart avers spend all.

Servants wages, buying and keeping of horses, and purchasing other utensils, eat up the product of a farm.

10. Cadgers has ay mind of load sadles.

Spoken when people bring in, by head and shoulders, a discourse of those things they are affected with, and used to.

Lat.—Navita de ventis, de tauris narrat arator.

11. Condition makes, condition breaks.

Particular conditions, agreed to, and condescended upon, binds a man in law.

Lat.—Pactio tollit legem.

12. Court to the town, and whore to the window.

Persuading our daughters to stay within, and not be gadding, and gaping after every new sight: for such practice looked liker a whore than a modest virgin.

Eng.—A maid oft seen, and a gown oft worn,
Are disesteem'd and held in scorn.

13. Clap a ^f carle on the cods, and he'll fart in your ^g loaf.

Shewing the ungrateful temper of mean and unmannerly curs, who often requite a kindness with an ill turn.

Lat.—Ungentem pungit, pungentem rusticus ungit.

Item.—Perit quod datur ingrato.

14. ^h Crooked ⁱ carlin, quoth the cripple to his wife.

15. Clipped arse, quoth ^k bunty.

Spoken, as several others, when a man upbraids us with what himself is guilty of.

---

^d A carle is any man under a gentleman.   ^e Horses.
^f Any man under a gentleman.   ^g Hand.   ^h Lame.   ⁱ Old woman.   ^k A hen without a rump.

Lat.—Quis tulerit Grachos de seditione querentes.

16. Can is eith carried about.

Eng.—Cunning is no burthen.

Lat.—Quævis terra alit artificem.

17. Clout upon a hole is good gentry, clout upon a clout is good yeomanry, but clout upon a clouted clout is downright beggary.

Facetiously spoken, to those who quarrel with a patch about you.

18. Carry a lady to Rome, and give her one [1] hatch, all is done.

A reflection upon the humours of great persons, whom if you oblige in a hundred things, and disoblige in one, All the fat is in the fire.

Lat.—Dulcis inexpertis cultura potentis amici.

19. Cold kail hot again, that lov'd I never.

Old love renewed again, that lov'd I ever.

Spoken when an old courtship is renewed. The first answers Crambe re cocta semi mors. The second, Amantium ira amoris redintegratio est.

Eng.—Old pottage is sooner heated than new ones made.

20. Cast you o'er the house [m] riggen, and you'll fall on your feet.

Spoken when one has a better fortune than either they expected, or deserved.

21. Confess debt, and beg days.

That is, own your debts, and request for a longer day of payment.

22. Cast a bone in the deel's teeth.

Gratify some squeezing oppressor, or some unconscionable officer, to save your self from his harm.

23. Corn him well he'll work the better.

Taken from usage given to horses. Apply'd to the giving of large fees that you may be the better serv'd.

24. Cast not out the foul water, till you bring in the clean.

Part not with that way of living you have, till you be sure of a better.

25. [n] Crabbed was, and cause had.

26. [o] Crab without a cause, and [p] mease without amends.

---

[1] Jolt. [m] Top of the house. [n] Angry. [o] Be angry. [p] Settle.

27. Cool in the skin you ᴾ hat in.

These three are spoken to them that are angry, and we know not for what: the first ironically, and the other two with resentment.

28. Come not to counsel uncall'd.

Spoken to officious persons, literally translated from,
Lat.—Ne accesseris ad consilium, antequam voceris.

29. Come it early, come it late, in May, comes the cow quake.

A cold rain oftentimes falls out in May, which makes the cows, which are then but poor and weak, to tremble.

30. Care not, would have it.

If you ask a man if he will have such a thing, and he answers I care not, it is a sign that he would have it.

31. Common fame ꝗ sindle to blame.

A man will seldom be under an universal ill report, unless he has given some occasion for it.

Eng.—No smoke without some fire.
Lat.—Rumor publicus non omnino frustra est.

32. Cast the cat o'er him.

It is believed that when a man is raving in a fever, the cat cast over him will cure him; apply'd to them whom we hear telling extravagant things, as they were raving.

33. Cold cools the love that kendles so hot.

A pretended observation that they, whose passions are too violent in the beginning, will soon alter, and grow coldrife.

Eng.—Hot love soon cold.

34. Cut dwells in every town.

Cut is a dog's name, and Cut is a publick tax, and few towns want that.

35. Cease your snow-balls casting.

Spoken to them who are throwing their taunts about.

36. Contentibus, quoth Tommy Tomson, kiss my wife and welcome.

Spoken facetiously when we comply with a project.

37. Clean ʳ pith, and fair play.

That is, without trick or cheat, taken from wrestling.

38. Cripples are good doers; break your leg and try.

The first is an assertion, the second an answer.

39. Cocks with red combs are good traders.

A jest upon a man that has red hair.

ᴾ Grew hot.   ꝗ Seldom.   ʳ Strength.

40. ^s Combsters are ay ^t creechie.
It is ordinary to see men look like their trade.

41. Call again, you're no ghost.
Spoken when one knocks at the door, upon supposition that a ghost will not call twice.

42. Counsel will make a man stick his own mare.
Spoken when we are over persuaded to do a thing.

43. Change of masters, change of manners.

44. Count like Jews, pay like friends.
A very good advice! and answers to that other proverb, Oft counting keeps friends long together.

45. ^uCaff and ^v drass is good enough for cart ^w avers.
Coarse meat may serve people of coarse conditions.
Eng.—No carrion will kill a crow.

46. Come up, my dirty cousin.
A reprimand to mean people, when they propose a thing that seems too saucy.

47. Careless folk cumbers the earth.
Spoken to those who, in a sullen mood (upon any disappointment, reproof or disaster) say they care not.

48. Cast your cloaths togither.
That is, marry, they will say you, and such an one will cast your cloaths togither.

49. Comb sindle, comb sore.
Taken from children's heads, which if long uncomb'd will become so entangled, that it will put them to pain. Apply'd to those who forbear for awhile, and then come with severity.

50. Children are certain cares, but uncertain comforts.
This proverb needs no explication to any that ever had children, and brought them up: they well know that we can have them no time without care; but often without comfort.

51. Custom is a second nature.
So strong is inveterate custom, that it often conquers, and bears down, nature itself.

52. Come with the wind, go with the water.
Lat.—Male parta, male dilabuntur.

53. Cut your cloak according to your cloth.
Let your expence be suited to your income.

54. Charge your friend, er'e you need him.

---

^s Wool-combers.   ^t Greasy.   ^u Chaff.   ^v Grains.
^w Horses.

F 2

That you may know what to expect from him, if you do.

55. Chalk is no [x] sheers.

Taken from taylors marking out their cloth before they cut it, signifying that a thing may be proposed, that will never be executed.

56. Confession of a fault is half amends.

It softens resentment, and signifies that a man is sorry.

Lat.—Ignoscere pulchrum, pœnæ genus est vidisse precantem.

57. Crack of wealth watty.

A jeering exclamation, when one has gotten something that they did not expect, or far'd better than was supposed.

58. Count again is no forbidden.

Spoken when we count the money we have received.

D.

1. Dogs bark as they are bred.

Spoken when people, vilely educated, behave themselves accordingly.

Eng.—It is hard to make a horse shite oats that never eat any.

Item.—Cat after his kind.

2. Death and marriage make term day.

Marriage frees a man from his service in Scotland; and death in all countries.

3. Daylight will peep through a little hole.

A little indication may discover a great design.

4. Dear bought and far sought is good for ladies.

Witness tea, coffee, china-wares, and the like, which if they were the natural product of these kingdoms would not be valued.

Lat.—Magis ea juvant quæ pluris emuntur.

5. Drunk at night and dry in the morning.

They are very temperate and abstemious people, who are not sensible of the truth of this proverb.

Eng.—Ever drink, ever dry.

6. [y] Dree out the inch as you have done the span.

Spoken to encourage people to continue in ill service, or bear ill circumstances, whose end is near at hand.

Lat.—Tu ne cede malis, sed contra audentior ito.

7. Draff is good enough for swine.

---

[x] Scissors.   [y] Bear, suffer.

Spoken jocosely when people refuse what is good, and fine, and feed upon that which is more coarse.

Eng.—A turd is as good for a sow, as a pancake.

Lat.—Sui gratius cœnum quam unguentum.

Item.—Asinus stramentum mavult quam aurum.

8. Dirten arse dreads ay.

When people are sensible that they have done amiss, they are still apprehensive of discovery.

Lat.—Heu quam difficile est crimen non prodere vultu.

Item.—Judicium metuit sibi mens male conscia justum.

9. Do on the hill as you would do in the hall.

Accustom yourself to act with discretion and good manners at all times; and it will become habitual and easy to you.

10. Dee'l made souters sailers, that can neither steer nor row.

Spoken to them that take a thing in hand that they have no skill of.

Lat.—Qui semitam non sapiunt, alteri monstrant viam.

Item.—Oportet rerum ducere qui didicit.

11. Dogs will rid swine.

A third opposite will make two contending parties agree.

12. Drive a cow to the hall and she'll run to the bayer.

Spoken when people of mean breeding, and low education do not take to, or become, a more honourable station.

Lat.—Fortuna non mutat genus.

13. Did you ever [b] fit accounts with him?

Spoken to them who lavishly commend some person, of whose honesty, and just dealing, they have had no proof.

Lat.—Qualem commendas etiam atque etiam aspic; ne mox, Incutiant tibi peccata aliena pudorem.

14. Double charge will [c] rive a canon.

Spoken when people urge upon you more than you can bear, be it meat, drink, work, or so.

15. Double drinks are good for drouth.

Spoken when we would have him that has drunk once drink again.

16. Doves and [d] domine's leave ay a foul house.

Pigeons will dirty every thing where they are: and these little fellows, whom gentlemen bring in to educate their children, will be entreaguing with the maids; and it is well if the daughters escape.

---

[b] Adjust.　　[c] Split.　　[d] Pedagogues.

v 3

17. Daughters and dead fish are no keeping wares.

If so! let the daughters be dispos'd of, and the fish eaten as soon as conveniently you can; lest the one miscarry and the other stink.

Eng.—Marry your son when you will, and your daughter when you can.

Item.—Marry your daughter lest she marry her self.

18. ᵉ Dummy will not lye.

Spoken to convince our servants, and others, of their ill usage of what has been among their hands: as if you would say, see my horse is lean, my utensils are broken, my grain is eaten. Nempe res ipsa loquitur.

19. Deed shews proof.

The thing done shews how it was done, and what was done with it.

Lat.—Exitus acta probat.

20. Dirt defies the king.

Spoken disdainfully to them that say they defy us.

21. Dee'l ᶠ mein you if your leg was broken.

Spoken to them who have gotten some signal good fo' une, as if it were no pity to see them get some mishap.

22. Dee'l speed them that speer's and ken's so well.

A spiteful return to those who ask an ensnaring question which we suspect they can answer themselves.

23. Death at one door and ᵍ hardship at another.

Spoken when the head of a family is dead, by whose industry they were upheld and kept together.

24. Draff he sought, but drink was his errand.

Spoken of them who make a sleeveless errand into a house where they know people are at dinner.

25. Do a thing well and no body will ask how long you was about it.

Spoken when men excuse their not doing a thing well, because they did not bestow time on it.

Eng. That which is well done is twice done.

26. Drink and drouth come not always togither.

27. Danger past and God forgotten.

In time of danger and affliction men will address themselves earnestly to God for relief; but too often when relieved forget to be thankful. As one says of the Pope's courtiers, Importuni ut accipiant, inquieti donec accipiant ; & ubi acciperint ingrati.

ᵉ That which cannot speak.   ᶠ Bemoan.   ᵍ Ruin.

Lat.—Simul ac miserum est perit gratia.

28. Dirt parts good company.

Spoken when unworthy fellows break in upon our company, which makes us uneasy, and willing to break up.

29. Dame [h] deem warily, ye wat no who [i] wiles your [k] sell.

Spoken to them who pass harsh censures upon others, while perhaps they themselves are as harshly censured.

30. Ding down the nests, and the rooks will flee away.

Destroy the places where villains shelter, and they will disperse. This proverb was unhappily apply'd at the Reformation to the destroying of many stately cathedrals and collegiate churches.

31. Do well and doubt no man.

But rest satisfied in the testimony of a good conscience.

Lat.—Conscia mens recti famæ mendacis ridet.

32. Do well and doubt all men.

Lest they malign and envy you.

33. Death defies the doctor.

Lat.—Contra vim mortis non est medicamen in hortis.

34. Do not sigh for him, but send for him; if he be unhang'd he'll come.

Spoken when a young maid sighs, alledging that it is for a sweetheart.

Lat.—Non luctu, sed remedio, opus est in malis.

35. Do as the maids do, say no and take it.

Spoken when we urge a thing upon them, who have already refused it.

36. [l] Daffen and want of wit makes old wives [m] kirn water.

Spoken when we alledge that nothing but egregious folly could tempt a man to do such a thing.

37. [n] Dast folk's no wise strow.

Spoken when people advise what is not prudent, or promise what is not reasonable.

38. [o] Ditt your mouth with your meat.

Spoken with resentment to our inferiors when they talk at table what they should not.

---

[h] Judge. [i] Blames. [k] Sell. [l] Jolly.
[m] Churn. [n] Foolish. [o] Stop.

39. Deel's in our bairns, they will not go to bed when
their belly is full.

Spoken with indignation, when people who are already
well enough, cannot hold themselves so, or be satisfied.

40. Deal small and serve all.

Spoken when we see a thing unequally divided.

41. Do well and have well.

That is, be a good man, and you will be kindly dealt by,
for, Bonis bona contingunt.

42. Do the likeliest, and hope the best.

43. Do as you would be done by.

Lat.—Quod tibi fieri non vis, alteri ne facias.

44. Do well, and dread no shame.

45. Do what you ought, and come what will.

These two, with others of that sort, signify that men should
act upon a steady principle of virtue, justice, and honesty;
not out of fear, interest, or shame: and this truly is the only
way to go through the world with ease, reputation, and honour.

46. Delays in love are dangerous.

For either party may alter their mind.

47. Damming and loving is sure fishing.

An advice to prefer a sure gain, though small, to the
prospect of a greater with uncertainty.

48. Dee'l be i'the pack sheet she comes in.

Eng.—I would not touch her with a pair of tongs.

E

1. EVER busy, ever bare.

It is not always found that they who pursue the world most
eagerly, gets the greatest share of it.

2. Every man to his mind, quoth the carle when he
kiss'd his cow.

The variety of men's affections, and aversions, has given
occasion to many proverbs.

Lat.—Denique non omnes eadem mirantur amantque.

Item.————Trahit sua quemque voluptas.

3. Experience is good, but often dear bought.

4. Experience teaches fools.

Both spoken when people find themselves, or others mistaken in some things, and courses, which they formerly lov'd,
and approv'd of, to their disadvantage.

Lat.—Experientia stultorum magistra.

5. Every man's nose will not be a shoeing horn.

Spoken to them who have found the man, with whom they were dealing, more sagacious and cunning than they expected : every man is not to be impos'd on, or made a property of.

6. Every crow thinks its own ª bard ᵇ bonniest.

Lat.—Suum cuique pulchrum.

7. Every play must be play'd, and some must be the players.

An excuse for a project that has miscarried, taken from fatality. As the rogue says in the play,

Quid si hoc quispiam voluit deus.

8. Every man wears his belt in his own fashion.

An apology for a man's acting differently from others: I have heard this proverb otherways express'd.

Lat.—Velle suum cuique est nec voto vivitar uno.

9. Every miller draws water to his own mill.

Men's eagerness upon self-interest has given occasion to this, and a great many other proverbs.

Lat.—Proximus sum egomet mihi.

10. Every man can guide an ill wife, but he that has her.

Often, and justly, apply'd in a literal sense ; but in a general when one apprehends that he could order such a station, post, or business, better than he that has it.

Lat.—Facile omnes, cum valemus, ægrotis consilia damus.

11. Every man for himself, and God for all.

The best meaning this will bear is, every man do his best endeavour, and leave the issue to God.

12. Every land hath its own ª laugh, and every corn its own ᵈ caff.

Every country hath its own laws, customs, and usages.

Eng.—So many countries, so many customs.

Lat.—Suus est mos cuique genti.

13. Enough is as good as a feast.

14. Enough is enough of bread and cheese.

Lat.—Satis est quod sufficit ; nimis est quod suffocat.

15. Every man ᵉ flamms the fat sow's arse.

ª Young one.   ᵇ Fairest, prettiest.
ᶜ Law, custom.   ᵈ Chaff.   ᵉ Basteth.

They will be sure to get most gifts that least want them.

Eng.—Every one basteth the fat hog, while the lean one burneth.

Lat.—Pauper eris semper, si pauper es Quintiliane.

Dantur opes nullis, nunc, nisi divitibus.

16. Eith to learn the cat to the [f] kirn.

An ill custom is soon learn'd, but not so soon forgotten.

Lat.—Canis a corio nunquam absterebitur uncto.

Item.—Periculum est canem intestina gustâsse.

17. Every dog hath his day, and a bitch two after-
    noons.

Every man hath his turn of good or bad fortune. Commonly spoken with a vindictive mind, when injur'd by those
in place or power; hoping that we will have our day about
with them.

18. Every thing hath a beginning.

Spoken to encourage a man to go on with a small business,
stock, or interest, in hopes of future advancement.

Lat.—Omne principium debile.

19. Either a man, or a mouse.

Either do strenuously, or give over.

Lat.—Aut Cæsar aut nihil.

20. Every man's man had a man, and that made the
    treve fall.

The treve was a strong castle built by black Douglass: the
governor left a deputy, and he a substitute, by whose negligence the castle was taken and burn'd. Spoken when servants employ other servants to do the business that they
were entrusted with, and both neglect it.

21. Every man for his own hand as John Jelly fought.

A proverb barring partners, two men was fighting, John
Jelly going by makes up fiercely to them, each of them ask'd
him which he was for, he answered for his own hand, and
beat them both.

22. Every day is not [g] Yule-day, give the cat a
    [h] castock.

Signifying that upon jovial occasions people should be
more free and liberal than ordinary, because they return not
often.

.23 Either live or die with honour.

---

[f] Churn.   [g] Christmas.   [h] A kail stock.

Do stoutly and bravely, and if you prevail, you live, and if you die, you die with honour.

Lat.—Emori per virtutem præstat, quam per dedecus vivere.

24. Every thing would fain live.

Spoken in excuse of man or beast, who make their best endeavour to get a living.

25. Eat well is drink well's brother.

Spoken when we have eaten well, and taken a large draught after.

26. Every thing has its time, and so has the ¹ rippling-comb.

The sense the same with the 17th.

27. Every best his ᵏ bottle.

This is only spoken when people are drinking, and propose that every man shall have his pint, quart, &c.

28. Eat your fill, and ¹ pouch none, is Gardiners law.

Spoken to them who pocket some of what is before them.

29. ᵐ Eild and ⁿ poortha is a sore burthen on one back.

No doubt age joyn'd with poverty is very afflicting, when a man wants support, and ability to procure it.

30. Ell and tell is good merchandise.

The best market is to get ready money for your wares, to the same purpose they say,

31. The best payment is on the peck bottom.

That is, when you have measured out your grain, to receive your payment on the peck that measured it.

32. Early master, soon ° knave.

When a youth is too soon his own master, he will squander his patrimony, and so must turn servant.

33. Evening oarts is good morning foder.

Spoken when a man breakfasts upon what he left for supper.

34. ᵖ Eith to keep the castle that was never beseeg'd.

Spoken with bitterness, by a handsome woman, when an ugly one calls her a whore. Intimating that no body will give her the tentation.

---

¹ An instrument to take the bolls of the lint.   ᵏ A bundle of straw or hay.   ¹ Pocket.   ᵐ Age.   ⁿ Poverty.   ° Servant.   ᵖ Easy.

Eng.—Easy keeping an orchard when no body robs it.

Lat.—Forma maligna pudicitiæ custos.

35. Every shoe fits not every foot.

Every condition of life, every behaviour, every speech and gesture, becomes not every body ; that will be decent in one, which will be ridiculous in another.

Eng.—A man in a doublet may make an ass in a cassock.

Lat.—Nam quod turpe bonis Titio Seioque decebat,
——Crispinum.

36. Early sow, early mow.

The sooner a man sets about a business, the sooner he finds the effects of it.

Eng.—The rath sower never borrows from the late.

37. Every thing is the worse for the wearing.

Spoken of persons, beasts, and things, when they are grown old and decay'd.

38. Either win the horse, or q tine the saddle.

Spoken as an encouragement to a noble attempt.

39. Early pricks that will be a thorn.

40. Early crooks the tree that in good b cammon will be.

Both these signify that children soon shew their propensities and inclinations.

Lat.—Protinus apparet qui arbores frugiferæ futuræ.

Item.—Adeo a teneris assuescere multum est.

41. Either the i tod or the k braken bush.

Spoken to silly people when they speak with uncertainty.

42. Every one loups over the dike where it is l laighest.

There are many proverbs to this purpose, signifying that poor people are run down by every body.

43. Every man to his trade, quoth the boy to the bishop.

A bishop asked a cabbin boy if he could say his prayers, he ask'd the bishop if he could say his compass, the bishop said no; why then, says the boy, every man to his trade.

Lat.—Tractent frabilia fabri.

Item.—Quam scit uterque liberis censebo exerceat artem.

44. Every flow hath its m ebb.

---

q Lose.   b A crooked stick with which boys play at cammon, shinny, or side ye.   i Fox.   k Furn.   l Lowest.
m Neep.

There is a time when families, and single persons thrive, and there is a time when they go backward.

Lat.—Variæ sunt fortunæ vices.

45. Eat and welcome, fast and twice as welcome.

A jocose invitation to our known friend to eat.

46. Even stands his cap to-day for all that.

It took its rise from a minister in our country, who for a sermon preach'd most fiercely against the supremacy of the Pope; and for a conclusion said, Even stands his cap for all that I have said, drinking good Romany wine this day. Apply'd when we signify that all that we can say against any great man, can do him no harm.

47. Early rising is the first thing that puts a man to the door.

In the Scottish phrase to be put to the door is to be ruin'd; so the jest lies in the double signification of the word, for when a man rises early he will soon go to the door.

48. Eating and drinking takes away a man's stomach.

A jest, but contrary to another.

49. Eating and drinking wants but a beginning.

Eng.—One shoulder of mutton drives down another.

50. ᵐEven your heels to your arse, and your arse to the ⁿmuck ᵖ midding.

A phrase of great contempt and indignation, to them that say, in anger, that they are as good as us, as if we should say, compare things that are alike ; compare your heels to your breech, and that to the dunghill.

51. Every man's dog will be as full of him as mine.

Spoken when we are blam'd for riding our horse too hard ; as if you would say, I'll get no other use of him, for when he is dead, he will be a common feast for every dog.

52. Every man as he loves let him send to the cook.

This is, let every man choose according to his liking.

53. Every man bows to the bush he gets ˢ beel of.

Every man pays court to him that he gains by.

54. ˢEild would be honoured.

Eng.—Age is honourable.

Lat.—Credebant hoc grande nefas, & morte piandum.
Si vetulo puer non assurrexerit.

55. Every man is a fool sometimes, and none at all times.

ᵐ Compare. ⁿ Dung. ᵖ Dunghill. ˢ Shelter. ˢ Age.

G

An apology for an imprudent action, in ourselves or others:
> Great wits to madness, sure, are near allied,
> And thin partitions doth their bounds divide.

56. Eith till that thy own heart will.

Eng.—Where the will is ready the feet are light.

57. Eith learn'd soon forgotten.

It is observ'd that they that come hard by any part of learning retain it long; and on the contrary they who suddenly learn, soon forget.

Lat.—Dediscit animus sero, quod dedicit diu.

58. Even as ye win't, so may you wear't.

Spoken to them who have gotten something by base and unjust means, and wish it may prosper with them accordingly.

59. Eaten bread is eith to pay.

Spoken of them who have bought something of me, and refuseth, or delayeth to pay me.

60. Every ᵇ dud bids another good day.

Spoken of people in rags and tatters.

Eng.—He is in the rag-man's hands.

61. Every man is blind in his own cause.

Eng.—Self-love is a mote in every man's eye.

62. Eat till you sweat, and work till you frize.

An upbraiding speech to lazy servants who love meat better than work.

Lat.—Sudant quando vorant, frigescunt quando laborant.

63. Eagles catches no flies.

Eng.—The gose-hawk beats not at a bunting.

Lat.—Aquila non captat muscas.

64. Eat pease with the king, and cherries with the beggar.

Pease are best when young, and cherries when ripe.

65. Every man's tale is good till another's be told.

Solomon hath it thus, When a man is first in his own cause he seemeth right, but his neighbour cometh after and trieth him.

66. Every man at thirty is a fool or a physician.

He is a fool who at that age knows not his constitution.

67. Every man is no born with a silver spoon in his mouth.

Every man is not born to an estate, but must labour for his support.

ᵇ Rag.

F.

1. For more acquaintance, as Sir John Ramsey drunk to his father.

Sir John Ramsey had been long abroad, and coming home he accidentally met with his father, who did not know him: he invites his father to a glass of wine, and drinks to him for more acquaintance. Apply'd jocosely, when we drink to our intimate friends or relations.

2. Fortune helps the hardy ay, and pultroons ay repels.

Out of the book call'd the Cherry and the Sloe; but ever since used as a proverb upon jovial occasions.

Lat.—Audentes fortuna juvat.

3. Foul fall nought, and then he'll get nothing.

A word of contempt to, or of, mean and unworthy persons, when they begin to be presumptuous.

4. Fools sets long ª trysts.

Spoken when people promise to do a thing a good while hence.

5. Folks dogs bark worse than themselves.

Spoken when our neighbours servants resent a thing we have done, worse than they would do themselves.

6. Fools haste is no speed.

Spoken when people make a great bustle, and yet put no work by their hand, but often by their too much haste spoil what they are about.

Lat.—Canis festinans cæcos parit catulos.

7. Fart on this side of the sea, and fart on the other side.

Change of climates doth not always change manners.

Lat.—Patriam quis exul, se quoque fugit.

Item.—Cœlum, non animum, mutat qui trans mare currit.

8. Fair ᵇ heights make fools ᶜ fain.

Eng.—Promise and give nothing is comfort for a fool.

Lat.—Promissis dives quilibet esse potest.

9. Fat fowls have fair feathers.

Spoken when people extol what they have heard or seen elsewhere, as giving little credit to them.

Lat.—Remoti colles virides procul esse videntur.

10. Feeling has no fellow.

ª Appointments.   ᵇ Promises.   ᶜ Glad.

I suppose in point of certainty, though I have heard it otherwise apply'd.

11. For as good again, like the Sundays milk.

A precise woman in our country would not sell her milk on
Sunday, but would give it for as good again. Spoken when we
suspect peoples kindness to be mercenary ; or when we promise to make either their kindness, or michief, a suitable return.

12. Friendship cannot stand ay on one side.

Friendship is cultivated by mutual good offices; spoken to
urge some instances of kindness on them to whom we have
been formerly oblig'd.

Lat.—Dedeous est semper sumere, nilque dare.

13. Frost and falshood has ay a foul hinder end.

When frost thaws, the ways are dirty ; and when falshood.
is discovered it causes shame and disgrace.

14. Fools, bairns, and drunken men tell all that is in
their mind.

The reflection is on the last.

Lat.—Cum verax aperit præcordia liber.

15. Friends agree best at a distance.

By friends here is meant relations, and they agree best when
their interests does not interfere.

16. Feeding out of course, makes metal out of kind.

Good pasture will make a small breed of cattel larger.

17. Fair fall the wife and well may she spin,
That reckens the [d] lawing with a quart to come
in.

A rhyme among drunken companions, who would have the
landlady put into her bill a bottle not yet called for.

18. Fools should not have [c] chapping sticks.

Spoken when we take a stick from a child, or when others
are doing harm with what they have taken up.

Lat.—Non prodest stulto virga nociva data.

19. Foul water [b] slockens fire.

It has but a foul meaning.

20. False folk should have many witnesses.

For otherways they will deny their bargain.   Spoken when
cunning knaves bid you prove what you alledge.

21. Fair folk is ay [i] fisonless,

---

[d] The Reckoning.   [c] Sticks in their hand to beat with.
[b] Quenches.   [i] Featless, feeble, niggardly.

A jest upon them who are of a fair complexion, as if such were weakly, niggardly, or little good with them.

22. Farewel frost, fair weather [k] nest.

Spoken when they go off, whom we are glad to part with. Eng.—Farewel frost, nothing gotten nothing lost.

23. Featless folk is ay fain of [l] other.

A jest upon two people who are glad when they meet.

24. Far from my heart my husband's mother.

Taken from the ill understanding that is often between mothers in law and their daughters in law, Spoken when a loss is mentioned in which we have little concern.

25. From the teeth forward.

That is, not inwardly, and from my heart, ore tenus.

26. Folks wat not, sometimes, whether to run fast or go at leisure.

For too much haste may spoil a business, as well as too much laziness.

Lat.—Fallitur in dubiis, humana solertia, rebus.

27. Fair exchange is no rob'ry.

Spoken when we take up one thing, and lay down another.

28. [m] Fair fall you and that's [n] a fleech.

An ironical commendation of them, whose words and actions we approve not.

29. For fault of wise men fools sit on benks.

Spoken when we see unworthy persons in authority.

30. Fools are fain of flitting, and wise men of sitting.

Spoken to them who are fond of altering their place, station, or condition, without good reason.

Lat.—Optat ephippia bos, optat arare caballus.

31. Fill full, and ha'd full, makes a stiff [o] weime.

Spoken when people eat between meals.

32. Far fra court, far fra care.

A real truth, but rarely believed, till confirm'd by experience.

Lat.—Procul a jove, procul a fulmine.

33. Fancy flees before the wind.

Love and liking are not always well grounded.

34. Fresh fish, and poor friends become soon ill [p] sar'd.

Spoken when we see poor relations slighted.

---

[k] Next. [l] One of another. [m] Blessing on you. [n] A piece of flattery. [o] Belly. [p] Savour'd, smell'd.

35. ^q Flaying a ^r burd is no the way to ^s grip it.

A vile intimation! that a man should conceal his ill intentions upon any, lest they provide against it, and so prevent it.

Eng.—Let not your mouse-trap smell of cheese.

Lat.—Quæ nimis apparent retia fugit avis.

36. Fat paunches bode lean pates.

A groundless reflection upon fat men, of whom I have known many ingenious, and but few ill-natur'd or malicious.

37. Fore warn'd half arm'd.

A man who expects a misfortune will prepare against it.

Lat.—Præmonitus, præmunitus.

38. Fair words will not make the pot ^t play.

Eng.—Fair words butter no parsnips.

39. Fast bind, fast find.

An encouragement to careful securing, and laying up, as the only way to keep and preserve.

40. Force, without forecaste, is little worth.

Strength, unless guided by skill and discretion, will avail but little.

Lat.—Vis consilii expers mole ruit suâ.

41. Follow love and it will flee thee:
Flee love and it will follow thee.

I do not understand this proverb; unless it answers to that of the flatterer in Terence: Novi ingenium mulierum; nolunt ubi velis; ubi nolis cupiunt ultro.

42. Fools tye knots, and wise men loose them.

Spoken when people, for want of skill and management, have spoil'd and entangled a business, which will require wisdom to set right again.

43. Forbid a fool a thing, and that he will do.

Apply'd for the most part to children, when they do what they have been forbid once, and again.

Lat.—Nitimur invetitum semper, cupimusque negata.

44. Freedom is a fair thing:
But often foully abused.

Eng.—No man loves his fetters though made of gold.

They say Sir William Wallace had always the following rhyme in his mouth,
Dico tibi verum, libertas optima rerum,
Nunquam servili sub nictu vivito fili.

45. ^u Fling at the ^v brod was ne'er a good ox.

---

^q Frightening. ^r Bird. ^s Catch. ^t Boil. ^u Kick.
^v Goad.

Taken from a drawing ox, who kicks when he is prick'd by the goad. Apply'd to them who spurn at reproof.

46. Far behind must follow the faster.

People whose business and labour is behind their neighbours, must be the more busy and industrious.

47. February fill dike either with black or white.

February brings commonly rough weather, either snow or rain.

48. For my own pleasure as the man ᵛ strake his wife.

A surlish answer to them who ask you why you do such a thing.

49. Fat flesh frizes soon.

Spoken when a fat person complains of cold.

50. Fools wonder ay at ˣ farlies.

A surlish answer to them that say that they wonder why you did so, or so.

51. Fann'd fire and forc'd love, never did well yet.

And indeed both flames burn brightest when they come freely.

Lat.—Omne ex necessitate molestum est.

52. Four and tuantie taylors cannot make a man.

The jest is in the word make, for though one taylor can shew himself a man, yet no number of them can frame one.

53. Flee never so fast you cannot flee your fortune.

Spoken by them who believe that all things come by fatality.

Lat.—Lanificas nulli tres exorare sorores
    Contigit; observant quam statuere diem.

54. Fools should not see half done work.

Many fine pieces of work will look clumsy, and aukward when it is a doing, which they who want judgment will be offended at.

55. Farts in ʸ erse is dirt in Latin.

A by word expressing contempt and scorn of any person, or thing.

56. Fair go they, fair come they, and ay their heels hithermost.

Originally apply'd to the fairies, about whom the vulgar Scots have strange stories and opinions. But now used when they speak of wicked and bad men, with whom they desire to have no concern or business.

ᵛ Beat.   ˣ Miracle.   ʸ Irish.

57. **Fine feathers make fine birds.**

Ornament and dress will set out a person, who otherways would look but coarse.

60. **Fair maidens wear no purses.**

Spoken when young women offer to pay their club in company, which the Scots never allow.

61. **Fair hair has fool roots.**

Alledging that children of a fair complexion will be apt to be lousy.

62. **For fashion's sake, as dogs goes to the market.**

Spoken when we see people declare for a party, or make a profession, which we suppose they would not do, if it were not in vogue.

63. **Fair offer no cause of [1] feud.**

Spoken when one refuses what we proffer them, signifying that it was the effect of our good will, and ought to be taken as such.

Eng.—He that bids me to meat wishes me to live.

64. **Faint heart never won fair lady.**

Lat.—Certandum est, nulli veniunt sine marte triumphi;
    Et nisi certanti nulla corona datur.

Item.—Timidi nunquam statuere tropheum.

65. **Fair words break no bone :**
    But foul words many a one.

Solomon hath it, A soft answer turneth away wrath: but grievous words stirreth up anger.

66. **For want of a nail the shoe may be lost.**

I have seen this run out to a great length, but the meaning is, that a little care, early bestowed, may prevent a great loss.

Lat.—Ehu quam levibus pereunt ingentia causis.

67. **Fools [2] big houses and wise men buy them.**

I knew a gentleman buy 2000l. worth of land, build a house upon it, and sell both house and land to pay the expences of his building.

Eng.—He that buys a house ready wrought,
    Has many a pin and nail for nought.

68. **Fools make feasts and wise men eat them.**

This was once said to a great man in Scotland, upon his giving an entertainment. Who readily answer'd,

69. **Wise men make proverbs and fools repeat them.**

70. **Fire and water are good servants, but ill masters.**

---

[1] Enmity.   [2] Build.

71. Fidlers wives, and gamesters ale, are free to all men.

The fidlers wives are brought in for the sake of the gamesters ale. Spoken when we are drinking what others have won at play.

72. Fidlers, dogs, and flesh-flies, come to feasts un-call'd.

Fidlers for money, the flies for a sip, and the dogs for a scrap.

73. Fair and foolish, black and proud,
Long and lazy, little and loud.

A groundless proverb upon womens different statures and complexions.

74. First come first serv'd.

75. Fancy may kill or cure.

There are many stories of the power of imagination to do good or evil, and, I am persuaded, the efficacy of these things that they call charms depend intirely upon it.

76. Fat housekeepers make lean executors.

Because they spend all in their life-time.

77. Fools are fain of nothing.

Spoken when we see people much taken up with fair promises, or improbable expectations.

78. Fish must swim thrice.

Viz. Once in water, once in sauce, and once in drink.

79. Fidler's fare! meat, drink, and money.

Spoken often when we have din'd with our friend, and after won some money from him at play.

80. Fall on the [7] fayest, the beetle among the bairns.

Spoken when we do a thing at venture, that may be good for some, and bad for another; and let the event fall upon the most unfortunate; answers to the English, Among you blind harpers.

G.

1. Give a bairn his will, and a whelp his fill, and none of these two will thrive.

The whelp will be fat and lazy; and the child will be perverse and froward.

2. God's bairn is [a] eith to [b] lear.

----

[7] They that have the most signs of death. [a] Easy.
[b] Learn.

A child endowed with grace and good nature will be easily taught.

3. Great barkers are no biters.

Great boasters are not always best performers.

Eng.—Dogs that bark at distance, bite not at hand.

Lat. —Canes timidi vehementius latrant.

4. Gold is good but it may be dear bought.

Spoken when an extravagant price is ask'd for a good thing.

Eng.—A man may buy gold too dear.

5. Get a name to rise early, and you may lye all day.

I would not have a man depend too much upon this proverb; for a good name is soon lost, and hardly to be retriev'd.

Eng.—He that once a good name gets,

May piss a bed, and say he sweats.

6. Classes and lasses are ᶜ bruckle wares.

Both apt to fall, and both ruined by falling.

7. Good enough has gotten a wise, and far better wants.

Spoken when unworthy persons are prefer'd.

8. God send you readier meat than running hares.

Spoken to those who have improbable expectations.

9. God help them that gets them with one, and brings them up with another.

Occasioned by the miserable condition of those who have motherless orphans under the cruel care of a step-dame.

10. Give a man luck, and cast him in the sea.

Spoken when a man is unexpectedly fortunate.

Lat.—Fortuna in omne re dominatur.

11. Give you an inch, and you'll take a span.

Spoken to shameless intruders upon your good humour.

12. God sends men cloth, according to their cold.

God supports and supplies men, according to their circumstances, stations, wants, and conditions.

Lat.—Deus nunquam deest in necessariis.

13. God send us some money, for they are little thought of that want it, quoth the Earl of Eglinton at his prayers.

14. God keep ill geer out of my hands, for if my hands once get it, my heart will never part with it.

The Earl of Eglinton turn'd off his chaplain, and said pub-

ᶜ Brittle.

ltok prayers in his own family; where these two proverbs
were two standing petitions.

15. Gut no fish till you get them.

Spoken to them who have pregnant expectations, and boast
of them as if they had them in possession.

Eng.—All the craft is in the catching.

Lat.—Ante victoriam triumphum ne canas.

16. God send water in that well, that people thinks
will never go dry.

Spoken when our poor kin, and followers, are always asking of us; as if we should never be exhausted.

17. Give over while the play is good.

Spoken to those who are like to fall from jest to earnest.
Also to those who are too wantonly jesting on you; advising
them to give over, lest they provoke you to make them a surlish return.

18. Gentle ᵈ poddocks has long toes.

Spoken to dissuade you from provoking persons of power
and interest; because they can reach you, though at a distance.

19. Giff gaff makes good fellowship.

Mutual obligations improve and continue friendship.

20. Give you an use, and you'll call't a custom.

Spoken when they, who have before received kindnesses
from us, importune for more, or when they who have been
permitted to intrude upon our interest, would continue so
to do.

Eng.—An ill custom is like a good cake, better broken
than kept.

21. ᵉ Geily is sing ᶠWallowways brother.

Spoken when we.ask how a thing is done, and are answered gaily, that is, indifferently, as if indifferent was next to bad.

22. Give you meat, drink, and cloaths, and you'll beg
work among your friends.

Spoken to lazy lubbers, who love idleness better than work.

23. Gone is the goose, that the great egg laid.

The man is dead who had the fund; spoken when people
expect that from us, which, by reason of some benefactor's
death, we are disabled to give.

24. God keep me from the man that has but one thing
to mind.

Because he will mind that thing to purpose. Spoken by

ᵈ Frogs.   ᵉ Indifferently.   ᶠ A word of lamentation.

great men, when poor people importune them about some special interest, which they have at heart.

25. Geer is easier gotten, than guided.

It may be gotten by chance, or inheritance, but must be guided by discretion.

Lat.—Non minor est virtus, quam quærere, parta fœri.

Casus inest illic, hic erit artis opus.

26. God send you the world you bode, and that's neither hunger nor scant.

Spoken when people speak magnificently, and liberally.

27. God be with the good Laird of ᶠ Bamagee, that took never more from a poor man than he had.

Spoken when we have gotten all from poor debtors that they could give, though not all they owed. The Laird of Balmaghie was a good man, and took any thing from his tenants that they could spare.

28. God doth not measure men by inches.

People of small stature may have stout hearts.

29. Gentle servants are poor men's ʰ hardship.

Because the conceit of their birth, and blood, will make them despise and neglect your service. Spoken also by way of merry excuse when a gentleman proffers to do you some mean service.

30. ᶦ Good your ᶦ common to kiss your ᵏ kimmer.

Spoken to them whom we see do service, or shew kindness to them, to whom they have great obligations.

31. God help you to a ᶦ hutch, for you will never win to a ᵐ mealing.

A disdainful repartee of a maid, to an unworthy courtier; meaning that he may be content with a meaner match.

32. Good to fish in muddy waters.

A cursed saying, of them who expect to find their private interests in the public disturbance.

33. Good ale need no wisp.

A wisp of straw stuck upon the top of a country house is a sign that ale is to be sold there: But if the ale be good, people will haunt the house, though there be none. Apply'd when we would signify that a thing, excellent in its self, need but little recommendation. Translated from the Latin.

Vino venali non opus est suspensâ hederâ.

ᶠ Spell'd Balmaghie.   ʰ Ruin.   ᶦ You have great obligations.   ᵏ The pot companion.   ᶦ Cottage.   ᵐ Farm.

34. Good chear, and good cheap, makes many haunt the house.

Eng.—Where men are well used, they'll frequent there.

35. God's help is nearer than the fair even.

God's immediate providence may sooner assist us, than any second causes, that we can propose.

36. Good will should be taken for part payment.

When people do their utmost to satisfy their debts, or repay kindnesses, it were a pity to urge them farther.

37. God never sends the mouth, but the meat with it.

Spoken to those that grudge their having many children.

38. ᵐ Girn when ye bind, and laugh when ye lose.

When people shew force and activity they grin: bind your sacks with care and cunning, and, at the journey's end, you will laugh to see them all safe.

39. Give a carle your finger, and he'll take your whole hand.

Suffer an unmannerly fellow to intrude upon you, and he will intrude more and more.

40. Good kail is half meat.

Good broth will, in some measure, supply the want of bread.

41. Give your own sea ⁿ maws your own fish guts.

If you have any superfluities give them to your poor relations, friends, or countrymen, rather than to others.

42. Give a greedy man a great bone.

Give a covetous man something that is bulky, although it be not so good. Spoken jocosely when we give a thing big in quantity, though coarse.

43. Good forecast makes work easy.

To forecast and contrive how a thing may be best done, and to lay in materials for the doing of it, is the way to make work go on apace.

44. 'Gree like dogs.

Ironically forbidding children to fall out about their meat.
Like dogs that snarl about a bone,
And play together when they have none.

45. ° Gaunting bodes wanting, one of three,
    Meat, sleep, or good company.

When people yawn they are either hungry, sleepy, or solitary. I have heard it more roguishly express'd.

ᵐ Grin.   ⁿ Gulls.   ° Yawning.

H

46. Get your spindle and ᴾ roke ready, and God will
send you ᑫ tow.

Use proper means, and depend upon God for the blessing.

47. Gentry sent to the market will not buy a peck of
ˢ meal.

Spoken when a bare gentlewoman is proffered in marriage
to the son of a wealthy yeoman.

48. Go hop and hang your self, and then you'll die
dancing.

An impertinent ill-mannered by-word.

49. Gape while you get it.

Spoken to those who expect a thing without reason.
Eng.—He that gapes till he be fed,
May gape till he be dead.

50. Great gains makes work easy.

Be sure! and will make workmen nimble, and busy.

51. Good memories have ill judgments.

Spoken to them who call to mind a past thing, at an unseasonable time, or before improper company.

52. Gar wood is ill to grow.

A return to them that say they will gar, that is, force you
to do such a thing; as if they would find it a hard task.

53. Go thy way, lad, and give thy wife nothing.

An exclamation when we pretend to admire some silly saying, or thing: and it will hit patter if the person has been
boasting of what he did, or designs to do.

54. Give a thing, and take a thing,
Is the ill ʳ man's ˢ goud ring.

A cant among children, when they demand a thing again,
which they had bestowed.

55. God send us something of our own when other folk
goes to their meat.

Spoken when we are disappointed of something that we
would have borrowed.

56. God send you more wit, and me more silver, for
we have both need of it.

Spoken when people propose, or say, what we think foolish
and improper.

57. God ᵗ sain your eye man.

Spoken when you commend a thing without blessing it,

ᴾ Distaff.　　ᑫ The coarse of flax.　　ʳ The devil's.
ˢ Gold.　　ᵗ Bless.

which my countrymen cannot endure, thinking that thereby
you will give it the blink of an ill eye: a senseless, but common, conceit. If the person commending be an unworthy or
inferior fellow, they will say, Dee'l be in your een, and a pickle salt togither.

58. God send us all to do well, and then have hap to
meet with * seil.

A sort of discontented wish, when we are suspicious that
some of us will not do well.

59. Give a going man a drink, and a rising man a
knock.

If a man's occasions call him away from company, make
him drink before he go: but if any rise up to breed a quarrel, knock him down.

60. Give it about, it will come to my father at last.

A young fellow was sitting in company with his father, who,
upon some provocation, gave him a blow; who immediately
gave his left hand man as much, and bad him give it about.
Spoken when we would have some ill turn done to some body,
but not immediately by our self.

61. Give my cousin kail ᵛ enow,
And see my cousin's dish be ʷ fow.

A senseless ridicule of servants to a poor relation, when he
comes to his rich friend's house.

62. Gentlemen are wondrous scarce, when a webster
gets a lady.

Spoken when we hear that a man pretends to an unlikely
and unequal courtship.

63. ˣ Gee ways, as ʸ Geily pish'd.

A senseless bauble when a thing is crooked, or looks awry.

64. God comes with leaden feet, but strikes with iron
hands.

Eng.—God is slow a coming, but strikes sure.

Lat.—Raro antecedentem scelestem deseruit pœna, pede
claudo.

65. God keep my tongue, for my tail was never.ᶻ sicker.

Intimating that you could say something, but that you
think it better to hold your tongue.

66. ᵃ Gaunting goes from man to man.

Spoken when we do a foolish thing in imitation of others.

Lat.—Oscitante uno, deinde oscitat et alter.

Salvation. ᵛ Enough. ʷ Full. ˣ Toward one side.
ʸ A woman's name. ᶻ Sure, staunch. ᵃ Yawning.

H 2

67. Give is a good man, but he is soon weary.

Men are soon weary of always giving, and receiving no return. Whereas giff gaff is good fellowship.

68. Good to fetch sorrow to a sick wife.

Spoken to them that stay long, when sent an errand.

69. Guess'd work is the best, when it is right done.

Because it saves the trouble of taking dimensions, but it is seldom well done. Spoken when a thing we did at a venture hit right.

70. God takes care of fools, and drunken men.

Taken from the strange escapes that both these sort of people meet with.

Eng.—Drunken people seldom take harm.

71. Good reason, and part of cause.

An ironical approbation of some foolish saying, action, or design.

72. Greedy folk has long arms.

People will make strange shifts, to get what they have a desire for.

73. God puts his best jewels in his finest cabinets.

As if handsome persons should have the greatest virtues.

74. Give a strong thief a stark name.

A ridicule upon the hard names that doctors give their remedies, as if Album Græcum, and Radix graminis were some fine things.

75. God keep the cats out of your way, for the hens can flie.

Spoken with disdain to them that threaten what they will do, when we know they dare do nothing.

76. God sends fools fortunes.

Eng.—Fortune favours fools.
Lat.—Fortuna favit fatuis.

77. Good to be merry and wise.

Spoken when people's mirth borders too much upon folly.

78. Good wares make a quick market.

79. Good watch prevents harm.

Lat.—Satius est initiis mederi, quam fine.

80. Give losing gamesters leave to talk.

Suffer men who have had losses and wrongs, to express their resentments.

81. God sends meat, and the dee'l cooks.

A passionate expression, when our meat is ill dress'd.

82. Good to begin well, better to end well.

83. Go to bed with the lamb, and rise with the [b] laverock.

This proverb was not invented by a courtier, or a rake.

84. Good words cost nothing.

And therefore may be the freelier given.

85. Great bodies move slowly.

Spoken of the deliberations of parliaments; and other great
assemblies, or in jest to them that go slowly on in their business.

86. God help the poor, for the rich can help themselves.

87. God help the rich, for the poor can beg.

The first of these is spoken in case of famine or scarcity of
bread. The second in case of publick disturbances.

88. Give a dog an ill name, and he'll soon be hang'd.

Spoken of those who raise an ill name on a man on purpose
to prevent his advancement. A cursed, but common, practice.

89. Good folks are scarce, you'll take care of one.

Spoken to those who carefully provide against ill weather,
or cowardly shun dangers.

90. Gray ey'd greedy, brown ey'd needy, black eye
never [c] blinn, till it shame all its een [d] kin.

Like the rest of the physiognomical observations, foolish,
and groundless.

91. Give her her will or she'll burst, quoth the good
man when his wife was [e] dinging him.

Spoken jocosely, upon wilful and perverse people.

92. God's will be done; but dee'l [f] bedrite the [g] spee-
man.

Spoken when people predict ill things to us.

H.

1. Help is good at all plays, but at meat.

And very good there too, if the entertainer be hearty, and
the table plentiful.

2. [h] Hooly and fair, goes far in a day.

Working constantly, though soberly, will dispatch a great
deal of business.

Eng.—Soft and fair goes far journeys.

---

[b] Lark. [c] Blind. [d] Kindred. [e] Beating. [f] Beshite.
[g] Fortune-teller. [h] Softly, quietly.

Item.—He that goes softly, goes safely.

Lat.—Da spatium, tenuemque moram: male cuncta ministrat.

Impetus.

3. He that is ill to himself, will be good to no body.

Qui sibi nequam, cui bonus?

4. He lov'd mutton well, that lick'd where the ewe lay.

Spoken to them, who will sip the bottom of a glass where good liquor was, or scrape a plate, after good meat.

Eng.—He lov'd mutton well, that dip'd his bread in wool.

Lat.—Certe extrema linea amare, haud nihil est.

5. He that never eat flesh, thinks a pudding a ⁱ dainteth.

A man not us'd to what is good, thinks much of what is indifferent.

6. He that gets his geer before his wit, will be short while master of it.

For want of sense and discretion to manage it.

Eng.—A fool and his money is soon parted.

7. Highest in court nearest the ^k widdie.

Witness the fatal fall of many courtiers.

8. He's a good horse that never stumbled,
   And a better wife that never grumbled.

Both so rare, that I never met with either: from the Latin.

Lat.—Bonus equus qui nunquam cespitet.

Item.—Bonus quandoque dormitat homerus.

9. Horses are good of all hues.

Eng.—A good horse never had an ill colour.

10. He that counts all the pins in the plough, will never yoke her.

11. He that counts all costs, will never put the plough in the ^l erd.

Both these signify that he that forcasts all difficulties, that he may meet with in his business, will never set about it.

Lat.—Quid tam dextro pede concipis, ut te conatus non poeniteat.

12. Hunger thou me, and I'll ^m harrie thee.

If servants get not their meat honestly and decently, they will neglect their master's business, or embezzel his goods.

ⁱ A fine bit.   ^k Gallows.   ^l Earth.   ^m Ruin.

Lat.—Equus suo defraudatus pabulo, ignavus est.

13. He that ⁿ speers all, gets but wit of part.

A repulse to curious impertinents, who are too busy at their questions.

14. He that has a mickle nose, thinks every body is speaking of it.

People that are sensible of their guilt, are always full of suspicion.

Lat.—Conscius ipse sibi, de se putat omnia dici.

15. Hunger is good ^o kitchin meat.

The same with the English, Hunger is good sauce. Both from the Latin.

Optimum condimentum fames.

Lat.—Latrantem stomachum bene leviet, cum sale, panis.

16. He sleeps as dogs do, when wives bakes; or when wives sift meal.

Apply'd to those who pretend to be asleep, or unconcern'd, who are all the while making their remarks.

17. Hunger is hard for a heal maw.

18. Hunger will break through hard stone walls.

Eng.—Hungry dogs will eat dirty puddings.

Lat.—Molestus interpellator venter.

19. Hang him that has no shifts, and hang him that has too many.

He that has no shift, is not worth hanging; and he that has too many, may be hang'd in time.

20. He is worth gold, that can win it.

Spoken to them who grudge the thriving condition of some neighbour, his decent apparel, or plentiful estate.

21. He that ows the cow, goes nearest her tail.

Every man is busy, and careful, about his proper interest.

22. He was the bee, that made the honey.

Spoken when a man is dead, whose industry procur'd what his family now enjoys.

23. He that follows ^p freets, freets will follow him.

He that notices superstitious observations (such as spilling of salt, Childermass day, and the like) it will fall to him accordingly.

Lat.—Multi ad fatum venere suum, dum fata timent.

ⁿ Asks.   ^o Whatever eat with bread, or take to make coarse meat go down, we call kitchin; as butter to bread, and milk to stir about, &c.   ^p Superstitious observations.

24. He that hews above his head, may have the
   ᑫ speal fall in his eye.

He that aims at things above his power, may be ruined by
his project.

Lat.—Dum petit infirmis, nimium sublimia pennis,
   Icarus, Icariis nimia fecit aquis.

25. He that hath but one eye, must look well to
   that.

Spoken when a man hath but one thing of a kind, and
therefore shy to lend it.

26. He that lives on hope, hath a slender diet.

Lat.—Qui spe aluntur pendent, non vivunt.

27. He's a ʳ sory good man, that's no mist.

The loss of the head of a family is considerable, be he
never so mean.

28. He that shews his purse, bribes the thief.

The English say, Longs to be rid of it.

29. He comes oftener with the rake, than the ˢ sho'el.

Spoken of a poor friend, whose business is not to give us,
but to get from us.

30. He may well swim that's held up by the chin.

Spoken of the thriving condition of those, who have some
to support, assist, and raise them.

31. He that sleeps with dogs, must rise with fleas.

If you keep company with base and unworthy fellows, you
will get some ill by them, or learn some ill from them.

32. His life, but not his honour, feal'd.

Spoken of those who bravely die in a good cause.

33. He that will not be counsell'd, cannot be help'd.

Spoken when your wholesome advice is rejected by a wilful, and obstinate man.   Vis consilii expers mole ruit sua.

34. He may ill run that cannot go.

In vain he attempts an uneasy task, who is not equal to an
easy one.

35. He goes away in an ill time that never comes
   again.

Spoken when we express our hope to see our friend, who is
gone from us.

36. He must rise early, that deceives the ᵗ tod.

Spoken to those that think to out-wit a cunning fellow,

ᑫ Chip.   ʳ Poor.   ˢ Shovel.   ᵗ Fox.

37. He that falls in the dirt, the longer he lies the fouler he is.

Spoken to those who lie under a slander, urging them to get themselves clear'd as soon as they can.

38. He that wrestles with a turd, fall he undermost or uppermost, he'll be sure to be bedirten.

Intimating the folly of contending with vile, or mean persons, by whom no honour is to be gotten.

Lat.—Demit honorem æmulus ajaci.

Item.—Hoc scio pro certo, ego si cum stercore certo,
Si vinco, aut vincor, certe ego maculor.

39. He's well worth sorrow, that buys it with his silver.

Spoken to them that have been at some pains, to inconvene themselves.

40. He that ᵗ lacks my mare, would buy my mare.

Buyers commonly discommend what they have a mind to; apply'd when a man discommends a maid, whom he would gladly marry, if he could get her.

41. He that seeks trouble, it were a pity he should miss it.

Spoken to, and of, quarrellers, who commonly come by the worst.

42. Had I wist, quoth the fool, or, beware of had I wist.

Spoken when people say, Had I wist what would have been the consequence of such an action, I had not done it.

Lat.—Stulti est dicere non putarem.

43. He fells two dogs with one stone.

Spoken when a man with one and the self same pains, effects two different businesses.

Lat.—Eadem fidelia duos parietes dealbare.

44. He's a proud horse that will not bear his own ᵘ provan.

An excuse for doing our own business ourselves; and it hits patter, if it belong to our own trade, profession, or way of living.

45. ᵛ Hae lad, and run lad.

Give ready money for your service, and you will be sure to be well served.

ᵗ Discommends.   ᵘ Provender.   ᵛ Here, take.

46. Hand in use is father of [w] lear.

Use in doing a thing acquires a habit, and that makes things be done easily, and readily.

Lat.—Usus adjuvat artem.

Item.—Fabricando fabrisimus.

Item.—Solus & artifices qui juvat usus adest.

47. He that has a dog of his own, may go to the kirk with a clean briest.

48. He is well eased, that has ought of his own.

He is best serv'd who has his own to do his own turn with.

49. He that has a goose, will get a goose.

A man that is wealthy, will be sure to get gifts, whereas he that is poor, will remain so.

50. His wit got wings, and would have flown,
    But poverty did keep him down.

Eng.—He would fain fly but he wants feathers.

Lat.—Haud facile emergunt quorum virtutibus obstat.
    Res angusta domi.

Item.—Sæpe sub attritâ, latitat sapientia, veste.

51. [x] Hame is a [y] hamely word.

Eng.—Home is seemly, if it was never so homely.

Item.—Better dry bread at home, than roast meat abroad.

Item.—The smoke of my own house is better than the fire of another's.

Lat.—Domus amica, domus optima.

Item.—Domi suæ quilibet rex.

52. He that's far from his geer, is near his [z] tinsel.

A man may be soon wrong'd when his back is turn'd.

53. He rode [a] sicker that never fell.

A man has gone through the world with a strange even hand, that never committed a blunder.

Eng.—It is a sound head that has not a soft piece in it.

Lat.—Nemo omnibus horis sapit.

54. Hall [b] binks are [c] sliddery.

Great men's favour is uncertain.

Lat.—Favor aulæ incertus.

Eng.—Hasty climb, suddain fall.

---

[w] Learning.   [x] Home.   [y] Familiar, easy, pleasant, it differs from homely in the English, which is coarse.
    [z] Loss.   [a] Sure.   [b] Benches.   [c] Slippy.

55. He's worth no well, can bide no wo.

Eng.—He deserves not the sweet, that will not taste the soure.   From the Latin,

Dulcia non meruit, qui non gustavit amara.

56. He that ^d tholes overcomes.

Lat.—Tandem patientia vincet.

57. He that will not thole, must fit many a hole.

58. He had need to have a heal ^e pow,
    That calls his neighbour nitty ^f know.

A man ought to be free of those faults that he throws up to others.

Lat.—Quis tulerit Gracchos, de seditione querentes.

59. ^g Hae will a deaf man hear.

Lat.—Allatoris adventus semper est gratus.

60. Hap, and a half-penny, is world's geer enough.

Lat.—Si fortuna volet, fies de rhetore consul.

61. He hides his meat, and seeks more.

Spoken when covetous people pretend poverty; and conceal their wealth, to plead pity.

62. He that deceives me once, shame fall him; if he
    deceives me twice, shame fall me.

It is my own blame if I trust a man again, that has deceived me once.

63. He would not sup kail with him, unless he broke
    the dish on his head.

A disdainful answer to them who compare our friend to some unworthy inferior fellow.

Lat.—Indignus, qui illi matulam porrigat.

64. He's free of fruit that wants an orchard.

Spoken to them who tell how free and liberal they would be, if they had such things, or were such persons.

65. He speaks in his drink, what he thought in his
    drouth.

Eng.—What sobriety conceals, drunkenness reveals.

Lat.—Quod in corde sobrii, more ebrii.

66. He bears with his heels, as the geese do in har-
    vest.

That is he heard, had he been pleased to answer.

67. He that's feard of a fart, should never hear
    thunder.

---

^d Suffers patiently.   ^e Head.   ^f A little hill full of nits.
^g Here take.

68. He that's [h] redd for windle straws, should not pish in [i] lays.

Spoken to those who are afraid of small, and far distant dangers. To the same purpose the English have several. As,

He that's afraid of every grass should not piss in a meadow.

He that's afraid of leaves should not come into a wood.

He that's afraid of the wagging of feathers must keep from among wild-fowl.

He that's afraid of wounds must keep from a battel.

69. Hope holds up the head.

Lat.—Vivere spe vidi, qui moriturus erat.

70. He will not lye where he's slain.

Spoken of timorous people, as if their corpse would flee from the place where they should be kill'd.

71. He knows what side his bread is butter'd on.

That is, he knows well where his interest lyes.

72. He [k] tarrows early that tarrows on his kail.

The Scots, for their first dish have broth (which they call kail) and their flesh-meat, boil'd or roasted, after. Spoken when men complain before they see the utmost that they will get.

73. He that gets forgets, but he that gives thinks on.

Spoken when you see a man, to whom you have been beneficial, careless of your interest and concern.

74. He will shoot higher that shoots at the moon, than he that shoots at the midding, though he never hit the mark.

Spoken as an encouragement to noble designs and endeavours.

75. He was scarce of news that told his father was hang'd.

Spoken to them that say something, that may tend to the disparagement of themselves, or family.

76. Hair and hair makes the carles head bare.

An estate may be ruined by small diminutions.

Lat.—Paulatimeve illitur cauda equina.

77. He's very full in his own house, that may not pick a bone in his neighbours.

An answer to him, who being bid to eat, excuses himself,

---

[h] Fear'd.   [i] Unploughed-land.   [k] To tarrow is to complain of meat as if it was too little.

because he had eaten at home. Though I have heard it more roguishly apply'd.

78. He's a wise bairn that kens his own father.

. If he be a Scottish man, their law says, Pater est quem nuptiæ monstrant. If English, let him but enquire, whether his mother's husband was within the four seas, when he was begotten; and if he was, he is his father, though he had been in Cathness, and she in Cornwal at the same time.

79. He streaks [1] ream in my teeth.

Spoken when we think one only flattering us, and not earnest, nor sincere in what they pretend.

Lat.—Os mihi oblinit.

80. He cares not whose bairn greet if his laugh.

Spoken of selfish people, whose endeavours terminate upon, and center in, themselves.

81. He that has one sheep in the flock, will like all the rest the better for it.

Spoken when we have a son at such a school, university, army, or society, we will wish the prosperity of these respective bodies, upon his account.

82. He's a silly man that can neither do good nor ill.

83. He can do ill, and he may do good.

Both used as a dissuasive from disobliging any, even the meanest, for sometime or other it may be in his power to do you service, or disservice.

84. He that marries a widow, and two daughters, has three back doors to his house.

85. He that marries a widow, and two daughters, marries three [m] stark thieves.

Because his wife will put things away to them, or for them.

86. He that has a wide [n] theim, had never a long arm.

Gluttonous people will not be liberal of their meat.

87. He's a hawk of the right nest.

He is like those he came of, always taken in an ill sense.

88. He's a [o] sarry cook that may not lick his own fingers.

Apply'd satyrically to receivers, trustees, guardians, and other managers. Signifying that they will take a share of what is among their hands. •

---

[1] Cream.   [m] Errant, very.   [n] Gut.   [o] Poor, mean.

89. He that well bides well betides.

He that waits patiently, may come to be well serv'd at last.
Lat.—Habent parvæ commoda magna moræ.

90. He left his money in his other breeks.

A taunt to him that wants money to pay his reckoning.

91. He's poor whom God hates.

A surlish return to them who, tauntingly, call us poor.

92. He eats the calf in the cow's belly.

Apply'd to them who spend their rent before it be due.
Eng.—He spends the Michaelmas rent in the midsummer moon.

93. He's o'er-shot in his own bow.

Eng.—He's beaten at his own weapon.

94. He should be ᴾ sindle angry, that has few to ᵠ mease him.

Eng.—He that has none to still him, may weep out his eyes.

95. He that has a wife, has a master.

He that's not sensible of the truth of this proverb, may blot it out, or pass it over.
Eng.—He that has a fellow-ruler, has an over-ruler.
Lat. ———— Vendes
    Hac obstante nihil, nihil, hæc si nollet, ematur :
    Hæc dabit affectus.

96. He that goes a borrowing goes a sorrowing.

He is a young house-keeper, or very well furnished, who knows not this to be true.

97. He's but Jock the laird's brother.

The Scottish lairds concern and zeal for the standing and continuance of their families, makes the provision for their younger sons very small.

98. Hungry stewards wear many shoon.

Because they bring so little at a time, they must go oft again for more.

99. He that never rode never fell.

Eng.—Nothing venture, nothing have.

100. He that talks to himself speaks to a fool.

Because none but fools will do so.

101. He was wrap'd in his mother's sark tail.

The Scots have a superstitious custom of receiving a child, when it comes to the world, in its mother's shift, if a male; believing that this usage will make him well-beloved among

ᴾ Seldom.   ᵠ Settle, please, still.

women.   And when a man proves unfortunate that way, they
will say,

102. He was [r] kep'd in a board-cloth; he has some
   hap to his meat, but none to his wives.

103. He that steals can hide.

Yes, and forswear too, a discouragement to search stol'n
goods.

104. He gets his kail in a [s] riven dish.

Spoken of them who are not much regarded.   For if his
broth be put in a split dish, he will get little good of them.

105. He that invented the [t] maiden, first [u] hanseled it.

Viz. James Earl of Morton, who had been for some years
governour of Scotland: but was afterwards cruelly, and unjustly, run down by a party, as many have been since.

Lat.—Nec lex est justior ulla.

   Quam necis artifices arte perire sua.

106. He that's not used to a sword, leaves't where
   he shites.

Spoken when people, advanced above their former condition, forget something proper to their station.

107. He's no wise man who cannot play the fool by a
   time.

Eng.—No man can play the fool so well as the wise man.

Lat.—Misce consiliis stultitiam brevem.

   Dulce est decipere loco.

108. He'll wag as the bush wags with him.

That is, he will comply with all changes of times, and
parties.

109. He that will to [v] Cowper, will to Cowper.

A reflection upon obstinate persons that will not be reclaim'd.

110. He is gone out of the [w] Cheswell he was made in.

A reflection upon persons who perk up above their birth,
and station.

Eng.—The priest forgets that ever he was a clerk.

Lat.—Majores nido pennas extendit.

111. He that would eat the fruit must climb the tree.

—112. He that would eat the kirnel must crack the nut.

Eng.—No pains, no gains.

Item.—No sweat, no sweet.

---

[r] Received.   [s] Split.   [t] An engine to behead people.
[u] Got the first of it.   [v] A town in Fife.   [w] Cheese-fat.

Lat.—Nil sine magno vita labore dedit mortalibus.

113. He has a sliddery gripe that has an eel by the tail.

Spoken to them who have to do with cunning fellows, whom you can hardly bind sure enough.

114. ˣHa'd your hand, your father slew a ʸ whaap.

115. Henry Cherk never slew a man till he come at him.

Both a ridicule upon them that threaten hard, and dare not execute. The last refers to him who threatens an absent person.

116. Had you such a shoe on every foot, you would ᶻ shochel.

A scornful return of a woman to a fellow that calls her she, and not by her name: she and shove hath both the same accent in Scotch.

117. Hawnkering, and hinging on, is a poor trade.

Spoken of the miserable condition of those who depend upon great men's promises, for places and preferments.

Eng.—He that waits on another man's trencher eats many a late dinner.

118. He that woos a maid, must come ᵃ sindle in her sight.

He that woos a widow must woo day and night.

I know nothing either of the truth, or reason of this proverb: they have another to that purpose.

119. How was Rome ᵇ bigged.

An answer to them that ask how such a thing will be done, intimating, that time and industry will do any thing.

120. Have you geer, have you none, ᶜ tine heart and all is gone.

Spoken to dissuade people from desponding in any case.

121. He that is first on the ᵈ midding, may sit where he will.

He that comes first has commonly the best choice.

122. ᵉ Hareships ᶠ sindle come single.

Spoken when one hardship comes upon the back of another.

123. ᵍ Heal sail is good sail.

ˣ Hold. ʸ Curlew. ᶻ Shove your foot along. ᵃ Seldom.
ᵇ Built. ᶜ Lose. ᵈ Dunghill. ᵉ Misfortunes. ᶠ Seldom.
ᵍ Whole.

It is good merchandising when we can put off all our wares in one bulk. Spoken jocosely when we take all that is before us.

124. He that strikes my dog, would strike myself if he durst.

Spoken with resentment to them who injure any thing that belongs to us. The English say in a benign sense, Love me and love my dog.

125. He that has not silver in his purse, should have silk on his tongue.

He that cannot pay his debts should at least give good words.

126. He that cannot make sport, should mar none.

127. He that's ill of his lodging, is well of his way-kenning.

Spoken when I ask my neighbour a loan, and he tells me that he cannot, but such an one can.

128. He never wrought a good [h] dark, that went grumbling about.

129. Half acres bears good corn.

Alluding to the half acre given to the herd, and commonly spoken in gaming, when we are but half as many as our antagonists.

130. He was never pleased with his work, who said, Now, when he had done with it.

Now, at the having done a thing, is a word of discontent.

131. He has cowp'd the mickle dish into the little.

The jest is in the different signification of the word cowp, which signifies to buy and sell grain, cattel, &c. and to turn one thing upon another. Spoken when people have fa'n behind in dealing.

Eng.—He has brought his noble to nine pence, and his nine pence to nothing.

Lat.—Ab equis ad asinos.

132. He can say [i] jo, and think it no.

That is, he can pretend kindness, where he has none.

133. He that drinks when he's no dry, will be dry when he gets no drink.

134. He had need to be twice skill'd, and once ground, that deals with you.

---

[h] Day's-work. [i] A word of flattery for joy.

I 3

Spoken to cunning sharpers, as if you would say, he had need to be well vers'd in business that will deal with you, and not be over-reach'd.

135. Hereafter comes not yet.

136. Hearken to the hinder end of it.

Both these are spoken when we suspect that such a project, or action, will have an ill consequence.

137. He that laughs when he's alone, will make sport in company.

Intimating that such an one is a fool.

138. He that's first up, is not always first serv'd.

Eng.—Desert and reward seldom keep company.

139. He has a hole under his nose that will never let him be ᵏ rough.

140. He has some wit, but a fool has the guiding of it.

It is known that wit and good sense may be separate. Spoken of them that have some flashes of wit, but want discretion.

141. He took the bog ˡ aslent.

I do not apprehend the expression, but the meaning is, he made his escape.

142. He has left the key in the cat hole.

143. He has left the key under the door.

144. He has taken a moon light flitting.

145. He has gone without taking his leave.

146. I wot not what he has done with his tripes, but he has taken his heels.

These five are only proverbial phrases, to signify that a man has run away for fear of his creditors: the last I heard only in Ireland, I suppose it is not used in Scotland.

147. Had I fish was never good to eat mustard.

An answer to them that say, Had I such a thing, I would do so, or so.

148. He must have leave to speak, who cannot hold his tongue.

Spoken against impertinent and indefatigable baublers.

149. He that trusts to ᵐ bon ploughs, will have his land lye ⁿ lazy.

150. He that is angry without a cause, must ᵒ mease without amends.

ᵏ Plentiful.   ˡ Run it diagonal ways.   ᵐ Borrowed.
ⁿ Fallow.   ᵒ Settle.

151. He that eats while he brusts, will be the worse while he lives.

A jocose return to them that urge us to eat.

152. He that borrows and bigs, makes feasts and thigs, drinks and is no dry; none of these three are thrifty.

153. He's a proud P tod that will not scrape his own hole.

A reproof to them who refuse to do their own proper business, or an excuse in them that do it.

154. He's o'er early up that is hang'd e're noon.

A jest upon them that boast of their early rising, or an excuse for them that lye long.

155. He loves me for little, that hates me for nought.

Spoken to those who are much displeased, upon a small provocation.

156. He is not the fool that the fool is; but the fool that with the fool deals.

Spoken against wanton boys, when they are playing upon an ideot.

157. He's a poor beggar that cannot go by one door.

Spoken to them that threaten never to do you service.

158. He's not the best q wright that casts the manyest r speals.

A return of a man that wants children, to him that upbraids him with it.

159. He that ill does, never good weens.

Lat.—Malus suspicax.

160. He that will not when he may, shall not when he will.

161. He that will not when he may,
    When he will he shall have nay.

Both spoken who refused a good offer, and then would have it again.

162. He will soon be a beggar, that cannot say nay.

Because people will make a prey of his liberal temper.

163. He had need of a long spoon that sups kail with the dee'l.

He that has to do with wicked and false men, had need to be cautious, and on his guard.

P Fox.   q Carpenter.   r Chips.

164. He that ᶠtheiks his house with turds, will find
   more teachers than reachers.

He that is engag'd in a difficult, and troublesome business,
will have more to give him their advice, than their assistance.

165. He that looks not e're he ᵗloup, will fall e're he
   wit.

A man without reasonable caution will meet with unfore-
seen inconveniences.

Eng.—Who looks not before will find himself behind.

166. Haste makes waste.

The English is the reverse.   Soft fire makes sweet malt.

Lat.—Qui nimium properat, serius absolvit.

167. He that marries a ᵘdaw eats mickle dirt.

168. He that marries e're he be wise, will die e're he
   thrive.

For want of skill to manage a family, he will put himself
so far behind, that he will not easily recover.

169. ᵛHaind geer helps well.

Eng.—A penny sav'd is a penny got.

170. He that sits on a ʷstane, is twice ˣfain.

That is, glad to sit down, because he is weary, and glad to
rise, because the stone is hard.

171. He that does his turn in time, sits half idle.

Because he is master of his business:

172. He goes long bare foot that wears dead men's
   ʸshoon.

Spoken to them who expect to be some man's heir, to get
his place, or wife, if he should die.

173. Honesty is no pride.

Spoken to them that go too careless in their dress; intimating, that it is no sign of pride to go decently.

174. He that fishes before the net, long e're he fish get.

Spoken to those who devour by expectation, what they have
not in possession, for the fish are not gotten till the net be
drawn ashore.

175. He never tint a cow, that ᶻgrat for a needle.

It is a token that a man had never a great loss, who is im-
moderately griev'd for a small one.

Lat. —— — Flagrantior æquo
   Non debet dolor esse viri, nec vulnere major.

ˢ Thatches.   ᵗ Jump.   ᵘ A slut.   ᵛ Sav'd.   ʷ Stone.
      ˣ Glad.   ʸ Shoes.   ᶻ Cry'd.

176. He that has no geer to tine, may have shines to pine.

He that has done a misdemeanour, if he be not able to pay a fine, may be put to corporal punishment. I have heard it pply'd by covetous creditors, to their insolvent debtors; but put in execution, it is vile, cruel, and ungodly.

177. He sits fow still who has a riven breck.

A man who is not very clamorous in his complaints, may lie under as great inconveniences as they that do. It took its rise from the Earl of Angus, who being in an engagement, and there wounded, stayed till all his men were drest, and then told them that he was wounded himself, by repeating this proverb.

178. He that does bidding, serves no dinging.

An apology, when we are told that we are doing a thing wrong, intimating that we were bid to do so.

179. He that blows best, bear away the horn.

He that does best, shall have the reward and commendation.

Lat.—Rex eris, si recte feceris.

180. He is sorest ᶻ dung whom his own wand ᵃ dingth.

A man is worst punished, when he bears the effects of his own folly.

181. He will never go well, for he was foundred in his feet.

Taken from horses; applied to them who have had an ill grounding in the beginning, whether in reading, or any other part of learning: where having laid the first foundation ill, the superstructure seldom proves firm, or solid.

182. He is well ʰ boden ᶜ there ᶜ benn, who will neither borrow nor lend.

A man must be well furnished indeed who needs not borrow, and will not lend.

Eng.—He may be contented, who needs neither borrow nor flatter.

183. He that has a good crop, may be ᵈ doing with some thistles.

If a man hath had a great deal of good conveniences, he may bear with some misfortunes.

184. He that pays last never pays twice.

Spoken in jest to one who is loth to pay his reckoning, as if it was out of a principle of prudence.

ᶻ Beaten.   ᵃ Beats.   ᵇ Furnished.   ᶜ In his house.
ᵈ Bears with.

185. He is deaf on that side of his head.

Spoken of those who like not, and therefore take no notice of, your proposals.

186. He will not give an inch of his will, for a span of his thriest.

Spoken of wilful and obstinate people, who will not comply with your most advantageous proposals, if contrary to their perverse humours.

187. He may be trusted with a houseful of unbor'd mill-stones.

That is, only with what he cannot carry away.

Eng.—I'll trust him no farther than I can throw him.

188. He can lie as fast as a dog can lick a dish.

189. He is not so dast, as he lets on him.

Spoken of knavish rogues, who pretend to be foolish when they have their interest in their eye.

190. He has turn'd his cloak on the other shoulder.

He has chang'd his side, party, or interest. The English say, He has turn'd cat i'the pan: the reason of which expression I do not know.

191. He's an Aberdeen's man, he may take his word again.

I do not know the original of this proverb. The people of that city say, that we mistake it, that it had its rise from a merchant in Dantzick, who having been never cheated by an Aberdeen's man, said that he would take an Aberdeen's man's word again; but in the mean time, we may apply it to them who deny what they have said.

192. He stumbled at a straw, and leap'd o'er a bink.

Spoken of them who are scrupulously doubtful about a small thing; and yet have large consciences in things of a higher nature: who will not say faith or truth, and yet will not stand to defraud the king of his revenue, of which I know many; like the pharisees, of whom our Saviour says, that they strain at a gnat, and swallow a camel.

193. He's a meer ᵉ cutchin carle, for all his manly looks.

Spoken of hectoring bullies, who look fierce, but yet are mere cowards at the bottom.

194. He has one face to God, and another to the devil.

Eng.—You carry two faces under one hood.

Item.—Laugh in my face, and cut my throat.

Lat.—Aliorum medicus, ipse ulceribus scates.

ᵉ Coward.

Lat.—Pelliculam veterem retines, & fronte politus.

Astulam vapido goras sub pectore vulpem.

195. [f] Hae is half full.

Having. abundance makes peoples stomachs less sharp, and craving ; whereas the sense and apprehensions of want, makes people more anxious, and solicitous.

196. He's a proud beggar that makes his own alms.

Eng.—Beggars should not be chusers.

197. Hanging goes by hap.

Eng.—Marriage and hanging goes by destiny.

198. He has't a kind, he [g] cost it not.

Spoken when people take after their parents in ill things.

199. He gave no green barley for it.

To the same purpose.

200. He has [h] fault of a wife, that marries [i] mam's [k] pet.

Maids that have been much indulg'd by their mothers, and have had much of their will, seldom prove good wives.

201. He was as hard with me, as if I had been the wild Scot of Galoway.

That is, he dealt with me rigorously and severely.

202. Happy is the wooing that's not long a doing.

There are Scottish proverbs downright opposite to this. As, a hasty meeting, a hasty parting. I must own, that I have seldom seen an oft interrupted courtship, or a suddain match, prove comfortable, or prosperous.

203. He that's [l] shor'd to death, should have a fart for his dead bell.

Spoken by stout men, when they are told of some man's threats, as if they were not much afraid.

204. Had I as mickle black spice, as he thinks himself worth of mice-dirt, I would be the richest man of my kin.

Spoken satyrically of proud beaus, whom we suspect to be highly conceited of their own worth.

205. He was worse [m] flay'd than hurt.

206. He kens his groats in other folks kail.

Spoken of those who are sharp and sagacious in knowing their own.

207. He will not give his bone to the dog.

208. He will not give the head for the washing.

---

[f] Here take.   [g] Bought.   [h] Need.   [i] Mam's.
[k] Darling.   [l] Threatened.   [m] Frightened.

Both these spoken of sturdy people, who will not readily part with their interest, or be bullied out of it.

209. He may grow better, but he cannot be worse.

Spoken of them who are extremely wicked, or extremely sick.

Eng.—If ever he alter it will be for the better.

210. He may laugh that wins.

Spoken when people laugh at your loss, or trouble.

Lat.—Tu rides, at ego ringor.

211. He rides with a sark tail in his teeth.

Spoken when a new married man has been abroad, and makes haste home.

212. He dare not say, Bo to your blanket.

That is, he dare not offer you the least injury.

213. He spoke to me as every word wo'd lift a dish.

That is, with great storm, and sturdiness.

214. He that spends his geer before he gets it, will get but little good of it.

He that spends his rent before it be due, will always be needy and penurious.

215. His purse and his palate are ill met.

Spoken when a poor man loves to eat good meat.

216. He that rides er'e he be ready, wants some of his grath.

Apply'd to him who goes about a business without proper tools to accomplish it.

217. Honesty keeps the crown of the [a] casway.

An honest man has nothing to be asham'd of, and so cares not whom he meets.

Eng.—Truth and oil are ever above.

Lat.—Veritas non quærit angulos.

218. He that laughs at his own jest, mars all the mirth of it.

219. Happy go lucky.

That is, let the fortunate get the fortunate share. Spoken when people venture upon an uncertain project.

Eng.—Happy man be his dole.

220. He came of the good, he cannot be ill.

A commendation of the good son of a good father.

Lat.—Dos est magna parentum virtus.

221. He is not the happiest man that has the most geer.

Worldly happiness requires many other ingredients as well

---

[a] Street.

as wealth, viz. Health, a good fame, a sound mind, and good relations: and, if any one of these be wanting, the whole composition is spoil'd.

Lat.—Non possidentem multa vocaveris recte beatum.

222. He has an ill look among lambs.

Apply'd to wanton young fellows casting an eye to the girls; alluding to a superstitious fancy among the Scots, that an ill eye may do harm; which opinion seems to be as old as Virgil,

Nescio quis teneros oculus mihi fascinat agnos.

223. He is wise that is wary in time.

That is, who foresees harm before it come, and provides against it.

Eng.—Take heed is good read.

224. He that gives all his geer to his bairns,
Take up a beetle, and knock out his [o] harns.

Taken from the history of one John Bell, who having given his whole substance to his children, was by them neglected; after he died there was found in his chest a mallet with this inscription,

I John Bell, leaves here a [p] mell, the man to fell,
Who gives all to his bairns, and keeps nothing to himsell.
Eng.—He that gives his goods before he be dead,
Take up a mallet and knock him on the head.
Item.—Keep your staff in your own hand.

225. He will go to hell for the house profit.

Spoken of them that will do any thing for gain.

Lat.—Quocunque modo rem.

226. [q] Heigh how is heavy some,
An old wife is [r] dowisome,
And courtesy is cumbersome,
To them that cannot shew it.

The whole is for the sake of the last, viz. that people who are not used to good breeding, and mannerly behaviour, perform it very untowardly.

227. He could eat me [s] but salt.

228. He loves no beef that grows on my bones.

Both these signify that the man hates me vehemently.

229. He that eats a boll of meal in bannocks, eats a peck of ashes.

That sort of bread is bak'd in the ashes.

---

[o] Brains. [p] Maul. [q] An interjection of sorrow.
[r] Tedious. [s] Without.

230. He has soon done that never ᵗ dought.

Spoken of weakly and feeble people, when they cannot perform what they have taken in hand.

231. He looked as if butter would not have melted
in his mouth.

Spoken of roguish fellows, who upon occasion, and design,
look and speak demurely.

232. Here comes John Black, and Gilbert Ram on
his back.

Spoken when we see black clouds portending rain.

233. He has the better end of the string.

That is, he has the advantage in this cause.

234. He shall either ᵘ girn, or man ᵛ fin.

Spoken in case of slander, that he that uttered it, shall give
his author, or be punished for it himself.

235. He gave me whitings, ᵚ but bones.

That is, he gave me fair words. The Scots call flatteries
whitings, and flatterers white people.

236. He would go a mile to flit a sow.

Spoken of sauntring persons, who would take any pretence
to go from their proper business.

237. He that will not hear Mother Hood, shall hear
Step-mother Hood.

That is, they who will not be prevail'd upon by fair means,
shall meet with harsher treatment.

238. He that is welcome fares well.

An apology for giving to, or receiving from, a hearty friend,
an ordinary entertainment.

Lat.—Super omnia vultus accessere boni.

239. Hotch, and help your self to get your bairns.

A senseless answer to them that bids us help them.

240. He that forsakes measure, measure forsakes him.

That is, he who is immoderate in any thing, design, or action, shall meet with treatment accordingly.

241. He that has two hoards, will get a third.

A man that has once got a stock, will find it an easy matter
to encrease it.

Lat.—Scilicet improbæ crescunt divitiæ.

242. He that is born to be hang'd, will never be
drown'd.

ᵗ Had ability.   ᵘ Grin.   ᵛ Fine.   ᵚ Without.

Spoken when ill persons escape some imminent danger, as if they ow'd their life to the gallows.

243. Happy man, happy * kevel.

Jocosely spoken when people are drawing lots, or when it has faln out well with us, or our friend.

244. Handle the pudding while it is hot.

That is, set about a business with care, while the present opportunity offers.

245. He's a weak horse that ⁊ dow not bear the saddle.

Spoken to them who complain that they cannot wear such a weighty suit as is offered them.

246. He has wit at will,
That with an angry heart can hold him still.

247. He that shames let him be ᶻ shent.

An old Scottish proverb not now used, scarcely understood; a wish that he who exposes his neighbour, may come to shame himself.

248. He knows not a B by a bull's foot.

That is, he is illiterate.

249. He who meddles with quarrels, gets the ridding stroke.

Solomon says, He that meddles with a strife that belongs not to him, is as if he took a dog by the ears.

Eng. He that blows in the dust will fill his eyes.

250. ᵃ Ha'ds a', quoth the herd's wife, kiss me first; for I am farrest from home.

A senseless bauble signifying no more so that we are all content.

251. Here's to you all, ᵇ arse ᵇ o'er ᵇ head, as the moor-bride drank to her maidens.

A comical jocose saying when we drink to the whole company.

252. He is a sowter, who sits on your nose and drites in your mouth.

A bitter reflection upon them that call a shoemaker Sowter, a word that they cannot abide.

253. He thinks himself no page's peer.

That is, he thinks no body comparable to himself.

254. Hell will never be full till you be in it.

ˣ Lot.....⁊ Is not able to. ᶻ Blam'd. ᵃ We are all content. ᵇ One with another.

A bitter reflection upon them who are covetous, or very malicious.

255. He help'd me out at a dead lift.

That is, he gave me a seasonable assistance in a proper time.

256. He is old, and cold, and ill to lye beside.

Spoken by a young maid, when jeer'd with an old man.

257. He is neither so old, nor yet so cold, but you may heat your nose in his nether end.

A satyrical return to the former proverb.

258. ᶜ Hout your dogs, and bark your self.

A sharp return to those that say, Hout, to us, which is a word of contempt; in Latin, apage!

259. ᵈ Hareship in the Highlands, the hens in the corn,
    If the cocks go in it, will never be shorn.

An ironical outcry upon a small loss.

260. He would fain have a fool, that makes a fool of himself.

261. He that has a full purse, never wanted a friend.

262. He that ows the mare, ows the bear.

Spoken when a man's own people, or cattel, do him harm.

263. He that has a mind to strike a dog, will never want a stick.

If a man resolves to do his neighbour a mischief, he will never want means to effect it.

Eng.—To him that wills, ways will not be wanting.

Lat.—Malefacere qui vult, nunquam non causam inveniet.

264. He lay in his scabbard, as many a good sword has done.

That is, lay with his cloaths on, did not strip and go to bed.

265. His horse got a bite of a cold bridle.

That is, got neither hay, nor oats.

266. He'll get enough one day, when his mouth's full of ᵉ mools.

Spoken of covetous people, who will never be satisfied while they are alive.

267. He has feathered his nest, he may flye when he will.

ᶜ A word used to dogs to make them give over barking.
    ᵈ Misfortune.   ᵉ Earth, mould.

Spoken of them who have had a good place so long, that they have gotten estates.

268. He had a finger in the pye.

That is, he had some concern in the matter as well as others.

269. He vapours like a ^f tike in a tedder.

A ridicule upon a swaggering, conceited young fellow.

270. Happy is she who marries the son of a dead mother.

There is rarely a good understanding between a daughter in law, and her husband's mother.

Lat.—Desperanda tibi salvâ concordia socru.

271. He is cooling, and supping.

That is, he has nothing, but from hand to mouth.

272. Honesty may be dear bought, but can never be an ill pennyworth.

For it will be sure to make a man a gainer at the last.

Lat.—Lætius, est quoties magno sibi constat, honestum.

273. He sits above that deals acres.

An appeal to the Divine Providence, justice and omniscience.

274. Hang hunger, and drown drouth, let the dog lick the cat's mouth.

Spoken jocosely when we deal liberally.

275. Hunting, and hawking, and paramours,
For one joy, hath a hundred displeasures.

This is in the old Scottish Collection, I have not heard it used. It signifies the mischief of unseasonable recreations, and unlawful pleasures.

Eng.—He that steals honey, should beware of the sting.

276. He is good that fail'd never.

A persuasion to bear the neglects of a friend, who has on other occasions been beneficial to you.

277. Hot love, hasty vengeance.

The love that's too violent, will not last long.

Lat.—Nihil vehemens durabile.

278. Heard you the crack that that gave.

Spoken when we hear an empty boast, or a notorious lye.

279. He that gives all, would give nothing.

When we ask a share of what one has, if they give us all, we alledge that it was in a pet, and with a grudge.

---

^f An old dog.

x 3

280. He'll not get leave to snoke where she pishes.

Spoken with disdain, when it is said such a man is courting such a woman, much his superior.

281. He that spends his geer upon a whore,
Both shame, and skathe, he must endure.

282. He is wise that knows when he's well enough.

That is a pitch of wisdom to which few attain.

283. His old brass will buy you a new pan.

An encouragement to a young woman to marry an old wealthy man: because his riches will get her a new husband, when he shall dye.

284. Ha'd your feet ᵍ luckied addie, old folk are not ʰ feery.

A foolish bauble when people stumble.

285. He never said an ill word, nor did a good thing.

Spoken of people who do not want sense, but are ill managers.

286. Hopers go to hell.

Spoken when they, whom we are reproving for their carelessness, and negligence, say they hope to do well enough.

Eng.—Hell is full of good meanings and good wishes.

287. He's well away, if he bides.

Spoken when we are glad to be quit of an ill man's company.

288. How came you and I to be so great.

Spoken when our inferiors are too familiar with us.

289. How by your self, burn'd be the mark.

The Scots when they compare person to person, or limb to limb, will say, Blist be the mark. This is spoken when other people throws up to us, what we think agrees better to themselves, and, instead of the blessing, add this imprecation.

290. He that refuses a groat for a crack, a horse for a
start, or a wife for a fart, will never be well
monied, well horsed, or well wived.

If a man will buy or have nothing but what is free from all imperfection, he must want.

291. He got his mother's ⁱ malison, that day.

Spoken of him that has got an ill wife.

292. He will never send you away with a sore heart.

Spoken of those who are ready at their promises, but slow in their performance.

ᵍ Grandfather.　ʰ Nimble.　ⁱ Curse, malediction.

293. He will get the poor man's answer.

That is, a flat denial; spoken when it is said that such a man will court a woman, whom we suspect he will not get.

294. He that's angry, is [k] sindle at case.

His impatient temper keeps him always on the fret.

295. He that loves law, will get his fill of it.

For such are sure of two things, an uneasy life, and a broken fortune.

296. Humph, quoth the dee'l, when he clip'd the sow,
A great cry, and little [l] woo.

Spoken of great pretences, and small performances.

Lat.—Parturiunt montes, nascetur ridiculus mus.

297. He'll let nothing go to the [m] odd for want of looking after it.

Spoken of scraping, careful people.

298. He that marries a maiden, marries a pokeful of pleasure,

299. He that marries a widow, marries a pokeful of [n] pleas sure.

These two are always joined together, and are a dissuasive from marrying a widow, because she is often involved in law-suits.

300. Here to day, and away to morrow.

Intimating the uncertainty of mortal life, and indeed of all sublunary things.

301. He owes me a day's shearing, the longest in harvest.

Spoken of one to whom I have done a signal good turn.

302. Had it come in your arse, you would have gone to the midding with it.

Spoken in anger to them, who, being ask'd why they did, or said such a thing, say, it came in my head.

303. He will think his breeks a burthen.

That is, he will be heartily wearied with such a thing.

304. He that has gold may buy land.

Lat.—Potentes potenter agunt.

305. He's a gentle horse that never [o] cust his rider.

He is a good servant that never disobliged his master.

306. Had you been in the midding, you would not have seen that.

---

[k] Seldom.   [l] Wool.   [m] Be lost.   [n] Law-suits.   [o] Threw.

Spoken with resentment when people say they saw such or such a thing, that was undecent.

307. He that speers all opinions comes ill speed.

Because their different advices will confuse, and distract him.

308. He that forecasts all perrels, will win no worship.

Because he will be frightened from any noble attempt.

309. He is but ᴾ daft that has to do, and spares for every speech.

These three last (as several others in this book) are taken out of an ingenious Scottish book, call'd, The Cherry and the Slae; a book so commonly known to Scottish men, that a great share of it passes for proverbs. It is written in native genuine Scotch, and, to them who understand it, very fine and taking.

310. He's a fool that marries his wife at � Yule.

For when the corn's to sheer, the bairns to bear.

If a woman be got with child in Christmas, it is like that she may lye in in harvest, the throngest time of the year.

311. He gives no other milk.

An answer to them that say you work your horse too sore, since his work is all that you will get of him.

312. He owes a pudding to the ʳ glade.

Spoken of a poor weak beast which we suspect to be a dying.

313. He is gone to seek his father's sword.

Spoken of idle vagrants who go a travelling without any good or worthy design.

314. He has nothing to crave at my hand.

Eng.—I have as good as I got.

Lat.—Par pari retuli.

315. Here the geer, but where's the money.

A proverbial exclamation, upon the shewing of any fine thing.

316. He that knows what will be cheap, or dear,

Need not be a merchant, but for a year.

Because in that year he will gain enough. Spoken of the uncertainty of prices, and markets.

317. He that liveth well, liveth long.

Because he has attain'd all the ends of living.

ᴾ Foolish.　　ᴠ Christmas.　　ʳ Kite.

Lat.—Ampliat ætatis spatium sibi vir bonus, hoc est, vivere bis, vità posse priore frui.

318. He is lifeless that's faultless.

Lat.—Nemo sine crimine vivit.

Item.—Nam vitiis nemo sine nascitur.

319. He was never a good ⁸ aver, that ᵗ flung at the ᵘ brod.

Spoken to them who spurn at reproof, or correction, whom Solomon calls brutish.

320. He that will cheat in play, will not be honest in earnest.

Eng.—Fair is fair, work or play.

321. He that does you an ill turn, will never forgive you.

The sense and conscience of his injustice, or unkindness, will make him still jealous of you, and so hate you.

322. He that may not as he will, must do as he may.

Lat.—Ut quimus, quando ut volumus non licet.

323. He that is mann'd with boys, and hors'd with colts, will have his meat eaten, and his work undone.

Because the boy will neglect his business, and the horse will throw him.

324. He that's not handsome at twenty, strong at thirty, wise at forty, rich at fifty, will never be handsome, strong, wise, or rich.

I have pass'd all these terms, and have never yet had any of these qualifications. De me conclamatum est.

325. He that looks with one eye, and winks with another,

I will not believe him, though he was my brother.

If the man naturally squint, my countrymen have an aversion to him, and all who have any thing disagreeable, if he wink, or nod, they look upon him to be a false man.

326. Half a word to a wise man.

Lat.—Verbum sapienti sat est.

327. He's a fool that forgets himself.

Lat.—Qui sibi nequam cui bonus?

328. He's a wise man who

When he's well, can hold him so.

---

⁸ Work-horse.　　ᵗ Winched.　　ᵘ Goad.

There are not many such men, for the mind of man is insatiable, either of wealth, or honour.

329. He [v] gangs early to beg, that cannot say nay.

Because men will make a prey of his liberal disposition.

330. He begs of them that borrowed of him.

Spoken of the man who by his liberal, or squandering temper, has ruined his estate.

331. He has mickle prayer, but little devotion.

Spoken of those men who make great pretences to religion, but shew little of it in their practice, of whom I have known many.

332. He has an eye in his neck.

Spoken of wary and cautious people.

333. Help, for help in harvest.

That is, help me now, and I will help you on your throngest occasions.

334. He sees an inch before his nose.

That is, he is a wary and cautious man.

335. He must needs run, whom the devil drives.

336. Hens are free of horse corn.

Spoken of those who are free of what is not their own.

337. He that counts [w] but his hostess, counts twice.

For men reckon their debts neither so many, nor so great, as really they are.

Lat.—Non respondet opinioni calculus.

338. His heart is in his hose.

Lat.—Cor in genua cecidit.

339. Happy the son, whose father goes to the devil.

Intimating that great estates are gotten by usury, or other ill arts.

Lat.—Omnis dives, aut iniquus est, aut iniqui hæres.

340. He that hath his hand in the lyon's mouth, must take it out as well as he can.

He that is under the distress of a severe person, must extricate himself as well as he is able.

341. He has gotten the boot, and the better horse.

That is, he has gotten the advantage in the exchange.

Lat.—Diomedes cum glauco permutavit.

342. He that once gets his fingers in the mud, can hardly get them out again.

---

[v] Goes. [w] Without.

Spoken of them who take a humour to building.

343. He may find fault that cannot mend.

Lat.—Carpet citius, aliquis, quam imitabitur.

344. He that does evil, hates the light.---Scripture.

345. He that speaks the thing he should not, shall hear the thing he would not.

Lat.—Si pergat ea quæ vult dicere, quæ non vult audiet.

346. He is not a merchant bare,
That hath either money, worth, or ware.

A good merchant may want ready money.

347. He has his nose in every man's turd.

Eng.—He has an oar in every boat.

348. He woos for cake and pudding.

Spoken when people pretend courtship, to promote another interest.

349. He counts his half-penny good silver.

That is, he thinks much of himself with little reason.

350. He that's born under a thrippenny planet, will never be worth a groat.

351. He is a wise man who
Can make a friend of a foe.

352. He would fain be forward if he wist how.

Spoken of pert aspiring fellows.

353. He that wears black must carry a brush on his back.

354. His arse makes buttons.

Spoken of him who is in a terrible fright, or as they say, Dirt flay'd.

355. He that plays more than he sees, forfeits his eyes.

An excuse for over-looking an advantage at game.

356. He that buys land, buys stones ;
He that buys beef, buys bones ;
He that buys nuts, buys shells ;
He that buys good ale, buys nought else.

357. He is poor that cannot promise.

358. He put it out of my eye, and into my arse.

That is, he conceal'd it out of my sight, but apply'd it to my profit; spoken when servants steal corn to feed their master's horse, or such like.

359. He that sells wares for words, must live by the loss.

Spoken when a man refuses to sell a trust.

360. He has spur metal in him.

361. He's of a ^{x} carie temper.

Both spoken of those who are soft and lazy.

362. He that kisses his wife at the market cross, will
have many to teach him.

Spoken when people are officiously instructing us in doing
what we are about.

363. He is upon his high horse.

Spoken when people fall into a passion.

364. He has more wit in his little finger, than you
have in your whole hand.

365. He plays least in sight.

Taken from a game at cards so call'd, that is he keeps himself conceal'd.

366. He looks like a wild cat out of a bush.

Spoken of him that looks fiercely and with anger.

367. He got the knights bone off her.

Intimating that he debauch'd her before she was married.

368. He look'd to me like the far end of a French
fiddle.

That is, with disdain and contempt.

369. He is gone off at the nail.

Taken from scissors when the two sides go asunder, means
that he is gone out of all bounds of reason.

370. Ha'd your hands off other folks bairns, till you
get some of your own.

Spoken by a girl, when a young man offers to teaze her.

371. He'll be a man before his mother.

Spoken to ill grown children.

372. He never lies, but when the ^{y} hollen is green.

Meaning that he lies at all times.

373. Have a care of the cattel.

An ironical caution upon a feign'd danger.

374. He has broken his face on the ^{z} ambry.

Spoken of bluff, fat cheek'd boys.

375. He is dead now, and it is better for me to eat of
him, than lie on him.

Intimating that it is a heinous sin to tell a lie of a dead
man, who cannot vindicate himself.

Lat.—Cum mortui non mordent, iniquum est ut mordeantur.
Item.—De mortuis, & absentibus, nil nisi bonum.

---

^{x} Soft like flummery. ^{y} Holly. ^{z} Cup-board.

376. He wats not whether he bears the earth, or the earth him.

Spoken of excessive proud people.

377. He'll put o'er the borrowing days.

Spoken upon some hopes of our sick friend's recovery; taken from weak caitel, who if they outlive the first nine days of April, we hope they will not die.

378. He's no steel to the back.

An allusion to iron tools, and signifies either that he is not thoroughly honest in his behaviour, or not firm in his health.

379. He that has an ill wife should eat mickle but'er.

The jest is in the identity of the pronunciation of butter and but her, that is, without her.

380. He rides not ay when he saddles his horse.

Spoken of them who make great pretences to haste, but yet linger long enough.

381. He'll pish i'the wisp.

I do not know the ground, or reason of the phrase: but it signifies that such an one will not thrive in that trade, business, or office that they have taken in hand. And answers to the English, He'll come home by weeping cross.

382. He has left his pack in Weakfield (Wakefield).

This is apply'd to those youths whom we send to England, to be pedlars, when they come home broken.

383. He has swallowed a flie.

Spoken of sots who are always drunk, as if there was a fly in their throat which they endeavoured to wash down.

I.

1. It is good to have our *coag out, when it rains kail.

It is good to be in the way when things are a going.

Eng.—It is good to make hay while the sun shines.

2. If you will not take what I will give you, take what you brought with you.

You brought nothing with you, so take what I give you, or want.

3. If you was as skitterfull as you are scornful, you would ᵇ file the whole house.

A bitter return to those who are too liberal of their taunts.

ᵃ Dish. ᵇ Dirty.

4. Ill won, ill c ward.

Eng.—Ill gotten ill spent.

Lat.—Male parta male dilabuntur.

5. Ill doers, ill d deemers.

6. He that ill did, never good e ween'd.

. Both these are very well express'd in that excellent English proverb, The old woman had never sought her daughter in the oven, if she had not been there herself.

: Lat.—Qui sibi male conscii, alios suspicantur.

7. Ill will never spoke well.

When people are known to have an aversion to any person, or party, what they say of them, must be received with some abatement. Or as we say, Cum grano salis.

Eng.—Where love fails we spy all faults.

8. It is a sore f dung bairn, that may not g greet.

. They are under great awe, that may not complain. Spoken when people take it ill, that we dare to complain of their hard, and severe usage.

9. I have seen more snow on one h dike, than now on seven.

. Spoken when people say they have seen things cheaper, dearer, better, or otherways: intimating that things, times, prices and seasons, are liable to change.

10. It is a tale of two drinks.

It is a thing that requires deliberation; at least as long as the glass may go twice about.

11. If you be not ill, be not ill like ;

If you steal not my kail, break not my dike.

Eng.—He that would no evil do,

Must do nought that's like thereto.

12. It is ill to be call'd a thief, and ay found i piking.

It is ill to have a bad name, and often found in a suspicious place, or posture.

Eng.—A dog that licks ashes, trust him not with meal.

13. If I cannot k kep goose, I'll k kep goslin.

If I cannot work my revenge upon the principal author of my injury, I will upon his children, relations, or friends.

14. It is good to have two strings to one's bow.

Eng.—Two anchors are good, as I have been told,

If one anchor breaks, the other may hold. .

---

c Laid out. d Suspecters. e Thought, believed, supposed. f Beaten. g Cry. h Ditch. i Picking. k Catch.

15. It is too late to spare, when the bottom is bare.

Lat.—Sera est in fundo parsimonia.

16. It is ill halting before cripples.

It is hard to put tricks upon them, who are as well vers'd in these things as yourself.

17. It's an ill pack that's no worth the custom.

It is a bad thing that is not worth any small pains, or cost that it may require.

Eng.—Forsake not the market for the toll.

18. I will never drite in my bonnet, and set it on my head.

I will never make a whore of the woman that I resolve to marry, or marry the woman I have made a whore of.

19. If wishes were horses, beggars would ride.

20. It is ill ¹ kitchin that keeps the bread away.

We may make the best of what we have, though not all we wish for: as if one should say, I have bread to give you, but nothing to eat with it? We answer, Let us have the bread however.

21. It is fair before the wren's door, where there is nothing within.

An answer to them who tell us that their house or doors are not clean enough, as if we should say you have children, cattel, and things going out and in.

22. If one sheep ᵐ loup o'er the ⁿ dike, all the rest will follow.

Shewing the influence of evil example.

23. If you had been another, I would have denied you at the first word.

Jocosely spoken when we give a flat denial.

24. I wish you had drunk water, when you drank that soup driuk.

Spoken when people say something out of the way; upon a jocose supposition that they are drunk, or they would not say so; sometimes they will say,

25. I wish you wist what you said.

Eng.—I wish you had never said that word.

26. It is ill to bring out of the flesh, that is bred in the bone.

It is hard to leave those ill customs to which we have been long inured.

ᵗ Any thing that we eat with bread. ᵐ Jump. ⁿ Ditch.

L 2

Lat.—Difficile est relinquere, quibus diu assueveris.

27. If you call me scabbed, I'll call you scal'd.

Lat.—Dixerit insanum qui me totidem audiet.

28. It is a true dream, that is seen waking.

It is easy to guess what appears plain and evident.

29. If I cannot do by might, I'll do by slight.

If I dare not attack my enemy openly, I'll do him an injury in a private and clandestine way.

Lat.—Ingenio pallet, cui vim natura negavit.

30. I am o'er old a cat, to draw a straw before my nose.

That is, I am too old to be imposed upon. A young cat will jump at a straw drawn before her, but not an old one; nothing being more playful than a young cat, and nothing more dull than an old one.

Eng.—Old birds will not be taken with chaff.

31. It is ° tint that is done to old men and bairns.

For the old men will die, and the children forget.

Lat.—In senem beneficiam ne contuleris.

32. It is well said, but who will bell the cat.

The nobility of Scotland entered into a conspiracy against Spence, the favourite of King James the 3d. It was proposed to go in a body to Stirling, to take Spence and hang him, and then to offer their service to the king as his natural counsellors. The Lord Gray says, It is well said, but who will bell the cat; alluding to the fable of the mice proposing to put a bell about the cat's neck, that they might be apprised of her coming. The Earl of Angus answered, I will bell the cat; which he effected, and was ever after call'd Archibald bell the Cat. The proverb is us'd when a thing of great difficulty is propos'd.

33. If you can spend much, put the more to the fire.

That is, if you have a great income spend accordingly. Some have it, Put the more to the fore, that is, lay up the more, and do accordingly.

34. It is a ᴾ sary hen that cannot scrape to one ᑫ bird.

Spoken of them that have but one child to provide for.

35. It is a ᴾ sary flock, where the ewe bears the bell.

It is a bad house where the wife commands. Though there are some such houses in the world.

36. I would not take a bite of his bed strow, for the love of his person.

A saucy answer of a maid, when told of a sweetheart whom she pretends to contemn.

° Lost.   ᴾ Poor.   ᑫ Chicken.

37. It is good baking beside meal.

That is, People may do well enough, when they have some to uphold and supply them.

38. If it will be no better, it is well that it is no worse.

Lat.—Est quoddam prodire tenus, si non datur ultra.

Item.—Contenti simus hoc catone.

39. It is a sary brewing, that's no good in the ʳ newing.

Spoken when people are much taken with new projects.

40. It is well ˢ hain'd, that is ˢ hain'd off the belly.

Spoken by them who are more fond of fine cloaths than good meat; as also, by penurious saving people, who are pleas'd how savingly they can put by a meal.

41. It is little of God's might, to make a poor man a knight.

Lat.—Si fortuna volet; fies, de rhetore, consul.

42. It is an ill bargain, where no man wins.

Lat.—Flet victor, victus interiit.

43. I have given a stick to break my head.

Heu patior telis, vulnera facta, meis.

44. I have other tow on my ᵗ roke.

Eng. —I have other fish to fry.

45. If one will not, another will; the ᵘ morn's the market day.

46. If one will not, another will; so are all maidens married.

The world was never so dull, but if one will not another will.

Lat.—Invenies alium, si te fastidit Alexis.

47. I'll sell my lad, quoth ᵛ Livistone: I'll buy't, quoth ᵛ Bamagee.

If a man have a good pennyworth to sell, he will still find a buyer.

48. I will say nothing, but I will ʷ yerk at the thinking.

49. I will keep my mind to my self, and tell my tale to the wind.

50. I will do as Mackissock's cow did, I'll think more than I'll say.

These three are to the same purpose, and signify that I will, at present, conceal my resentments; but I will watch an opportunity for retaliation.

ʳ When it is new. ˢ Sav'd. ᵗ Distaff. ᵘ To-morrow.
ᵛ The title of two lairds, the last is spell'd Balmaghie.
ʷ Be busy.

L.3

Lat.—Manet altâ mente repostum..

51. I have a good bow, but it is in the castle.

Spoken to them who say that they have a thing very proper for that business, but it is not at hand.

Eng.—All is not at hand that helps.

52. It is ill to take breeks off a bare arse.

Eng.—Where nothing is, nothing is to be had.

Lat.—Quid quæso erripias nudo.

53. It is needless to bid a wood man run.

Spoken when people urge us to hasten, when we are doing all that we can.

Lat.—In planitiem equum provocas.

54. I like his room, better than his company.

55. It eith crying ˣ Yule, under another man's stool.

The words are hardly sense; but it is spoken when we see people spend liberally, what is not their own.

56. I know your meaning by your mumping.

I know by your motions and gestures what you would be at, and what you design.

Lat.—Nutis signisque loquuntur.

57. If marriages be made in heaven, some had few friends there.

An answer of him that has an ill wife, to them who say, Marriages are made in heaven.

58. I wo'd be very loth, and ʸ scant of cloth, to sole my ˣ hose with dockans.

59. I will never ᵃ lout so ᵇ leagh, and lift so little.

60. I had better kail in my ᶜ coag, and never gave them a catch.

These three last are returns of a haughty maid, to them that tell her of an unworthy suitor. The latter alludes to an art among the Scottish reapers, who, if their broth be too hot, can throw them up into the air, as they turn pancakes, with-out losing one drop of them.

61. I cannot sit, and run, and pish, and gather ᵈ speals.

Spoken when we are bid to do many things at once.

Lat.—Simul sorbere, & flare, est difficile.

Item.—Non omnia possumus omnes.

62. If the doctor cures, the sun sees it ; but if he kills, the earth hides it.

ˣ Christmas.   ʸ Scarce.   ᶻ Stockings.   ᵃ Stoop..
ᵇ Low.   ᶜ Dish.   ᵈ Chips.

Spoken to dissuade ignorant people from quacking, because they cannot kill with license, as doctors may.

63. It will be a good fire when it burns, quoth the tod when he pish'd on the ice.

Nothing but a ridicule upon a bad fire.

64. It's a bare ° moor that you'll go o'er, and no get ' prick to your ' blanket.

Spoken of getting, scraping fellows, who will be making something of every thing.

65. It is long to Lammas.

Spoken in jest, when we forget to lay down bread at the table, as if we had done it designedly, because it will be long e'er new bread come.

66. If you take my fair daughter, take her foul tail.

If you get some great advantage, take some small inconveniences that may attend it.

67. If it will not be a good shoe, let it go down i'the heel.

If a thing would not do as you would have it, do the next best with it.

68. If you had all the wit in the world, fools wo'd ' fell you.

Spoken disdainfully, to them that think themselves very wise.

69. If the lad go to the well against his will, Either the cann will break, or the water will spill.

Spoken when people mismanage a business, that they were forc'd to go about against their mind.

70. It is ill to waken sleeping dogs.

It is foolish to stir up a quarrel, that has been long forgot; or provoke a person, to whom you are not a match.

Lat.—Irritare canem noli dormire volentem.

71. If the laird slight the lady, so will all the kitchin-boys.

If people despise their own, so will other persons.

72. I will never put the carle above the gentleman.

Spoken when we offer ale to them that have been drinking claret.

73. It is a poor kin, that has neither whore nor thief in it.

74. It is a sary wood, that has never a withered bough in it.

° Heath.   ' A bodkin to pin your cloth about you.
      ' Knock you down.

Both these spoken when some of our relations, who have done an ill thing, is cast in our teeth.

75. It is a ʰ soure ⁱ reek, where the good wife ᵏ dings the good man.

A man in my country coming out of his house with tears on his cheeks, was ask'd the occasion; he said, There was a soure reek in the house; but, upon farther inquiry, it was found that his wife had beaten him

76. It is a sore ⁱ field, where all is slain.

Spoken when we have something remaining, after a great loss.

77. If strokes be good to give they are good to get.

Spoken to those whom we beat for beating of others.

78. If you brew well, you'll drink the better.

If what you have done be good, and right, you will find the effects accordingly.

Eng.—Hot sup, hot swallow.

Item.—Every bird must hatch its own egg.

Item.—Even as you brew, so let you bake.

Lat.—Tute hoc in tristi, tibi omne exedendum est.

79. Ill hearing makes wrong rehearsing.

Spoken when we hear one give a wrong account of a matter of fact.

Eng.—Misunderstanding brings lies to the town.

Eat.—Judicium reddit verum, narratio vera.

80. It is a good poor man's blade, it will bow e're it break.

Spoken commonly of an ill-tempered knife, that will stand as it is bent, or the like.

81. Ill bairns are best heard at home.

A discouragement to extravagant boys, who are fond of travelling.

Lat.—Fœlix qui propriis, ævum transegit, in arvis,

Ipsa domus puerum, quem vidit, ipsa senem.

82. I'll take no more of your counsel, than I think mete for me.

An answer to them that advise in jest.

83. It may betrue that some men say; but it must be true that all men say.

84. It is not the cowl that makes the frier.

Lat.—Cuculla non facit monachum

85. It is fair in hall, where beards wag all.

ʰ Bitter.   ⁱ Smoke.   ᵏ Beats.   ˡ Battel.

Spoken when we give a share of what is going to every body, that all may eat alike.

86. If you love me, ^m kythe that.

If you have a value for me, shew it by your deeds. When one professeth kindness for another, he will answer, What says the bird? alledging that there is a bird whose note is Kythe that.

Eng.—He is my friend who grinds at my mill.

87. It is a ⁿ thrawn fac'd bairn that is gotten against the father's will.

Kindness extorted comes always with an ill grace.

88. If you be angry, ^o claw your ^p weime.

89. If you be angry, sit ^q leagh and ^r mease you.

Both these spoken to them whose anger we value not.

Eng.—If you be angry, turn the buckle of your belt behind.

90. I brought him off the moor for God's sake, and he begins to bite the bairns.

Spoken when they whom we have supported make unhand-some and unthankful returns.

Eng.—He has brought up a bird to pick out his eyes.

Item.—Put a snake in your bosom, and it will sting when it is warm.

91. I'll make a shift, as Macwhid did with the preaching.

Alexander Macwhid was a knowing countryman, and a great stickler for the king and church, in the time of the late anarchy. At the Restoration, clergymen being scarce, Bishop Taylor ask'd him if he thought he could preach; he answered that he could make a shift; upon which he was ordain'd, and got a small living near Lisburn. The proverb is spoken when we promise to do as well as we can.

92. ^s Juck, and let a ^t jaw go o'er you.

That is, prudently yield to a present torrent.

Lat.—Is sapiens, qui se ad casus accommodat omnes.

93. It was never ill said, that was not ill ^u ta'n.

Intimating that we had no ill design in what we said, only the man took it ill.

94. It is good to be sure, quoth the miller, when he ^v moultered twice.

---

^m Make it appear.   ⁿ Distorted.   ^o Scratch.   ^p Belly.
^q Low.   ^r Settle.   ^s Down with your head.   ^t A wave.
^u Taken.   ^v Took the tool.

Eng.—He that leaves certainty and sticks to chance,.
When the fool pipes, he shall dance.

95. It's a ᵂ sary collop that's got off a capon.
One cannot take much where there is but little.

96. I'll serve you all with one met vessel.
That is, I'll serve you all alike, or rather I will give nothing
to any of you.

97. It is no sin to sell dear, but a sin to give ill measure.
When you sell the buyers are on their guard, but measures.
and weights are left to your conscience.

98. It is no more sin to see a woman greet, than to
see a goose go barefoot.
Eng.—A woman laughs when she can, and cries when she
will.

Lat.—Uberibus semper lachrymis, semperque paratis.
In statione sua, atque expectantibus illam,
Quo jubeat manare modo.

99. It's a good goose that's ay dropping.
It is a good friend that is always giving; spoken to dissuade us from too much importuning a friend.

100. Ill gotten goods will not enrich the third heir.
Eng.—Ill gotten goods seldom prosper.
Lat.—De male quisitis non gaudet tertius hæres.

101. I'll get a better ˣ lorspeaker than you, for nought.
Spoken to them whom we expected to favour us, and yet
appear against us, and our interest.
Eng.—You are good to help a lame dog o'er a stile.

102. If it be a fault, it is no ʸ farlie.
Spoken in excuse for doing a thing, bad indeed, but common, and usual.

103. It is a good sport that fills the belly.
Spoken when people eat heartily, and pretend to be in jest.
Though I have heard it more roguishly apply'd.

104. I have lick'd my self clean.
Spoken when one has managed a bad bargain, so as not to
lose by it.

105. It is a shame to eat the cow, and ᶻ worry on the
tail.
It is a shame to perform a great task all but a little, and
then give over.
Lat.—Turpe, devorato bove, est hærere in cauda.

ᵂ Poor.   ˣ Advocate, proctor.   ʸ Miracle.   ᶻ Choak.

106. It is a good world, if it hold.

Spoken to them who take their ease and pleasure now without respect to their future condition.

107. It is a good world, but they are ill that are on't.

The word world is sometimes taken for the universe, and sometimes for mankind; in the first sense it is good, in the second bad.

108. It is ^a eith to learn you a good use.

109. It is eith to learn the cat to the ^b kirn.

Lat.—Rei malæ consuetudo pessima.

110. If any man ^c speer at you, you may say you wat not.

A sharp return to a curious asker.

111. It is an ill wind that blows good to no body.

Things that are bad in general, may be good to some in particular.

Eng.—It is an ill air where nothing is to be gain'd.

112. If you touch dirt, it will stick to your fingers.

A dissuasive from medling with vile or mean persons.

113. I'll ^d wad a turd against your tongue; I care not whether I win, or lose.

A sarcastical answer to him who impertinently offers to lay wagers.

114. I thought all my meal dough.

I thought all my pains ill bestowed. Spoken when we are disappointed of our expectation.

Lat.—Pro thesauro carbones.

115. I had rather my bannock should burn, than you should turn it.

Spoken to those, whose intermedling with our business we think not for our profit; sometimes when a service is proffered which we think not proper to be accepted.

116. I will not make a toil of a pleasure, queth the good man, when he buried his wife.

A man going under his wife's head to the grave, was bid go faster, because the way was long, and the day short; answered, I will not make a toil of a pleasure.

117. Ireland will be your hinder end.

Foreboding that he will steal, and go to Ireland to escape justice.

118. It is by the head that the cow gives the milk.

---

^a Easy.　　^b Churn.　　^c Ask.　　^d Wager.

Every thing is able for its business, as it is kep't.

119. If you had stuck a knife to my heart, it would not have bled.

Intimating that the thing was a great surprize.

120. If you would be a merchant fine,
  Beware of old horse, herring, and wine.

Old horses will die, herrings stink, and wine soure; but the whole is for the sake of the first; the second and third has made many a rich merchant.

121. Ill weed waxeth well.

Eng.—Ill weeds grow apace.

122. It is good to be good in your time, for you wat not how long it will last.

Spoken to those who are now in credit, power, and authority; that they should not be proud, or insolent; for they may meet with a change.

123. I would not fother you for your muck.

That is, all you do is not worth your keeping.

124. It is hard to make an old mare leave * flinging.

It is hard to reclaim those, who have been long and habitually wicked.

125. I ken by my ʃ coag, who milks my cow.

Spoken by a woman who is jealous of her husband.

126. It may come in an hour, that will not come in a year.

Lat.—Plus enim fati valet bora benigni,
  Qnamsi te veneris commendet epistola Marti.

127. I wish it may come through you like ꜰ tags ꜰ otscate.

128. I wish it be the first sight you see.

129. I wish it may do you as much good, as grass does dogs.

These three are ridiculous imprecations to them who have eaten something that we design'd for our self.

130. If I come, I must bring a stool with me.

An answer to them who desires you to come where you are not invited.

131. It is a sin to put foul hands on it.

Spoken of some fine clean thing, commonly in jest.

132. I would have something to look to on Sunday.

133. I would have my eye full.

---

* Kicking.   ʃ Pail.   ꜰ The rumps of ray.

Both these spoken when we complain of one's wife, or husband, that they are not big, comely, or sightly.

134. I cannot believe you, you speak so fair.

Spoken when people promise us what they are not likely to perform.

135. I'll make a rope of [h] draff hold you.

Signifying that he has no great mind to go away.

136. It is ill to bring [i] butt, that's no there [i] benn.

One cannot produce what he has not.

137. It sets not a haggish to be roasted, for burning of the bag.

High stations become not mean persons, for they will misbehave in them.

Eng.—The higher the ape goes, the more he shews his tail.

138. I have seen as full a haggish toom'd on the midding.

Spoken, with great resentment, to wealthy people, who are insolent and purse-proud. I have seen as rich people brought to poverty.

139. It is hard to sit in Rome, and strive against the pope.

It is foolish to strive with our governours, landlords, or those under whose distress we are.

Eng.—He that draws his sword against his prince, must throw away the scabbard.

140. If you sell your purse to your wife, give your breeks into the bargain.

For if your wife command your purse, she will certainly have the mastery in every thing else.

141. I will never [k] cast [k] off [k] me, before [l] I go [l] ly.

I will not give my goods away before my death.

142. I wish you was a laird of your word.

A common expression, when we wish that what they say would prove true: I wish you a laird on that condition.

143. If he be old, he has the more wit.

An apology for marrying an old man, but a very lame one.

144. I wish you lamb in your [m] lair; as many a good ew has done.

145. I hope your early rising will do you no harm.

---

[h] Grains.   [i] Butt is towards the door; benn is into the house.   [k] Strip my self.   [l] Go to bed.   [m] The place where you lye.

M

Both spoken to those who lye too long a bed.

146. Ill ª deem'd half hang'd.

A man that is vehemently suspected, will soon be found guilty.

Eng.—One man had better steal a horse, than another look over a hedge.

147. If she serve me to live with, she may serve you
     to look at.

An answer to them that discommend our wife, but may be apply'd to any thing else that we have.

148. I had rather go by his door, than o'er his grave.

Nothing but a wish that our sick friend should recover.

149. If it had been a wolf, it would have worried you.

Spoken when one hath, to no purpose, sought a thing, that was afterwards found hard by them.

Eng. If it had been a bear it would have bit you.

150. I have good broad shoulders.

I can bear all the calumnies that you can load me with.

151. If the dee'l be laird, you'll be tenant.

Eng.—If the dee'l be vicar, you'll be clerk.

Spoken of trimmers, turn-coats, and time-servers.

152. Ill layers up make many thieves.

Eng.—How can the cat help it if the maid be a fool.

Item.—Opportunity makes the thief.

Lat.—Occasione duntaxat opus improbitati.

153. It is good fighting under a bucklar.

The meaning is roguish, the English say,

Eng.—It is safe taking a shive of a cut loaf.

154. It is good walking with a horse in one's hand.

It is good when a man of any art, trade, or profession, has an estate to support him, if these should fail.

155. It is something to be º sub to a good estate.

Because at the long run it may fall to us.

156. If it get you with bairn, I'll father it.

Spoken to urge a modest girl to take a glass of wine, or any such thing.

157. It is a sin to lye on the dee'l.

It is wrong to call bad people worse than they are.

Eng.—Give the devil his due.

158. It is no time to ᴾ stoup when the head's off.

ª Suspected.   º Akin.   ᴾ Bow down yourself to escape what is thrown at you.

That is, care, wariness, and saving, is to no purpose when all is gone.

159. If ever I get his cart ꝗ whemling, I'll give it a ʳ putt.

If I get him at a disadvantage, I'll take my revenge on him.

160. It is kindly the poke ˢ sa're of the herring.

It is no uncommon thing to see children take after their parents. Always meant in ill things.

Eng.—Like father, like son.

Lat.—Crimina nostra sequuntur a nobis geniti.

161. It is dear bought honey, that's lick'd off a thorn.

Spoken of the ill effect of unlawful pleasures.

Eng.—Sweet meat has soure sauce.

Item.—If you steal the honey, take a care of the sting.

Lat.—Vina, venusque nocent.

162. It is not long since louse bore ᵗ langett, no wonder she fall and break her neck.

Spoken when one has suddenly started up to a high station, and behaves himself saucily in it.

163. It is no play where one greets, and another laughs.

Spoken when a patrimony is unequally divided.

164. It is no ᵘ tint, a friend gets.

165. I never sat on your coat tail.

That is, I never spent at your cost.

166. It goes as much into my heart as my heel.

Spoken with disdain, signifying that what is said or done does not affect us in the least.

167. It is ᵛ well ᵛ war'd that ʷ wasters want geer.

168. It is no sin to see wasters want.

Both spoken when we see them in need, who have squander'd their patrimony.

169. If ever you make a good pudding, I'll eat the ˣ prick.

That is, I am much mistaken if ever you do good.

170. If you wanted me, and your meat, you would want one good friend.

Facetiously meaning by, the one good friend, his meat.

ꝗ Overturning. ʳ A push, a thrust. ˢ Savour, smell.
ᵗ A rope or chain to bind a horse's fore foot to his hind one.
ᵘ Lost. ᵛ But just. ʷ Spendthrifts. ˣ Skiver.

171. Ill flesh was never good [y] bruise.

Signifying that ill natured people seldom do a good thing: the Scots call an ill-natured boy ill flesh.

Eng.—Of evil grain no good seed can come.

172. I wat how the world wags,
     He is best belov'd that has most bags.

Lat.—Et genus, & formam regina pecunia donat.

173. It is ill your kytes [z] common.

That is, I have deserv'd of you, because I have often fill'd your belly.

174. I am not so blind, as I am blear ey'd.

I may think it proper to hold my tongue, but yet I can very well observe how things go.

175. I'll never live poor, to die rich.

Eng.—I had rather die a beggar, than live a beggar.

Lat.—Cum furor haud dubius est, cum sit manifesta phrenesis,
     Ut locuples moriare, egenti vivere fato.

176. If a man be once down, down with him.

If fortune frown upon a man, his friends will lessen, and his enemies multiply.

Eng.—If a man once fall, all will tread upon him.

Lat.—Vulgus sequitur fortunam ut semper & odit damnatos.

177. It was never for nothing that the cat lick'd the stone.

178. It was never for nothing the [a] gled whistled.

People who officiously offer their service, may be suspected to have some selfish end in it.

Eng.—The cat knows whose lips she licks.

179. It is gone I lov'd you for.

Jocosely spoken by girls to their courtiers, when they have had any loss or disaster.

180. It is good to fear the worst, the best will be the welcomer.

Fearing the worst will make us careful, and cautious; and if things succeed better than we expected, the surprise will be pleasant.

Lat.—Grata superveniet quæ non sperabitur hora.

---

[y] Broth.   [z] Ill your common, or good your common is,
there lies great obligations on you to do so, or other ways.
     [a] Kits.

181. It shall not be for your ease, and honour both.

Spoken when we threaten to make a thing done in opposition to us, either uneasy, or disgraceful to the authors. This does not come up to the English, Honour and ease are seldom bed-fellows.

182. I wish I could put my finger, where you can put your whole hand.

Intimating that they had much money.

183. It is ill medling between the bark and the rind.

It is a troublesome and thankless office to concern ourselves in the jars, and out-falls of near relations, as man and wife, parents and children, &c.

184. It was but their cloaths that ᵇ cast out.

That is, the quarrel was not real, but only with design, in order to accomplish some end.

185. If you will tell your secret to your servant, you have made him your master.

For having that hawnk over you he will be saucy.

Lat.—Charus erit verri, qui verrem, témpore quo vult,
     Acousare potest.

186. If you laugh at your own sport, the company will laugh at you.

187. If your errand come my gate, you shall be as well serv'd.

Either a promise, or a threatening, but rather the last.

188. I once gave a dog ᶜ handsel, and he was hang'd e'er night.

Jocosely spoken to them who ask us handsel, that is, the first money for such a parcel.

189. Ill comes often upon worse back.

Spoken when one misfortune succeeds another.

190. I never lik'd a dry bargain.

Spoken when people that are about a bargain, propose to take a glass of ale.

Lat.—Venalia, sine vino, expediri non possunt.

191. I am speaking of hay, and you of horse corn.

Spoken when people answer cross purposes.

Lat.—Ego de alliis loquor, tu de cæpis respondes.

192. It's a sary mouse that has but one hole.

Eng.—The mouse that has but one hole is soon taken.
Lat.—Uni cubili non fidit mus.

ᵇ Fell out, at variance.   ᶜ The first bit in the morning.

M 3

193. If a lye had worried you, you had been dead long since.

194. If that had been the first lye you had told, I could have charm'd you.

It is alleg'd that when people take the falling sickness the first time, that some charm may be apply'd to them, that will hinder them to take it again: jocosely pretending that if you had catch'd him when he told his first lie, you could have apply'd a charm to him that would have hindered him to have told another; but that his many lies put a stop to that.

195. I know he'll come, by his long tarrying.

Jocosely, as if his long stay was a token that he would come at last.

196. It is time to rise, if you be clean under you.

That is, if you have not beshit the bed; for in that case you would be ashamed to rise.

197. If all be well, ^d I's be ^e wyteless.

Spoken with a suspicion that all will not be well, and if so, I have no hand in it.

198. It is ill to make a silk purse of a sow's ear.

199. It is ill to make a ^f blawer horn of a tod's tail.

Both signify, that one cannot make fine work out of bad materials.

Eng.—Every block will not be a bedstead.

Lat.—Ex quovis ligno non fit Mercurius.

200. I ken him as well as I had gone up through him, and down through him, with a light candle.

201. I ken it as well, as fill ^g bayer kens her stake.

Eng.—I know him as well as the beggar knows his dish.

Lat.—Ego te intus, & in cute novi.

202. I'll ken him, by a black sheep, hereafter.

Spoken with indignation, of one that has deceived me, and whom I will not trust again.

203. I'll never keep a dog and bark myself.

If I keep servants, they shall do my work for me.

204. It sets you well to ^h slaver, you let such ⁱ gaadys fall.

Ironically signifying that what he is saying, or doing, is too assuming for him.

---

^d I will be. ^e Blameless. ^f Blowing. ^g A cow's name.
^h Slabber. ⁱ Hauks.

205. I had no mind I was married, my briddal was so
fectless.

The thing was of so small importance, that I never once
thought of it.

206. I will not lye in my own dish.

I will not say I have gotten meat when I have not.

207. I'll tell the ᵏ bourd, but not the body.

I will tell you the story, but not name the person.

Eng.—I'll name no names.

208. I had rather my friend should think me ˡ framet,
than ᵐ fashious.

Lat.—Malim in hanc peccare partem, ut desiderer, quam
ut obtundam.

Eng.—Better be unmannerly, than troublesome.

209. If I live another year, I'll call this year ⁿ tarn
year.

That is, I will order my affairs so, that the next year shall
appear quite another year.

Lat.—Semper agricola, in novum annum, dives.

210. I had but little butter, and I cast that on the
coal.

That is, the little thing I had, I mismanaged.

Eng.—I threw the helve after the hatchet.

Lat.—Post omnia perdere naulum.

211. It is time enough to cry, Oh, when you are hurt.

Spoken to dissuade people from groundless fears.

212. I have a cold coal to blow at.

Spoken after some great loss, or disappointment of expectation.

213. It is God that feeds the crows,
    That neither tils, harrows, nor sows.

214. I have brought an ill comb to my own head.

That is, I have engag'd myself in a troublesome business.

Eng.—I have brought an old house on my head.

215. It is an ill cause that none dare speak in.

Eng.—It is a bad cloth that will take no colour.

216. I will not go about the bush with you.

That is, I'll tell you my mind freely, without fear, flattery,
or circumlocution. Always said in anger.

ᵏ Jest, story.   ˡ Strange.   ᵐ Troublesome.
            ⁿ Last year.

217. I never lov'd 'bout gates, quoth the good wife, when she [o] harl'd the good man o'er the fire.

The second part is added only to make it comical; it signifies no more, but I always lov'd plain dealing.

218. It is good that mends.

Spoken when we hear that a person, or thing, is better, or does better.

219. If you had as little money, as you have manners, you would be the poorest man of your kin.

Spoken to wealthy people, when they behave themselves rudely, haughtily, or insolently.

220. It is a world that will not give us a bitt, and a brat.

If a man be honest and industrious, he can hardly miss food and raiment.

221. I cannot sell the cow, and sup the milk.

Eng.—I cannot eat my cake, and have my cake.

222. I scorn to make my mouth my arse.

Spoken with indignation to them who would have us deny what we have said.

223. It is not the way to [p] grip a [q] burd, to cast your bonnet at her.

A vile, malicious proverb, persuading to conceal your resentment, 'till a proper time of revenge offer, lest your enemies, being appriz'd of your design, arm against you.

224. Ill to take, and eith to tire.

Apply'd to horses, alledging them to be jades who are hard to be catch'd.

225. I'll never brew drink, and [r] treat drinkers.

I will not be at the pains to procure such, and such things, and then to urge them upon people against their wills.

226. I never lov'd meat that crow'd in my [s] crop.

Spoken when people have done you service, and afterwards upbraid you with it.

227. It would be a good sight for a blind man to see.

Spoken with contempt, when we despise any person, or thing, which we were ask'd if we had seen.

---

[o] Trail'd. [p] Catch. [q] Bird. [r] Intreat, urge, force. [s] Craw.

228. It would have done a blind man good, to have seen it.

Spoken to the same purpose, but more jocosely.

229. I bake no bread by your shins.

I do not understand the phrase, but it means, I get no advantage by you.

230. I think more of the sight, than the ᵗ farlie.

Spoken disdainfully, when you are ask'd if you saw such a person, or thing, or what you thought of him, or it: I was better pleas'd that I had my eyes to see it, than any pleasure I had in seeing of it.

231. I care not whether the ᵘ tod ᵛ worrie the goose, or the goose the tod.

Spoken when two people are contending, whom we equally undervalue.

Eng.—For my peck of malt set the kiln on fire.

232. I will speak to my lord about your business.

A senseless saying, when we see a thing past remedy.

233. I think more of your kindness than it is all worth.

Spoken with resentment, to them who have neglected our business.

234. In harvest time, lairds are labourers.

Spoken to urge them to work in harvest, who perhaps think it below them.

Eng.—They must hunger in winter, that will not work in harvest.

235. It is come to mickle, but it's no come to that.

Spoken when we reject the proffer of a mean service, match, or business, we are not come so low as that yet.

236. If you will not hold him, he'll do't all.

Spoken ironically, when we suspect the person not so earnest upon the business, as he pretends.

237. I'll make the mantle meet for the man.

That is, I'll pay you according as you serve me.

238. It will make a ʷ bra ˣ show, in a ʸ landward kirk.

A jest upon a girl when we see her fond of a new suit.

ᵗ Wonder.   ᵘ Fox.   ᵛ Kill.   ʷ Fine.   ˣ Sight.
ʸ Country.

239. It begins to work like soap on a sow's arse.

Spoken tauntingly when a business grows more involv'd, intricate, and troublesome.

240. I draw it from you, like a fart from a dead mare.

Spoken of them who will not do, or say, a thing but with force, and constraint.

241. I will not creep in his arse, for a week of his fair weather.

That is, I'll scorn to creep or cringe to him for any thing that ever I will get by him.

Eng.—I'll not creep in his arse to bake in his oven.

242. I'll learn you to lick, for supping is dear.

A senseless saying when we correct our children, servants, or scholars.

243. I never saw a foul thing so cleanly.

Spoken when they, who us'd to be dirty enough, pretend to cleanliness.

244. I'll do as the cow of Forfar did, I'll take a standing drink.

Spoken when we come into company by chance, or refuse to sit down. A woman in Forfar set out her wort to cool, a cow came by and drunk it out. The owner was sued for damages, but was acquit because the cow took but a standing drink. They have another proverb to this purpose.

245. It will come out yet, like the holm corn.

I do not know the reason of the expression, but it is used when we see a young man, and a young woman too oft in company, we suspect there will be some effects of that familiarity hereafter.

246. I'll put dare behind the door, and do it.

Spoken when people say, we dare not do such a thing.

247. If, and an, spoils many a good charter.

Spoken when a thing is promised upon such a condition, if they can, if they have time. Taken from the clauses irritant in a conveyance.

Lat.—Suppositio nihil ponit in re.

248. It is hard for a greedy eye to have a [z] leal heart.

Because such act against the bent of their inclinations.

249. I hold bleuch of him.

An allusion to the different tenures by which lairds hold

[z] Honest.

their land, some ward, some black ward, some blench. This
last pays no service.

250. I have more ado than a dish to wash.

I have business of importance and concern on my hands.

251. I prick'd not louse since I soled your hose, where
I might have prick'd a thousand.

An answer of a taylor to him that calls him pricklouse.

252. If you will not come you'll bide,
As Bog said to his bride.

Spoken when we are indifferent whether they come or not.

253. I had rather have a groat, than a ª grip of your
coat.

Spoken by young fellows, when girls run away from them ;
as if they were careless.

254. If you be hasty, you'll never be lasty.

Spoken ironically to lazy people.

255. If all ᵇ heights hitt.

If what I propos'd be attain'd ; if what was promised be
accomplished.

256. I will take the best first, as the priest did the
plumbs.

257. It is a stanch house that there is never a drop in.

The insufficiency, and unsatisfactoriness of all human
things has given occasion to this, and many other proverbs.

258. I have taken the sheaf from the mare.

That is, I have stop'd my intended journey. A man going
a journey, gave his mare a sheaf of oats, that she might perform the better : but altering his mind, he ordered his sheaf to
be taken from her.

259. If it be ill, it is as ill ᶜ rused.

Spoken to them that discommend what we have.

260. It is no shift to want.

Spoken when in necessity we take what we have use for ;
they say also, Want is the worst of it.

Eng.—A bad bush is better than an open field.

261. It is better to sup with a cutty, than want a
spoon.

It is better to have a thing, not quite so good in its kind,
than to want altogether.

Eng.—Better play small game than stand out.

ª Catch.　　ᵇ Promises.　　ᶜ Commended.

262. It is good fish, when it is ^d gripped.

Eng.—All the craft is in the catching.

263. It is not every man that feels the stink of his own fart.

Every man is not sensible of his own defects.

Lat.—Suus cuique crepitus bene olet.

264. I think you have taken the bumple feist.

Spoken, with contempt, of those who are become unreasonably out of humour.

Eng.—You are sick of the mulligrubs with eating chop'd hay.

265. It is a hard task to be poor and ^e leal.

Because poverty is a great temptation to steal.

Lat.—Magnum pauperies opprobrium, jubet quidvis facere aut pati.

266. It is good to nip the brier in the bud.

It is good to prevent, by wholesome correction, the vicious inclinations of children.

267. I am going the errand you cannot go for me.

Eng.—I am going to my uncle John's house.

268. It is but a true jest at best.

Spoken when people discommend themselves, on purpose to be praised.

269. I cannot find you both tale and ears.

Spoken, with resentment, to those that will not listen to us.

270. I neither got stock, nor ^f brock.

That is, neither money, nor interest.

Lat.—Sors, cum usura, perit.

271. I am ^g wae for your skathe, there is so little of it.

A mock condoleance.

272. Just enough, and no more, like Jannet Herris ^h shearers meat.

Spoken when people have eaten all that is before them.

273. It is mickle that makes a taylor laugh; but sowters ⁱ girns ay.

A ridicule upon shoemakers, who at every stitch grin with the force of drawing through the thread.

274. I wist I had a string at his lug.

Spoken of those that tarry long, for had you a string at his ear, you would pull hard.

275. I'll draw the belt nearer the ribs.

| ^d Catch'd. | ^e Honest. | ^f Offalls. | ^g Sorry. |
| | ^h Reapers. | ⁱ Grins. | |

That is, 1 will retrench my expences; spoken upon the occasion of some unlook'd for loss or expence.

276. I have his cods in a cleft stick.

Spoken when we have people at an advantage.

277. If a louse miss its foot on his coat, it will be sure to break its neck.

Signifying that his coat is thread-bare.

278. It is good to be out of harm's way.

279. If I cannot keep my tongue, I can keep my money.

Spoken when we have proffered to lay a wager, but refuse to lay down.

280. If she was my wife, I would make a queen of her.

That is, 1 would leave her the whole kingdom to herself, leave her, and go to another.

281. I will be your servant, when you have least to do, and most to spend.

The true meaning of that common phrase, Your humble servant, Sir.

282. I have my meat, and my ᵏ mense.

Spoken when we proffer meat, or any thing else, to them that refuse it.

283. I think we will be all chapmen, quoth the good wife, when she got a turd on her back.

A reprimand to those who perk up with their superiors, pretend to equal them in cloaths, &c.

284. I could have done that my self, but not so handsomely.

Spoken when people do a thing amiss, as snuffing out the candle, overturning the glass, or the like.

285. It ˡ were telling your kin, your ᵐ craig was broken, that you was like him.

Spoken with indignation, to them that disparage your friend.

286. If you win at that, you'll lose at nothing.

Spoken to them that are about an ill thing, which will undoubtedly prove to their damage.

287. If we have not the world's wealth, we have the world's ease.

Spoken by those who live happily, in a mean condition.

288. I had rather see't, than hear tell of it.

Eng.—Better have it, than hear of it.

ᵏ Here it signifies good manners. ˡ It were to the advantage of. ᵐ Neck.

N

289. It will hold out an honest man, but nothing will hold out thieves.

290. I will pay you and put nothing in your pouch.

I will bring an account upon you, that will balance your demand, or I'll keep you out at law.

291. If you will have the hen's egg, you must bear her cackling.

If you will have a good thing, you must bear with the inconveniences that attend it.

292. I will not tell a lye for scant of news.

293. If it will not sell, it will not soure.

Spoken when people will not give a price for those wares that will keep without loss.

294. It is well, that all our faults are not written in our face.

Spoken to them who upbraid us with some faults that we have been guilty of; alledging if theirs were as well known, they would look as black.

295. If he had spew'd as oft as he has rued, he would have a clean stomach.

Intimating that he has often repented the doing that thing, saying that word, or undertaking that project.

296. It will be a hot day that will make you [o] startle.

Spoken to settled, sober, grave people, who are not easily mov'd.

297. If I have done amiss, I'll make amends.

298. It would be a hard task to follow a black [p] cutted sow through a new burn'd [q] moor this night.

A comical indication that the night is very dark.

299. I [r] tint the staff I herded it with.

Spoken surlishly, when we are asked what is become of such a thing: arguing that we were not oblig'd to keep it.

300. Is there any mice in your arse?

A senseless surlish return to them that speak of themselves in the plural number. As if you would say, Whom do you speak of beside yourself.

301. If I had you at [s] Meggy Mills's house, I would get my word about.

Spoken when we are in a presence where it does not become

---

[o] Run as cattel does when sting'd by wasps. [p] Dock'd. [q] Heath. [r] Lost. [s] A woman's name, a diminutive of Margaret.

as to speak. It took its rise from a country fellow, who hearing his minister, in the pulpit, say something that he thought reflected on him, bawl'd out this proverb. Thinking that if he was at the ale-house with him, he would tell him his own,

302. I can see as far in a mill-stone, as he that pick'd it.

I understand very well how things go, and what you aim at.

303. If you had given a six-pence for that word, you would not have spoken it.

Because it is to no purpose, and can do you no good.

304. I heard you lately commended.

305. It is a friend that ᵗ ruses you.

Spoken both in jest, when we hear people speak well of themselves.

306. If we have little geer, we have the less care

Lat.—Bene est cui dens obtulit parcâ quod satis est manu.
Item.—Misera est magni custodia census.

307. It has no other father but you.

Spoken when people commend what they are selling.
Lat.—Laudat venales, qui vult exponere merces.

308. It is ill to put a blythe face on a black heart.

It is hard to pretend mirth, when the heart is sorrowful.
Lat.—Difficile est tristi, fingere, mente jocum.

309. If he be not a sowter, he's a good shoe clouter.

If he cannot make new, he can mend old.

310. It were a pity to refuse you, you ask so little.

Spoken to modest cravers: sometimes ironically to them, that ask too much.

311. It is neither far nor foul ᵘ gate.

And therefore the journey may be undertaken with ease.

312. It ᵛ sets you not to speak of him, 'till you wash your mouth with wine, and wipe it with a lawn towel.

A proud, haughty vindication of our friend, when we hear him ill spoken of by mean persons.

313. I wish he and I h. d a peck of gold to ᵂ deal, there should be ˣ scarted backs of hands, and hinging by the ʸ wicks of the mouth.

Spoken when such an one is said to be stronger than us; intimating that, upon a good occasion, we would not yield to him.

314. I have seen many a smaller madam.

ᵗ Commends.   ᵘ Way.   ᵛ Becomes.   ᵂ Divide.
ˣ Scratch'd.   ʸ Jaws.

N 2

Used in former times, by ordinary women, to them who call'd them Mistress. The jest lies in the double signification of the word smaller, which may mean less in bulk, or lower in station.

315. It is but a year sooner to the begging.

Facetiously spoken, when we design to be at a little more expence than we thought.

316. If I was at my own bairn foot.

I am now among strangers, but if I was at home among my friends, I would not suffer myself to be insulted.

317. I'll give you a bone to pick, that will stick in your ᵃ ha'se.

I'll tell you of something, that you will not easily digest.

318. If better were within, better would come out.

Spoken when people speak vile and opprobrious words, signifying that their base education can furnish them with none better.

319. It is the poor man's office to look, and the rich man cannot forbear it.

A return to them who ask us what we look at, or why we look at them.

320. If your tail was as ready as your tongue, you would shame all your kin.

A reprimand to scolds, and talkative women.

321. It is ill prizing of green barley.

It is ill prizing these things who have not yet had an occasion of shewing themselves; spoken of boys, colts, &c.

322. I will sooner see you ᵃ sleip ey'd, like a French cat.

A disdainful rejecting of an unworthy proposal; spoken by bold maids to the vile offers of young fellows.

323. I am not small beer thirsty, nor gray bread hungry.

I am not in so great need as to be content with a small or mean thing.

324. It is drink will you, but not drink shall you.

My beer is so bad, that I will not urge it upon you, but you may drink it if you please.

325. I'll do as the man did that sold the land.

That is, I will not do it again, for selling of an estate is a fault that few are twice guilty of.

326. It is a good tree that hath neither ᵇ knap nor ᶜ gaw.

ᵃ Throat.   ᵃ With the inside turn'd out.   ᵇ Knob.   ᶜ Want.

*There is nothing altogether perfect.

327. It will be a dirten ^d pingle.

Spoken when two cowards are going to fight, or the like.

328. It will be the last word in his *testament.

That is, he will not be induc'd to do it.

329. I am ^fflyting free with you.

I am so far out of the reach of your tongue, that though we should scold, you have nothing to say to me.

330. It is worth all you have offered for it.

Spoken when we refuse to buy a thing, as being too dear; so they would have us tell what we will give for it.

331. I am not oblig'd to summer and winter it.

Spoken when we would have told a thing, and they would have us tell it over again.

332. I would rather strive with the great rig, than with the ill neighbour.

An apology of him that takes a larger farm than we suppose he can manage: that he would rather do his best with it, than be vex'd with the contentions of an ill partner.

333. If he bind the poke, she'll sit down on it.

Spoken when a niggardly man is married to a more niggardly woman. The Scots call a niggardly man, A bind poke.

334. It had been a pity to have spoil'd two houses with them.

Spoken when two ill-natur'd people are married.

335. I must do as the beggars do, when I am full go away.

Spoken when we have din'd with our friend, and upon some urgent occasions must needs be gone.

336. I am not so scarce of clean pipes, as to ^gblow out of a burn'd ^h cutty.

Spoken by a young girl, when they tell her of marrying a widower; intimating that she had choice of young batchelors at her service.

337. If this be a feast, you have been at many.

An apology for a small dinner.

338. Ill herds make fat wolves.

This is in the old collection, I have not heard it used; it signifies that careless keepers give thieves occasion to steal.

339. It is not in your breeks.

---

^d Competition.   ^e Latter will.   ^f Scolding.   ^g Smoak.
^h A short pipe.

An allusion to money in our pockets; signifies our inability to effect, or procure such a thing.

340. It is hard to please all parties.

Eng.—He that wou'd please all, and himself too,
    Takes more in hand than he can do.

From the Latin, Durum est omnibus placere.

Lat.—Jupiter, neque pluens, neque abstinens, omnibus placet.

341. It is a filthy bird that files its own nest.

An angry reprimand to one that speaks ill of his country. In the north of Ireland they will say,

342. Sik a word out of a Crawford's mouth.

343. I will not make fish of one, and flesh of another.

Lat.—Tros tyriusve mihi nullo discrimine agetur.

344. It is good sleeping in a sound skin.

An apology of, or a reflection upon, him that shuns dangers.

345. Ill to day, and worse to morrow.

Lat.—Qui non est hodie, cras minus aptus erit.

346. It is ill to strive against the stream.

Lat.—Difficile est contra torrentem niti.

Item.—Stultus pugnat in adversis ire natator aquis.

347. If you would live for ever, wash the milk from
    your liver.

348. It is a pity fair weather should ever do harm.

349. It is hard both to pray and pay.

350. It is hard both to have, and want.

That is, to have a thing and not to make use of it.
    The rich poor man's emphatically poor.—Cowley.

351. It goes in at the one ear, and out at the other.

352. If things were to be done twice, all would be
    ᵏ wise.

353. If the devil find a man idle, he'll set him on
    work.

Eng.—An empty brain is the devil's shop.

Lat.—Otium diaboli pulvinar.

354. I will not buy a pig in a poke.

355. If I had a dog as doft, I would shoot him.

356. It is a lamb in the one taking; but it will be an
    old sheep e'er you get it off.

Eng.—Light burthens far heavy.

ᵏ The Scots pronounce it wie.

Often apply'd to debts, which are easier to be contracted than paid.

357. It shall never ride, and I gang.

That is, I will not eat it.

358. Ill news are ay o'er true.

359. I'll never buy a cow, when I can have milk so cheap.

360. It is ill to make an unlawful oath, but worse to keep it.

361. I deny that with both my hands, and all my teeth.

362. I have seen more than I have eaten.

Intimating that you have seen and convers'd with the world. Eng.—All the bread that I have eaten was not bak'd in one oven.

363. I have mickle to do, and few to do it for me.

364. I wish you may have Scotch to carry you to bed.

Spoken when our companions, beginning to take with the drink, begin to speak Latin; a common custom there, believing that by and by they will be at that pass that they will be able to speak no language.

365. I never heard it worse told.

A kind of exclamation when people say something of you, that tends to diminish the opinion the world has of you.

366. I wish you had a brose to lay the hair of your beard.

A disdainful return of a saucy maid, to a courtier that she thinks unworthy of her.

367. It is a good tongue that says no ill, and a better heart that thinks none.

Used when we have no inclination to speak our mind freely, concerning courts, or great men.

368. I'll make his own [1] garlans bind his own hose.

That is, what expence his business requires I will take out of his own money.

369. Just as it falls, quoth the wooer to the maid.

That is, as my affairs and circumstances allow. It took its rise from a courtier, who went to court a maid; she was dressing supper with a drop at her nose, she ask'd him if he would stay all night, he answered, Just as it falls; meaning if the drop fell among the meat he would go, if it fell by, he would stay.

---

[1] Garters.

370. It is the best spoke in his wheel.

371. I'll be [m] dady's bairn, and [n] minies bairn.

Spoken by them who have no intention to embark into the interest of any of the contending parties.

372. I spoke but one word, give me but one knock.

Spoken by those who being reprimanded for offering their opinion in a business, excuse themselves, by saying that they will proceed no farther.

373. It has neither arse nor elbow.

Spoken of a thing that is wholly unshapely.

374. I was like a cow in an [o] uncouth [p] loan.

That is, every body look'd strange to me.

375. I never lov'd water in my shoon, and my weime's made of better leather.

Jocosely spoken by them who refuse to drink water.

376. I would not have you cackling, for your egg.

I would not have your trouble and noise for all the advantage you bring me.

377. I never lov'd them that find fault with my shoon, and give me no leather.

Apply'd to them that find fault with some part of our habit, yet contribute nothing to make it better.

378. It's a bra thing to be honest.

Commonly a preface to the telling of some thievish, or knavish action.

379. I wish you were able, [q] why you never did it.

Spoken tauntingly to them that threaten to beat you, or boast of what they can do.

380. I have a workman's eye in my head.

Spoken when we nicely discern a thing a little wrong done.

381. I'll give you a meeting, as Mortimer gave his mother.

A threatening to be up with us, when occasion shall offer, but I know not the original.

382. I would sooner see your nose cheese, and my self the first bite.

To the same purpose with 322.

383. It is far to seek, and ill to find; like [r] Meg's maidenhead.

Spoken of a thing that's quite lost.

---

[m] Papa's.   [n] Mamma's.   [o] Strange.   [p] Milking-place.
[q] Upon condition that.   [r] A diminutive of Margaret.

384. It is not what is she, but what has she.

Spoken of the choice of wives, where the portion is often more look'd after than either the person or the virtues.

385. I wou'd not call the king my cousin.

Added when we say, Had I such a thing, could I get such a place, or effect such a project: I would think myself so happy, that I would flatter no body. They say also, I would be out of all my een kins mister.

K.

1. KISSING goes by favour.

Men shew regard, or do service, to people as they affect.

2. Kings are out of play.

It is not right, in subjects, to jest upon kings, or to pry narrowly into their determinations, and actions.

3. Kings have long hands.

Their power, and authority, reaches over all their dominions.
Lat.—An nescis longas regibus esse manus.

4. Keep your tongue within your teeth.

Lat.—Quod de quoque viro, & cui dicas, sæpe caveto.

5. Know when to spend, and when to spare,
   And you need not be busy, and you'll never be
   bare.

Eng.—To give and keep there is need of art.

6. Keep your kill-dry'd taunts, to your mouldy-hair'd
   maidens.

A disdainful return to those who are too liberal of their taunts.

7. Kiss you me 'till I grow white, and that will be an
   ill web to bleech.

A scornful answer to a saucy proposal.

8. Kindness will creep, where it cannot gang.

They who dare not shew their love openly, will find a way to convey the knowledge of it privately.

9. Kindness comes awill.

That is, love cannot be forc'd.

10. Kings and bears oft * worry their keepers.

Witness the tragical end of many courtiers.

11. Kings chaff is worth other men's corn.

The perquisites that attend kings service is better than the wages of other persons.

---

* Devour.

12. Kill the cock the laird's coming; well I wot he's
welcome.

A senseless bauble, spoken by servants, when they see the
laird a coming, whose original I do not know.

13. Kings cheese goes half away in parings.

A great deal of it goes to the officers of the revenue.

14. Keep something for the sore foot.

Preserve something for age, distress, and necessity.

Eng.—Keep something for him that rides on the white
horse.

15. [b] Keek in the [c] stoup was ne'er a good fellow.

Spoken when one peeps into the pot, to see if the liquor
be out; whereas a jolly good fellow should drink about, and
when the pot's empty call for more.

16. Kindness cannot be bought for geer.

But rather by mutual good offices; and therefore,

17. Kindness cannot stand ay on one side.

Spoken when you offer an instance of kindness to them who
have been formerly kind to you.

18. Kiss you her all but the mouth, and then you will
not miss her arse.

A surlish return to them that jeer you with being too familiar with such a woman.

19. Kail [d] hains bread.

Good broth will, in some measure, supply the want of
bread.

20. [e] Kitty [e] Swerrock where she sat, come [f] reik me
this, come [f] reik me that.

Spoken by mothers to their lazy daughters, when they call
to any body to reach them what they want, thinking it more
proper that they should rise, and go for it.

21. [g] Kae me, and I'll [g] kae thee.

Spoken when great people invite and feast one another,
and neglect the poor.

22. Keep that at home with you.

Spoken when people unawares upbraid us with what some
of their own near relations are guilty of.

23. Kiss my arse Kilmarnock, I am as little in your
[h] common, as you are in mine.

Spoken to people who have been rigorous to us, and ex-

---

[b] Peep. [c] Pot. [d] Saves. [e] Kate the lazy. [f] Reach.
[g] Invite. [h] To be in ones common, is to be oblig'd to them.

acted upon us, to whom therefore we think ourselves not oblig'd.

24. Keep the feast till the feast day.

An advice to maidens, not to dispose of their virginity 'till they be married ; or, as they say, Get kirk mense.

25. ¹ Keek in my kail pot, ᵏ glower in my ambry.

Spoken to them who officiously pry into our actions. Commonly used among children.

26. Kiss a ᵐ carle, and ⁿ clap a carle, and that's the way to ᵒ tine a carle.

27. Knock a carle, and ᵖ ding a carle ; and that's the way to win a carle.

Both these are join'd together, and signify, that people of mean breeding are rather to be won by harsh treatment, than civil.

28. Kiss my foot there's more flesh on it.

Spoken to them who tauntingly say, I kiss your hands.

29. Kitchin well is come to the town.

Spoken by mothers to their children, when they would have them spare what they give them to their bread ; for they have no more to give them.

30. Keep lint and it will be dirt : keep wool and it will be silk.

Lint mellows and improves by keeping, but wool rots.

31. Kissing is cry'd down to shaking of hands.

Spoken by a girl when ask'd a kiss. Alluding to proclamations for lowering the value of money : there is a proclamation that nobody should kiss hereafter, but only shake hands.

32. Keep as mickle of your Scots tongue as will buy your dog a ᵠ leaf.

A reprimand to conceited fellows who affectedly speak English, or, as they say, begin to knap.

33. Kiss my niry-nary, that's my arse in English.

A ridiculous taunting bauble.

34. Keep your breath to cool your brose.

Spoken to them who talk much to little purpose.

35. Kiss the hare's foot.

This is spoken to them who come too late to dinner : but I know not the reason of the expression.

ⁱ Peep. ᵏ Look sparingly. ˡ Cup-board. ᵐ Carle is every man not a gentleman. ⁿ Sooth, make of. ᵒ Lose. ᵖ Beat. ᵠ Loaf.

36. Keep your foot out of the fire, and I'll keep that from you.

Spoken to them who expect a thing, that they are not likely to get.

37. Kiss a slate-stone and that will not [r] slaver you.

An answer of a girl to him that asks her a kiss.

L.

1. LOVE me little, love me long.

A dissuasive from shewing too much, and too sudden kindness.

Lat.—Nihil vehemens durabile.

2. Little knows the wife that sits by the fire,
How the wind blows in Hurle-burle-swyre.

Hurle-burle-swyre is a passage through a ridge of mountains, that separate Nithsdale from Twadale and Clydsdale: where the mountains are so indented one with another, that there is a perpetual blowing. The meaning is, that they, who are at ease, know little of the trouble that others are expos'd to.

3. Little wit as mickle travell.

Spoken when people, for want of skill, put themselves to more trouble than they need.

4. Leave is light.

A reproof to them who intrude upon your interest, without your permission.

5. Look e'er you [a] loup, and you'll ken the better where you light.

Consider well before you undertake a thing of weight.

6. Long e'er the dee'l lye dead by the [b] dike side.

Spoken when we are told that some wicked persons is like to die.

Lat.—Mors optima rapit, leterrima relinqnit.

7. Little Jock gets the little dish, and it holds him ay long little.

Poor people are poorly serv'd, which prolongs their poverty.

8. Long [c] leal, long poor.

9. [d] Lala is long and [e] dwigh.

Two cursed proverbs to encourage people to dishonesty. As if honest and fair dealing were too tedious to procure worldly prosperity. The English say also,

---

[r] Slaber. [a] Leap. [b] Ditch. [c] Honest.
[d] Honesty. [e] Tedious.

Plain dealing is a jewel, but they that use it die beggars.

Lat.—Probitas laudatur, & alget.

I like another proverb far better, because far truer, viz.

10. Leal folks never wanted geer.

11. Live, and let live.

Deal so equally, and so fairly, that you may gain, and others may gain by you.

12. Love, and raw pease are two ill things, the one breaks the heart, and the other brusts the belly.

13. Love and raw pease will make a man speak at both the ends.

Eng.—Love and pease pottage will make their way.

14. Little said soon mended.

15. Little geer soon spended.

These two are often pronounced together for the rhyme's sake.

16. Lightly come, lightly go.

Lat.—Quod cito fit cito perit.

17. Long e'er the King of France get wot of that.

Spoken when people make a great talk of some little accident.

Lat.—Id populus curat scilicet.

18. Like to like, a scabbed horse to an old dike.

Like to like, quoth the devil to the collier.

19. Let the morn come, and the meat with it.

Spoken to them who are solicitous for to-morrow's provision.

Lat.—Lætus in præsens animus quod ultra est. Oderit curare.

20. Long tarrying takes all the thanks away.

Eng.—He loseth his thanks that promiseth, and delayeth.

Lat.—Qui cito dat, bis dat.

Item.—Gratia ab officio, quod mora tardat, abest.

Item.—Longa mora est nobis omnis, quæ gaudia differt.

21. Light burthens break no bones.

An excuse for not taking more in hand than we can well manage.

22. Let every man be content with his own f kevel.

Lat.—Sorte tuâ contentus abi.

Item.—Spartam nactus es, hanc orna.

23. Lads will be men.

An apology for giving sufficient meat to boys.

Lat.—Tandem fit surculus arbor.

---

f Lot.

o

24. Lips go, laps go, drink and pay.

If you put your lip to the cup to drink, put your hand to your lap to take out your purse.

Eng.—Touch pot touch penny.

25. Law makers should not be law breakers.

Lat.—Patere legem quam tulisti.

26. Like a sow playing on a ᵍ trump.

Spoken when people do a thing ungracefully.

Eng.—Like pigs playing on organs.

Lat.—Asinus ad lyram.

27. Leaches kill with license.

An argument dissuading people, of no skill, from quacking; for if any that they administer to die, they will be blam'd: but if any die under the hands of a physician, no notice is taken of it.

28. Leave off while the play is good.

Lest, if it be continued, it may come to earnest. Spoken also by people of age and gravity, when young people jest upon them, intimating that they will not bear it.

29. Let his own wand ding him.

Let him reap the fruits of his own folly.

Lat.—B's interimitur qui suis armis perit.

30. Little dogs have long tails.

People of a low stature may perform their business well enough. Other ways apply'd sometimes.

31. Like is an ill mark.

Lat.—Omne simile est dissimile.

Item.—Omnis similitudo claudicat, alioquin esset identitas.

32. Little intermedling makes fair parting.

When we do not busy ourselves about other men's interest and concerns, we can have little occasion to fall out with them.

Eng.—Of little medling, comes great ease.

33. Long e'er like to die fill the kirkyerd.

Eng.—Almost was never haug'd.

34. Loud in the ʰ loan was ne'er a good milk cow.

A reprimand to noisy girls.

35. Let alone makes many a ⁱ lown.

Want of correction makes many a bad boy.

Lat.—Deteriores omnes sumus licentia.

36. Learn your goodam to make milk kail.

Spoken to them who officiously offer to teach them who know more than themselves.

ᵍ Jew's harp.　　ʰ Milking-place.　　ⁱ Rogue.

Eng.—Teach your father to get bairns.

Lat.—Sus minervam.

37. Long e'er four bare legs heat in a bed.

To dissuade people who have no stock from marrying.

Eng.—More 'long to a bed than four bare legs.

38. Let one dee'l ding another.

Spoken when two bad persons quarrel.

Lat.—Fallacia alia aliam trudat.

39. Let the plough stand, and slay a mouse.

Lay aside, for a little, that business that you are so earnest upon; and take a little divertisement: Master Palmer has one directly contrary, viz.

Never let the plough stand to slay a mouse.

Which also has a good signification, to wit, that we be not taken off from our proper business, by every obvious divertisement.

40. Leave the court, e'er the court leave thee.

A good advice in its literal sense, if courtiers would take it, but it signifies that we should mortify our vicious inclinations, by consideration and religion, before old age make them forsake us.

41. Lye down with the lamb, and rise with the ᵏ laverock.

Eng.—Early to bed, and early to rise,

Makes a man healthy, wealthy, and wise.

42. Like a dog's turd broken, and look in both ends of it.

Spoken when two persons, equally vile, and base, are compared together.

Eng.—You may wink and choose.

43. Little to few, when taylors are true.

Lat.—Raro, ad tempus, fidem præstant artifices.

44. Let the earth ˡ big the ᵐ dike.

Let the expence that attends a thing, be taken out of the profit that it yields.

45. Little may an old horse do, that may not ⁿ nigher.

Spoken of over-grown decayed rakes, that speak bawdy.

Eng.—He's an ill horse that can neither whinny, nor wag his tail.

Item.—The old coachman loves the crack of the whip.

ᵏ Lark.   ˡ Build.   ᵐ Ditch.   ⁿ Neigh.

46. Let him that is cold blow at the coal.

Let them drudge about business that want it, and expect benefit by it.

Lat.—Lucernâ qui indigent, oleam infundant.

Item.— Eat, zonam qui perdidit.

47. Long standing, and little offering, makes a poor priest.

Spoken by hucksters, pedlars, and the like, when they have an ill market.

48. Lik'd geer is half bought.

For in that case a man will give a little more for his fancy.

Eng.—The bargain is soon made where wares please.

49. Light winning makes a heavy purse.

Because, when men sell at conscionable rates, they make quick returns, and that makes a rich merchant.

50. Loth to drink, and loth from it.

People of a narrow and niggardly spirit, when they treat they will be very profuse.

51. Little wats the ill willy wife, what a dinner may hold in.

For a handsome treat may procure good friends and great interest.

52. Laugh, and lay down again.

Spoken when one hath picked up any thing, as if you would say, give it back again, and pretend that you did it in jest.

53. Love lives in cottages, as well as in courts.

Conjugal love much more, for they who live in cottages keep no whores : and seldom marry for interest, wealth, or court favour, those whom they do not love.

54. Like butter in the black dog's ° ha'se.

That is, past recovery.

55. Lie you for me, and I'll swear for you.

Spoken of two rogues who combine to carry on a cheat.

56. Let the tail follow the skin.

Let the appurtenance follow the main bulk.

57. Little geer, less care.

Lat.—Misera est magni custodia census.

58. Live in measure, and laugh at the mediciners.

Nothing contributes more to health, than a temperate diet. Whereas, Nimia gula morborum mater.

Eng.—He that lives fast, cannot live long.

° Throat.

59. Long P ment, little dint.

Spoken when men threaten much, and dare not execute.

60. Let him come to himself, like Mackibbon's ᑫ crowdy.

Spoken when people are angry without a cause ; as if you would say, let him settle himself, for I value not his anger.

61. ʳ Lacking breeds laziness, praise breeds ˢ pith.

Discommend a boy and you discourage him, but commend him, and it will spur him on.

Lat.—Virtus laudata crescit.

Item.—Excitat auditor studium, laudataque virtus
Crescit: et immensum gloria calcar habet.

62. Lordships changes manners.

When people grow rich, and powerful, they grow proud.

63. Little ken'd, less car'd for.

Spoken of such of our relations as dwell at a distance.

Lat —Non sunt amici, amici qui vivunt procul.

64. Like the Orkney butter, neither good to eat, nor to ˢ creich wool.

A minister having in these words compar'd the covenant. made it a proverb; apply'd to a thing that is useful no way.

65. Loth to bed, and loth out of it.

Eng.—Lubbers guise, loth to bed, and loth to rise.

66. Last in bed best hear'd.

Spoken when they who lye longest are first serv'd.

67. Likely lies in the mire, and unlikely gets over.

Good likelihood is not always an infallible token of great strength, skill, or fortune.

Lat.———Viribus ille.
Confisus periit, admirandisque lacerti.

68. Long and small, like the cat's elbow.

A disparaging reflection upon slender people.

69. Let your horse drink what he will, but not where he will.

Often drinking in a journey, makes a horse faint.

Eng.—He that lets his horse drink at every water, and his wife go to every feast, will never have a good horse, or a good wife.

P Offering, threatening. ᑫ Brose. ʳ Discommending.
ˢ Force. ˢ Grease.

70. Like a magistrate among beggars.

Spoken of them that have some little authority, and make a great bustle with it.

71. Love your friend, but look to yourself.

Lat.—Nulli te facias nimis sodalem.

72. Longest at the fire soonest finds cold.

They who are used to ease, softness, and plenty, will soon be sensible of a contrary condition.

Lat.—Quem res plus nimio delectavere secundæ,
        Mutatæ quatiunt.

73. Long may you pish, and fart.

A ridiculous, dirty way of wishing people long life. From another old Scottish proverb, Pish and fart sound at the heart.

They have another wish of that sort, but I shall not trouble the reader with it.

74. Lay the sweet side of your tongue to it.

An answer to them that ask what they will get to their hasty-pudding. And if a boy ask what he will get to his bread? They will say, Slaver and sharp teeth. That is, your teeth to bruise it, and your spit to moisten it.

75. Learn young, learn fair.

Lat.—Tenacissimi sumus eorum, quæ rudibus annis percepimus.

Item.—Quo semel est imbuta recens servabit odorem.
        Testa diu.

76. ᵘ Lippen to me, but look to your self.

A modest refusal of what we importun'd for.

77. Lick thy ᵛloof, and lay't to mine, dry leather ᵂ gigs ay.

This signifies no more but kiss your hand and give it: spoken facetiously, upon some good fortune, unexpected.

78. ˣ Lean to your dinner.

Spoken to them that loll upon us.

79. Long straws are no moles, quoth the good wife when she harl'd the cat out of the kirn.

Spoken facetiously, when we get a long mole in our meat.

80. Long tongued wives go long with bairn.

Baubling wives will tell every tatling gossip that they have conceived; which makes them long expect their lying in. Apply'd to those who discover their projects, designs, and intentions, long before they are put in execution.

ᵘ Trust.   ᵛ Palm.   ᵂ Cracks.   ˣ Loll upon.

Lat.—Quod facturus es ea ne dixeris, frustratus enim rideberis.

81. Love most, least thought of.
Spoken when our love and friendship meet with neglect.

82. Let every sheep hing by his own shank.
83. Let every herring hing by its own head.
Every man must stand by his own endeavour, industry, and interest.

Eng.—Let every tub stand on its own bottom.

84. Lay up like a laird, and seek like a lad.
Spoken to them that take no care to lay up what they had in their hands, and so must drudge in seeking of it.

85. Love has no lack, if the dame was ne'er so black.
Lat.—Balbinum delectat polypus agnæ.

86. Little can a long tongue ᵞ lein.
Spoken as a reproof to a baubler.

87. Laugh at leisure, you may greet e'er night.
A reprimand to them that laugh intemperately.

88. Let him take a ᶻ spring of his own fiddle, and dance to it when he has done.
Let him go on in his own way, and bear the effects of it.

89. Let the world ᵃ shogg.
Spoken by them who have a mind to do as they have resolved, be the issue what will.

90. Lend your money, and lose your friend.
It is not the lending of our money that loses our friend; but the demanding it again, and that will lose a friend to my certain knowledge. They have a proverbial rhyme to this purpose.

I had a		and a		as many of this land,
I lent my		to my		when he did it demand.
I sought my	} penny {	from my	} friend {	when he had kept it long,
I lost my		and my		and was not that a wrong?
Had I a		and a		as I have had before,
I wo'd keep my		and my		and play the fool no more.

91. Like lips, like lettuce,
This is in the old collection from the Latin, Similes habent labra lactucas.

Eng.—Like priest like people.

Item.—A thistle is a fit sallad for an asse's mouth.

ᵞ Conceal. ᶻ Tune. ᵃ Shake from one side to the other.

92. Lay the ª sub side undermost, and reckon when ye rise.

An answer to him that objects against marrying a woman, because she is akin to him.

93. Long e'er you cut Falkland wood with a penknife.

Spoken when people set about a work without proper tools.

94. Let all trades live

Spoken when we have broken an utensil, which must employ a tradesman to mend it, or make a new one.

95. Love is never without jealousy.

Lat.—Z lotypiam parit amor

96. Let a friend go with a foe.

A bad proverb! for nothing should ever induce a friend to part with his friend. I would rather spare a foe for a friend's sake.

97. Let not the cobler go beyond his last.

This from the Latin, Ne sutor ultra crepidam. Taken from the famous story of Apelles, who could not bear that the cobler should correct any part of his picture beyond the slipper.

98. Like a dog in a manger; neither eat hay, nor suffer the horse to eat it.

99. Let him put in his finger, and he'll put in his whole hand.

An advice not to meddle with covetous and designing persons; who will screw themselves into your interest and property by degrees.

100. Long look'd for comes at last.

101. Love, and lordship, like no ᵇ marrows.

Lat.— Nec regna ferre socium, nec tædæ sciunt.

102. Little d.fference between a feast and a full.

103. Love and light cannot be hid.

Lat.—Amor & tussis non celatur.

104. Let never sorrow come so near your heart, unless for sin.

Spoken heartily when we have made our friend drink.

105. Lay by the book.

Signifying that we firmly believe what they say; so that they need not swear it.

106. Light suppers, long life days.

The English say, Light suppers make clean sheets.

ª Akin.   ᵇ Partners.

M.

1. MANY one kisses the bairn for love of the ^c nurrish.

That is, shew their kindness to the companions, friends, or relations, of those upon whom they have a design, which they hope by their influence to effect.

2. ^d Mickle fails that fools think.

Lat.—Fallitur augurio, spes bona, sæpe suo.

3. Many masters, quoth the ^e poddock to the harrow, when every ^f tin gave her a ^g tig.

Spoken by those whom persons, inferior to their masters, presume to reprove, command, or correct.

Eng.—Where every hand fleeceth, the sheep go naked.

4. Many say well, when it never was worse.

Spoken to them that say, Well, by way of resentment.

Eng.—Well, well is a word of malice.

5. Money will make the pot play, if the dee'l pish in the fire.

6. ^h Moyen does mickle, but money does more.

The vast influence that money has upon mortals, has given occasion to these two, and many other, proverbs.

Eng.—Money makes the mare go.

Lat.—Quid si dolosi spes refulserit nummi
    Poetas corvos, poetriasque picas,
    Cantare credas pegaseum melos—perseus.

Item.— ——Omnis enim res
    Virtus, fama, decus, divina, humanaque, pulchris
    Divitiis parent, quas, qui construxerit, ille
    Clarus erit, fortis, justus, sapiens, etiam & rex,
    Et quicquid voluit.

7. Meat is good, but ⁱ mense is better.

Let not ones greediness on their meat intrench upon their modesty.

8. Many excuses pishes the bed.

When men make many excuses it argues their guilt.

9. Many a good tale is spoil'd in the telling.

Apply'd often when a good sermon is ill delivered, to my certain knowledge.

Lat.—Nihil est quin, male narrando, possit depravarier.

---

^c Nurse.   ^d Much.   ^e Frog.   ^f Tooth.   ^g A little blow.   ^h Interest.   ⁱ Modesty.

10. Many hands make slight work.

Because, while every one trusts to another, the work is neglected.

11. Many hands make light work.

Because it is but little to every one.

Lat.—Multorum manibus grande levatur onus.

12. Metal is dangerous in a blind mare.

And so is bigotry, and blind zeal, in an ignorant fellow.

13. My daughter is my daughter all the days of her life,

My son is my son 'till he get him a wife.

A mother has seldom so good treatment from a daughter-in-law, as from a son-in-law.

14. Might overcomes right, by a time.

Lat.—Nam quid agas cum te furiosus cogat & idem
———Fortior.

15. [k] Mister makes man of craft.

Eng.—Make virtue of necessity.

Lat.—Necessitas rationum inventrix.

Item.—Magister artis ingeniiq ; largitor—venter.

16. My next neighbour's skathe is my present peril.

Lat.—Tum tua res agitur, paries cum proximus ardet.

17. Many hounds me soon [l] worry one hare.

Spoken when a potent family, with their friends, relations, and followers, bear hard upon a poor man.

Eng —Two to one is odds at foot-ball.

Lat.—Multis ictibus dejicitur quercus.

Item.—Ne Hercules ipse contra duas.

18. Mickle would ay have more.

This, and many others, are spoken of the insatiable desire that rich men have after wealth.

Lat.—Crescit indulgens sibi dirus hydrops.

19. Marry a beggar, and get a louse for your [m] togher good.

A dissuasive from joyning in trade, or farm, with a poor man, where the whole loss must lye on you : the following English has another invention : Sue a beggar and get a louse.

20. Mickledom is no virtue.

It is no virtue for a man to have a large body, or brawny limbs ; for a man of less stature may have more stoutness.

Lat.—A cane non magno sæpe tenetur aper.

---

[k] Need. [l] Kill. [m] Portion,

21. Messengers should neither be headed nor hang'd.

An excuse for carrying an ungrateful message.

Lat.—Legatus neo violatur, neo læditur.

22. My tongue is not under your belt.

You can say nothing of me that can make me hold my tongue.

Lat.— ———Hic murus ahenius esto
Nil conscire sibi, nullâ pallescere culpâ.

23. Meddle with your match.

Spoken by people of age, when young people jest upon them too wantonly: or by weak people, when insulted by the more strong, and robust, in that case they will say, You dare not meddle with your match.

24. Many fair promises in marriage making, but few in ⁿ togher paying.

People will flatter you with fair promises and proposals; 'till they get you engaged in some project for their interest, but after alter their tune.

Eng —Between promising and performing a man may marry his daughter.

Item.—He promises like a merchant, and pays like a man of war.

Lat.—Fistula dulce canit, volucrem dum decipit auceps.

25. Meat feeds, cloth cleeds, but manners makes the man.

And indeed good meat, and fine cloaths, without good breeding, are but poor recommendations.

Eng.—Manners often make fortunes.

26. Met and measure make all men wise.

Spoken when people would have what they buy weighed, or measured.

Eng.—Weight and measure take away strife.

27. Many heads are better than one.

Lat.—Plus vident oculi quam oculus.

28. Make friends of ᵉframet ᵉ folk.

Spoken to dissuade people from marrying their near kinswomen, thinking it better to procure new interests, and new alliances, by marrying into a stranger's family.

29. Maidens must be mild and meek,
Swift to hear, and slow to speak.

A rhyme much canted by mothers to their daughters in former times; but now almost antiquated.

ⁿ Portion.   ᵉ Strangers.

30. Muck bodes luck, dame go drite P there P benn.

Eng.—Shitten luck is good luck.

31. Make the best of a bad market.

Since you have faln into a troublesome business, mend it by your cunning and industry.

32. Make no baulks in good bearland.

Spoken when it is proposed to marry the youngest daughter, before the eldest.

33. q Mair in a r mair dish.

That is, a great deal more; an answer to them who ask you if you will have any more, when you have gotten but very little.

34. Murther will out.

Taken from the strange discoveries of murther. Spoken jocosely when something is like to be discovered, which we would gladly have conceal'd.

35. More by good luck, than by good guiding.

Spoken when a thing, ill managed, falls out well.

36. Maidens s toghers, and ministers t stipends, are ay less than they are call'd.

Maidens portions are magnified to procure them suiters. And ministers livings are call'd larger, by them who grudge that they are so large.

37. Many purses hold friends long together.

When every man pays his equal club, we are not burthensome to our friends, and so continue our friendship.

38. Many care for meal that have bak'd bread enough:

Spoken against whining, complaining people, who have enough, and yet are always making a moan.

39. Man propones, but God dispones.

Eng.—Man doth what he can, but God what he will.

Lat.—Non omnia eveniunt quæ animo statueris.

40. Many one serves a thankless master.

Spoken when you have done service to one, who seems not sensible of it, or thankful for it. Often too when we urge our service upon them that care not for it.

41. Many one u tines the v half v mark w whinger for the half-penny x whang.

P Into the inward part of the house.   q More.   r Bigger.
s Portions.   t Livings,   u Loses.   v Bought for six-pence.
w Dagger.   x Thong.

There are many to this purpose; spoken when people lose a considerable thing, for not being at an inconsiderable expence.

42. Wives, and mills, are ay wanting.

It requires much to keep a mill useful, and a wife fine.

43. Many one do [y] lack what they would [z] fain have in their pack.

Men will seem to discommend what they have a great mind to, in order to get it cheaper.

44. Marry in haste, and repent at leisure.

In a business of so great an importance as marriage, we ought to use great deliberation, and good advice.

45. Mickle corn, mickle care.

Lat.—Crescentem sequitur cura pecuniam.

46. Men speak of the fair, as things went there.

Men speak of men, or things, as they find them.

47. Malice is ay mindful.

Spoken when people rip up old sores, and think, with resentment, upon old disobligations.

48. More nice than [a] wise.

Spoken when people out of bashfulness leave a thing unsaid, or a person unspoken to, which would have contributed to their interest.

49. Money is welcome in a dirten clout.

Lat.—Dulcis odor lucri ex re quâlibet.

50. Mickle spoken, part split.

Eng.—Talk much err much. From the Spanish.

Lat.—Non est ejusdem multa, & opportuna, dicere.

51. Many one blames their wife, for their own unthrift.

I never saw a Scottish woman who had not this at her finger's ends.

52. Men [b] loup the dike where it is [c] leaghest.

That is, oppress and over-run those who are least able to resist them.

53. Many dogs will die e'er you'll be heir.

Spoken to them who shew themselves interested about a thing, in which they have no concern.

54. Money would be gotten, if there were money to get it with.

Intimating that the man would thrive, if he had a stock.

---

[y] Discommend.   [z] Gladly.   [a] In Scotch pronounced wice
     [b] Jump over.   [c] Lowest.

P

Eng.—He that lacketh a stock, his gain's not worth a chip.

55. Mutton is sweet, and gars folks die e'er they be sick.

That is, make people steal sheep and so be hang'd.

56. Man's mouth is no measure, unless his throat was stop'd.

Spoken when we chuse rather to drink out of a glass, than out of the pot; or, as they say, by word of mouth.

57. Many one's geer is many one's [d] death.

Spoken when oppressive, and covetous sheriffs condemn rich men for small crimes, and take their forfeitures.

Lat.—Raro venit in cœnaculo miles.
　　　　Sed plures nimià congesta pecuniâ curâ
　　　　Strangulat.

58. More hamely than welcome.

59. Mickle sorrow comes to the [e] screa, e'er the heat come to the [f] tea.

Spoken when one holds his shoe to the fire to warm his foot.

Eng.—While the leg warmeth the boot harmeth.

60. [g] Mint e'er ye strike.

Spoken to them that threaten us; give me fair warning, and do your best.

61. Many aunts, many [h] emms, many kinsfolk, few friends.

Spoken by them that have many rich friends, and are little the better for them.

62. March comes in with adder heads, and goes out with peacock tails.

Eng.—March comes in like a lyon, and goes out like a lamb.

63. Many good nights is loth away.

Spoken by those who, by reason of some accident, return after they had taken their leave.

64. [i] Mastery mows the meadow down.

Spoken when people of power and wealth effect a great business in a short time.

65. Many words fill not the [k] farlet.

66. Many one's coat saves their doublet.

Spoken when clergymen use you saucily, whom, in deference to their profession, you will not beat, as if you would say, Were it not for your coat, sir, &c.

---

[d] In Scotch dead.　　[e] Shoe.　　[f] Toe.　　[g] Make an offer.
　　[h] Relations.　　[i] Might, power.　　[k] A dry measure.

67. Mercy! mother! the bed's pish'd!

68. Married! ruin'd! and undone!

Both of them silly exclamations, upon some ridiculous accident.

69. Mickle pleasure, some pain.

Lat.—Ut rebus lætis par sit mensura malorum.

70. March borrowed from Averil

Three days, and they were ill.

It is alledg'd that the first three days of April are commonly rough and intemperate, like March, and these we call the borrowing days.

71. Marry above your match, and you get a master.

A wife, above our station and condition, will be apt to despise us, think her self disgrac'd, and prove insolent.

Lat.—Non honos est sed onus.   Species læsura ferentem.

Si qua voles apte nubere nube pari.

Item.—Malo te, Venusina, quam te Cornelia Mater

Grachorum, si cum magnis virtutibus adfers,

Grande supercilium. & numeres in dote triumphos.

72. Make a kirk, and a mill of it.

That is, make your best of it: it does not answer to the English, Make a hog or a dog of it: for that means, bring it either to one use, or another.

73. May bees fly not this time o'be year.

A return to them that say, May be, such a thing will come to pass; alluding to the identity of May be, and May bee.

74. Meat and mass never hindered man.

Eng.—Prayers and provender stop no journies.

75. Mickle, but not manful.

Lat.—Nulla, in tam magno corpore, mica satis.

76. Mickle must a good heart [1] thole.

77. Mickle head, little wit.

A groundless reflection: an eminent instance to the contrary was John Duke of Lauderdale.

78. Make not mickle of little.

Lat.————— Flagrantior æquo

Non debet dolor esse viri, nec vulnere major.

79. Many ways to kill a dog, and not to hang him.

There be many ways to bring about one and the same thing, or business.

80. Mickle power makes many enemies.

Occasion'd partly by envy, partly by fear.

---

[1] Suffer.

Lat.—Necesse est ut multos timeat, quem multi timent.

81. Mickle mouth'd folk are happy to their meat.

Spoken by, or to them who come opportunely to eat with us.

82. Maidens should be meek 'till they be married, and then burn kirks.

Spoken often by way of reflection, when we say that such a one is a good humour'd girl, as if you would say, Observe how she'll prove when she is married.

83. ᵐ Minting gets no bairns.

Only offering to do a thing, is not the way to effect it.

84. Must is for the king.

Spoken to them that say, You must do such a thing; such absolute commands become no subject.

85. Make one wrong step, and you fall to the bottom.

A business may be mismanaged, at first, by some unlucky turn, so as not easily to be retriev'd.

Eng.—He that would climb the ladder, must begin at the first step.

86. Many littles make a mickle.

Lat.—Ex granis fit acervus.

Item.—Adde parum parvo, magnus acervus erit.

87. ⁿ Mows may come to earnest.

What you speak in jest, may come to be done in reality.

88. March ᵒ whisker was never a good fisher.

An old proverb signifying that a windy March is a token of a bad fish year.

89. Mickle may fall between the cup and the lip.

This is an old Greek proverb, signifying that a project may come to be spoil'd just at the point of finishing. Some servants, being oppressed making a new vineyard, one of them told his master, that he should never taste the wine of it. When the wine was ready, the master takes a glass of it in his hand, but would not drink it till that servant should be call'd, but before he drunk there came word in, that a wild boar had broken into his vineyard; upon which he set aside the cup, and went to chase him out, but was kill'd by him.

Lat.—Multa cadunt inter calicem supremaque labra.

90. Make not two mews of one daughter.

This is in the old Scottish Collection, the sense I do not understand, unless it be spoken to them who think to oblige two different persons with one and the same benefit, taken from the Latin,

---

ᵐ Offering.　　ⁿ Jesting.　　ᵒ Blusterer.

Eædem filiæ duos generos parare.

91. Many a dog dead since you were a whelp.

92. More shew than substance.

93. Many irons in the fire, some must cool.

When men have too many works in hand, too many offices, or employments, some must be neglected.

94. Many one talks of Robin Hood that never shot in his bow:

And as many of Little John that never did him know.

Many talk of these exploits that they know little of.

Lat.—Non omnes, qui cytheram tenent, cytherædi.

95. Measure twice, cut but once.

Take good deliberation before you fall to actual execution.

96. Mocking is catching.

Spoken to discourage people from mimicking any man's imperfections, lest you contract a habit of them. A memorable instance I know of this just now, in a boy who got a habit of winking by mimicking a boy that did so; a habit of snuffing ungracefully with his nose, by mimicking his usher; and a habit of stammering, by imitating my self.

97. Much good do't you, and a merry go down, with every lump as great's my thumb.

A facetious wish to our companions when they are eating.

98. My P minnie has the leave o't.

Spoken jocosely, when we have no mind to tell a thing all out, or sing a song to the end.

99. Many a time have I gotten a wipe with a towel; but never a q daub with a dish clout before.

Spoken by saucy girls, when one jeers them with an unworthy sweetheart.

100. Mickle water goes by that the miller wats not of.

That is, people who have much among their hands, will have things broken, lost, and purloyned, of which they will not be sensible.

Lat.—Exigua est domus ubi non & multa supersunt,
Et dominum fallunt, & prosunt furibus.

101. Men is no mice.

An encouragement to act bravely.

102. My dancing days are done.

P Mamma.   q A dash.

N.

1. No fool to an old fool.

Spoken when men of advanc'd age behave themselves, or talk youthfully, or wantonly.

2. Never a barrel of better herring.

Lat.—Maxima pars hominum morbo jactatur eadem.

3. Narrow gathered, widely spent.

Wealth, gotten by too much sparing, comes often to be widely squander'd.

4. Need makes a naked man run.

Eng.—Need makes the old wife trot.

Lat.—Durum telum necessitas.

5. No rule so good as rule of thumb, if it hit.

But it seldom hits! Spoken when a thing falls out to be right, which we did at a venture.

6. Nothing is a bare man.

A jocose answer to children, when they say they have gotten nothing.

Lat.—Non entis nullæ sunt affectiones aut partes.

7. No longer pipe, no longer dance.

A reflection on those who have been advantaged by us heretofore, whose kindness continues no longer than they are getting by us.

Eng.—No longer faster, no longer friend.

Lat.—Dum fervet olla vivit amicitia.

8. Near my ^a sark; but nearer my skin.

Lat.—Omnes sibi melius esse quam alteri.

Item.—Tunica pallio proprior.

9. Nature passes nurture.

Lat.—Naturam expellas furcâ licet, usque recurret.

10. ^b Nipping and ^c scarting is Scots folks wooing.

When we see boys and girls jarring, we suspect them of some intrigue.

Eng.—By biting and scratching cats come together.

Lat.—Amantium iræ amoris redintegratio est.

11. Nearer God's blissing, than Carlisle fair.

You need but go to your closet for the one, but you must go out of the kingdom for the other.

12. None worse sho'd than the shoemaker's wife, and the smith's mare.

---

^a Shirt.   ^b Pinching.   ^c Scratching.

Spoken when people are scarce of what they might have plenty of, if they pleased.

13. Never shew your teeth when you cannot bite.

Never shew your resentment when you cannot do it to purpose.

14. Never bite, unless you make your teeth meet.

This, and the former, savour too much of malice and revenge. Vile unchristian vices. The more noble way is to forget and to forgive.

15. No man can live longer in peace than his neighbour pleases.

For an ill neighbour, with his scolding, noise, complaints, law-suits, and indictments, may be very troublesome.

Eng.—You must ask your neighbour if you'll live in peace.

16. Never came a hearty fart out of the wren's arse.

Spoken when niggardly people give some insignificant gift.

17. No ᵈ farlie dirt go dear, when a fart cost five shillings.

A satyrical expression of great folks, when those, of a meaner birth, pretend to education, breeding, or fine cloaths.

Lat.—Si tanti vitrum, quanti margaritum.

18. Never shew me the meat, but shew me the man.

If a man be fat, plump, and in good liking, I shall not ask what keeping he has had.   And on the contrary,

Lat.—Non verbis, sed factis probari vult græcia.

19. No penny, no pater noster.

20. No pains, no gains.

21. No profit, ᵉ but pains.

There are many others to this purpose.

Eng.—No pay, no service.

Item.—No sweat, no sweet.

Lat.—Non fit sine periculo facimus memorabile & magnum.

Item.—Nil sine magno —— vita labore dedit mortalibus.

22. Nobility, without ability, is like a pudding wanting ᶠsuet.

Both want the principal ingredient.

Lat.—Et genus & forma, nisi cum re, vilior alga est.

23. No worse happen you, than your own prayers.

Spoken to them that curse you, wishing that it may happen so ill to them as they wish to you.

24. Never scald your lips in other folks kail.

ᵈ Wonder. |ᵉ Without.   ᶠ Fat.

Do not officiously meddle in other folks business.

Lat.—Quod tuâ nil refert, percunctari desinas.

25. Never a poor man of his kin.

Spoken of those who, in their cups and airs boast mightily, and talk highly.

Lat.—Quid non ebriatus designat, aperta recludit,
    Spes jubet esse ratas, in prælia trudit inermem,
    Facundi calices quem non fecere disertum.

Item.—Quis post vina pauperiem crepat.

26. Never marry a widow, unless her first husband was hang'd.

Lest she upbraid you with him, and sing you an old Scottish song : You will never be like our old good man.

27. New lords, new laws.

The sense of this proverb is pretty well known.

Lat.—Novus rex, nova lex.

28. Never is a long term.

29. No body will come after you, that will set a longer term.

Both spoken to them that say they will never get such a thing effected.

30. Nothing comes fairer to light, than that which has been long hid.

Spoken when people unexpectedly find what has been long hid, or discover what has been long conceal'd.

31. Never break out of kind, to make your friends ᵍ farlie on you.

Spoken to them that follow the ill qualities of their parents.

32. Nearest the kirk, farrest from God.

Spoken to them who do not take these advantages, that they might easily have had.

33. No haste, but of well fair.

34. No more haste than good speed.

35. Nothing to be done in haste, but gripping of fleas.

These three spoken when we are unreasonably urged to make haste.

Eng.—Let us take more time, that we may have the sooner done.

Lat.—Festina lente.

Item.—Canis festinans cæcos parit catulos.

36. Never say ill fellow deals thou.

ᵍ Wonder at you.

I have made you so good a proffer, that you have no reason to call me an ill fellow.

37. No great loss [h] but some small profit.

Lat.—Nil adeo fortuna gravis miserabile fecit.

Ut minuant nulla gaudia parte malum.

Item.—Malo aliquis fuit usus in illo.

38. No safe wading in [i] uncouth waters.

It is no wisdom to engage with dangers that we are not acquainted with.

39. No friend to a bosom friend; no enemy to a bosom enemy.

40. No friend to a friend in [k] mister.

Lat.—Amicus certus in re incerta cernitur.

Eng.—A friend is never known 'till a man have need.

41. No fault but the cat had a clean band, she [l] sets a bonnet much so weel.

Ironically spoken to them who pretend to do, have, or wear, what does not become them.

42. Never trust much to a new friend, or an old enemy.

You know not how far the one may extend his love, or the other has suppress'd his enmity.

43. Nothing ill to be done, when will is at home.

Will is a readiness to act, and Will is a diminutive of William. They will say facetiously, I wish that lad was at home; meaning Will,

Eng.—Nothing difficult to a willing mind.

44. Never open your pack, and sell no wares.

Never proffer your service, where it is not likely to be accepted.

45. Never [m] let on you, but laugh.

Spoken when people are jeering our projects, pretensions and designs. As if you would say, Laugh you on, but I will effect it.

46. Nothing gotten [n] but pains, but an ill name.

I have seen people at pains and cost too, to get that itself.

47. Nothing like stark dead.

A vile malicious proverb! first used by Captain James Stewart, against the noble Earl of Morton; and afterwards apply'd to the Earl of Strafford, and A. B. Laud.

Lat.—Mortui non mordent.

48. Never good egg, or [o] burd.

---

[h] Without. [i] Strange. [k] Need. [l] Becomes. [m] Trouble yourself about it. [n] Without. [o] Chicken.

Spoken of bad boys, when they become worse men.

49. Nothing to do, but draw out, and loup on.

Spoken ironically to them who think a thing easy to be done, where yet they may meet with great difficulties.

50. No more to do but p ba'se, and go to q gody.

Taken from the fondling words of nurses to their children. Spoken when people, all of a suddain contract a friendship and familiarity, which we suspect will not be lasting.

51. No sooner up, but her head in the r ambry.

Spoken of or to maidens, who have too early a stomach.

52. Never kiss a man's wife, nor wipe his knife, for he will be likely to do both after you.

53. Neither fish nor flesh, nor good red herring.

That is, stark naught.

54. Nothing so s crouse, as a new washen louse.

Spoken of them who have been ragged and dirty, and are proud, and fond of new or clean cloaths.

55. Nothing enters into a close hand.

Niggardly people will not procure much good will.

56. No body t riving your cloaths.

No body will force you against your will ; apply'd to several things, especially to maidens who declare against marriage.

57. No body will make a bore, but you'll get a pin for it.

Spoken of those who are ready with their answers and excuses.

Eng.—Find you without an excuse, and find a hare without a muse.

58. Never look for a wife, 'till you have a house, and a fire to put her in.

The jest is in a fire to put her in, a house to put her in, and a fire to set her by.

Eng.—Before thou marry, be sure of a house where to tarry.

59. Never go to the dee'l, and a dish-clout in your hand.

If you will be a knave, be not in a trifle, but in something of value. A presbyterian minister had a son who was made archdeacon of Ossery ; when this was told to his father, he said, If my son will be a knave, I am glad that he is an arch-knave. This has the same sense,

As good be hang'd for an old sheep as a young lamb.

---

p Come in arms. q Godmother. r Cap-board.

s Merry, hearty. t Tearing.

Lat.—Aude aliquid brevibus gyaris, vel carcere dignum,
Si vis esse aliquid.

60. Never put a sword in a wood-man's hand.

Lat.—Ne puero gladium.

61. Never meet, never pay.

Spoken when we supply a friend in his need, and with a
free heart.

62. Nothing makes a man sooner old like, than sitting
    ill to his meat.

Spoken when people sit inconveniently at table. To sit ill
to one's meat, in Scotch, is to be ill kept.

63. Never came a wife well pleas'd from the mill but
    one, and she broke her neck.

A word commonly said to wives when they come from the
mill, but the occasion, sense, or meaning of it I know not.

64. Never say go, but ‡ gang.

Eng.—If you would have your errand done, send your servant;

If you would have it well done, go yourself.

65. No ⁈ farlie you say so to me, you said many times
    so to your mother.

A satyrical answer to those that call us by opprobrious
names, as if they used to call their mothers by such names.

66. Need makes greed.

Want is a temptation to covetousness.

67. No man can find his marrow in the ᵛ kirn so well
    as he that has been there himself.

Spoken to those who suspect us guilty of a thing, in which
they take measure of us by their practices and inclinations.

68. Nearest the heart, nearest the mouth.

Spoken to them who, designing to name one person, by mistake names another, perhaps a mistress or sweetheart.

69. None to you, but our dog Sorkie, and he's dead,
    and you're matchless.

A taunt to them that boast what they can do.

70. No body should drink, but them that can drink.

A reflection upon them that are soon drunk, or ill-natured
in their cups.

71. Never take a stone to break an egg, when you
    can do it with the back of your knife.

Lat.—Frustra sit per plura, quod, æque commode, fieri
potest per pauciora.

---

‡ Go yourself.   ⁈ Wonder.   ᵛ Churn.

72. Never take the * taws, when a word will do the turn.

Severity ought never to be used, where fair means will prevail.

Lat.—Pudore & libertate liberos retinere satius esse credo quam metu.

73. No body will ever take you for a conjurer.

Spoken to them who look blockish and sheepish.

74. Necessity has no law.

Spoken when people are forc'd upon a method, which otherways they would not take.

Eng.—No fence against a flail.

75. Nothing so bold as a blind mare.

Eng.—Who so bold as blind Byard.

Lat.—Dulce bellum inexpertis.

76. No man hath a lease of his life.

Lat.—Vita mancipium nulli, omnibus usui, datur.

77. No weather ill, if the wind be still.

78. Neck or nothing, for the king loves no cripples.

A prophane jest upon those who are like to fall, wishing that they may either break their neck, or come off safe; for breaking a limb will make them useless subjects.

79. Never too late to learn.

Lat.—Nunquam sera est ad bonos mores via.

80. None can play the fool so well as the wise man.

Lat.—Misce consiliis stultitiam brevem.

Dulce est desipere in foco.

81. No flying without wings.

A man cannot thrive and prosper in the world, that has no stock or support.

82. Not God above gets all men's love.

Lat.—Jupiter neque pluens, neque abstinens, omnibus placet.

83. No butter will stick to my bread.

Spoken when all means we use to thrive miscarry.

84. Never pour water on a drown'd mouse.

Never insult over those who are down already.

85. Nothing freer than a gift.

86. No jesting with edg'd tools·

It is no safe jesting with powerful men, or sacred things.

Lat.—In re seria jocandum non est.

Item.—Noli ludere cum sacris.

---

* A leather used instead of a rod.

87. Never strive against the stream.

Lat.—Dum furor in cursu est, currenti cede furori.

88. Neither rhyme nor reason.

89. Nature hates all suddain changes.

It is not safe for a man to change in his diet, behaviour, or way of living suddainly, from one extreme to another.

90. No man can make his own hap.

91. No reply is best.

Spoken by sedate and even-temper'd men, when abused by others.

92. Need makes virtue.

93. Never make ˣ toom ʸ rusie.

Never boast, or brag of that, which you have not, or cannot do.

94. Nineteen nay says of a maiden is but half a grant.

Spoken to encourage those who have had a denial from their mistress to attack them again.

95. Now is now, and yule's in winter.

A return to them that say Now, by way of resentment; a particle common in Scotland.

O.

1. ONE beggar is ay wo, that another by the ᵃ gate go.

Eng —Two of a trade will never agree.

Lat.—Figulus figulo invidet.

2. Out of the ᵇ peat-pot into the mire.

Eng.—Out of the frying pan into the fire.

Lat.— E fumo in flammam.

There is an English proverb that I have seen to this purpose, but I do not understand it, viz.

Out of God's blessing into the warm sun.

3. One man may lead a horse to the water, but four and twenty will not make him drink.

You may force the outward compliance, but not the will.

Lat.—Voluntas non potest cogi.

4. O'er mickle of ᶜ yee thing is good for ᵈ nething.

Eng.—Too much breaks the bag.

Lat.—Ne quid nimis.

5. O'er strong meat for your weak stomach.

Commonly spoken to old men, when they incline to marry young girls.

ˣ Empty.   ʸ Commendation.   ᵃ Way.   ᵇ The hole you dig peat or turf out of.   ᶜ One.   ᵈ Nothing

6. One scabbed sheep will ^e smite all the flock.
And one facetious fellow will mislead a whole community.
Lat.—Uvaque conspecta livorem ducit abuvà.

7. One wit bought is worth two for naught.
Eng.—Wit once bought is worth twice taught.

8. One man's meat is another man's poison.
Eng.—One man's breath is another man's death.

9. Oft ^f etle, whiles hit.
People who have made many trials to do a thing, may hit
right at last.

10. Old men are twice bairns.
Lat.—Bis pueri senes.

11. Old sins breed new shame.
It were well they always would ; for then they might breed
repentance also.

12. One good turn deserves another.
Lat.—Beneficium, qui dare nescit, injusta petit.

13. Out of debt out of danger.

14. Out of sight out of langour.
Eng.—Long absent, soon forgotten.
Lat.—Qui procul ab oculis, procul est a limite cordis.

15. One pair of heels is worth two pair of hands by a
time.
Especially to them who are better at fleeing than fighting.

16. Open confession is good for the soul.
Spoken ironically to them that boast of their ill deeds.

17. O'er mickle hameliness spills courtesy.
In the old Scottish Collection it is,

18. O'er great familiarity genders despite.
From the Latin, Nimia familiaritas contemptum parit.
Eng.—Play with your servant at home, and he'll play with
you abroad.

19. One year a nurse, and seven years a ^g daw.
Because that year will give her a habit of idleness.

20. Old wives, and bairns are fool the physicians.
Children cannot tell where their ailment lies, and old women are sick of a disease past the physicians skill.

21. One hand is no hand.
In the Scottish dialect, Yee hand is nee hand ; that is, one
hand, where there is no help, can dispatch but little work.
Lat.—Unus vir, nullus vir.
Eng.—One and none is all one.

---

^e Infect.   ^f Aim.   ^g Slut, or a lazy drab.

22. One fool makes many.

By diverting them from their proper business.

23. Once paid never crav'd.

In the Scottish dialect, Anes pay't ne'er cree't; pay your debts, and prevent dunning.

24. Of all ills the least is the best.

Lat.—E malis minimum eligendum.

25. Old wives was ay good maidens.

Old people will always be boasting what fine feats they did when they were young. The character of the old man in Horace is,

—— Laudatur temporis acti
Se puero, censor, castigatorque minorum.

26. Once a whore and ay a whore.

Lat.—Læsa pudicitia nullâ est reparabilis arte.

27. Oft counting keeps friends long together.

Old and intricate accounts are often the cause of misunderstanding, which often adjusting prevents.

28. Of all sorrows a full sorrow is the best.

Spoken when friends die and leave good legacies.

29. One thing said, and another thing seen.

Spoken when we convince a man of his mistake by plain matter of fact.

30. Once [b] wood and ay the [i] warr.

They who have once been mad will seldom have their senses sound and well again.

31. O'er [k] hally was hang'd; but rough and [l] sonsie [m] was away.

Spoken against too precise people; as if those of less pretensions were more to be trusted.

Quisquis plus justo non sapit; ille sapit.

32. O'er seiker, o'er lose.

The method taken to secure a thing often makes it miscarry.

33. Of enough men leave.

They who leave no scraps can hardly be said to have enough.

34. One does the skathe, and another gets the scorn.

Spoken when one is blam'd for another man's mistake.

Eng.—He struck at Tib, and down fell Tom.

Lat.—Faber cadit, cum ferias fullonem.

35. One may think that dares not speak.

Lat.—Opinionis pœnam nemo pendit.

_____

[b] Mad. [i] Worse. [k] Holy. [l] Lucky. [m] Got.

Q 2

36. Once an use and ever a custom.

Therefore an ill use ought to be early broken off.

Eng.—An ill custom is like a good cake, better broken than kept.

37. One of the court but none of the counsel.

One of the party, but not admitted into their secrets and intrigues.

38. O'er fine a purse to put a ᴺ plack in.

Spoken when one builds a magnificent house upon a small estate.

39. Oft times the ° cautioner pays the debt.

Not only a caution against suretiship, but often a return to them who say they'll be caution (that is, bail) that we will come to some ill accident. In the first sense it answers the English,

He that would be master of his own must not be bound for another

40. O'er late to spare, when the bottom is bare.

Lat.—Sera est in fundo parsimonia.

41. Old ᴾ springs give no price.

Spoken when old people or things are despised.

42. On painting and fighting look ᵠ abigh.

It is dangerous to be near the one, and if we look near the other it loseth much of its advantage.

43. Our sins, and our debts, are often more than we think.

We are too apt to have too good an opinion of our condition, both in reference to this world and another.

44. Out the high gate is ay fair play.

Downright honesty is both best and safest.

Solomon, He that walks uprightly, walks surely.

Eng.—Honesty is the best policy.

45. One ᴿ scon of a baking is enough.

It is unreasonable to expect two gratuities out of one thing.

46. Old use and wont, legs about the fire.

A reflection on them who persevere in a bad custom.

47. O'er narrow counting ˢ culzies no kindness.

When people deal in rigour with us, we think ourselves but little oblig'd to them.

48. Of ill debtors men take oaths.

ᴺ Two sixths of a penny. ° Surety. ᴾ Tunes. ᵠ Off at a side. ᴿ Cake. ˢ In Scotch pronounced culyies, it signifies to elicit, draw forth, or procure.

That is, swearing to pay you such a time: and men must take these promises when they can get no more.

49. One half of the world kens not how the other lives.

Men bred to ease and luxury are not sensible of the mean condition of a great many.

50. Once away, and ay away.

This is both a proverb and a proverbial phrase; as a proverb it signifies that no private authority can stop that which has once been allowed to be a publick road. As a phrase, it signifies that a thing is quite gone.

51. Of bairns gifts be not [t] fain.

No sooner they give them but they seek them again.

52. Our [u] sowins are ill sowr'd, ill [v] seil'd, ill salted, ill soden, thin, and few o'them. You may stay all night, but you may go home if you like. It is well ken'd your father's son was never a [w] scambler.

This was a speech of a country woman of mine, to a guest that she would gladly have shaken off, and being so oddly express'd, it became a proverb, which we repeat when we think our friend does not entertain us heartily.

53. Out of [x] Davy Lindsey into Wallace.

Spoken when people run out of one subject into another.

54. Of all meat in the world, drink goes the best down.

A facetious bull when we drink heartily after meat.

55. O'er mickle cook'ry spills the [y] bruise.

When people would do a thing too well, they often spoil it.

Eng.—A right Englishman! He knows not when a thing is well enough.

Lat.—Curando fieri quædam pejora videmus,

Vulnera; quæ melius non tetigisse fuit.

56. Of all the fish in the sea, herring is the king.

57. One good turn will meet another, if it were at the bridge of London.

58. One never loses by doing a good turn.

Both spoken by them who make a return for former favours.

---

[t] Glad. [u] Flumm'ry. [v] Strain'd. [w] One that goes about among his friends for meat, by the Irish call'd a sosherer. [x] Two Scottish books that children learn to read by. [y] Broth, a word that a Scottish man cannot spell, nor an Englishman pronounce.

59. Owe the mare, owe the bear, let the filly eat there.

Spoken when we see a man's goods squandered by his own people.

60. Of all wars peace is the end.

Spoken by them that would compose a law suit, or reconcile those who have had an outfall. It is not the same with the following,

Lat.—Pax quæritur bello.

61. Old debts are better than old sores.

The one may be paid, and the other will ake.

62. One swallow makes no summer.

Lat.—Una hirundo non facit ver.

63. One hand will not wash the other for nothing.

Lat.—Manus manum fricat.

64. One beats the bush, and another grips the bird.

Spoken when one reaps the effects of another man's labour.

65. Oppression will make a wise man mad.

66. One hour's cold will spoil seven years warming.

67. Of a little take a little.

68. Oh for a drop of gentle blood, that I may wear a black bit above my brow.

In Scotland no woman is suffered to wear a silk hood, unless she be a gentlewoman, that is, a gentleman's daughter, or married to a gentleman. A rich maid having the offer of a wealthy yeoman, or a bare gentleman, wish'd for the last to qualify her to wear a black hood. It is since spoken to such wealthy maidens, upon the like occasion.

P.

1. PEEL the kirk, and ᵃ thick the quire.

Eng.—Rob Peter and pay Paul.

2. Pride never left his master without a fall.

Proud people often meet with very humbling circumstances.

Lat.—Sequitur superbos ultor a tergo deus.

3. Pride and grace dwelt never in one place.

4. Pride, in a poor briest, has mickle dolour to ᵇ dree.

5. Pride and laziness would have mickle upholding.

Pride requires ornament, and laziness service.

6. Pride finds no cold.

Spoken heretofore to young women, when, in compliance with the fashion, they went with their breasts and shoulders

---

ᵃ Thatch.   ᵇ Suffer.

bare ; and may now be apply'd to beans with their open breasts, and ladies with their extravagant hoops.

7. Pride ^c but profit, wear shoon and go bare foot.

Spoken when people have something fine about them, but the rest shabby.

8. Play is good, but ^d daffin ^e dow not.

Spoken to them who are silly and impertinently foolish in their play.

9. Puddings, and paramours, should be hotly handled.

Puddings, when cold, are uneatable, and love, when cold-rife, is near the breaking off.

10. Put your hand no farther than your sleeve will reach.

That is, spend no more than your estate will bear.

Eng.—Stretch your legs according to your coverlid.

Lat.—Metiri se quemque suo modulo ac pede verum est.

Item.—Messe tenus propriâ vive.

Item.—Intra tuam pelliculam te contine.

Item.—Sumptus censum ne superet.

11. Poets and painters have leave to lye.

Eng.—Poets and painters lye with license.

Lat.—Pictoribus atque poetis

Quidlibet audendi semper fuit æqua potestas.

12. ^f Poortha parts friends.

At least makes them very coldrife.

13. Put your hand in the creel, and take out either an adder or an eel.

Spoken of taking a wife, where no cunning, art, or sense can secure a good choice, but must be taken for better and worse.

14. Pay beforehand was never well serv'd.

It is common to see tradesmen and labourers to go about a piece of work with great uneasiness, which is to pay a just debt, and say, grudgingly, I work for a dead horse.

15. Pray to God to help you, and put your hand to work.

Lat.—Manus admoventi fortuna imploranda est.

16. ^f Poortha is a pain, but no disgrace.

Unless it be the effects of laziness and luxury.

17. Poor be your meal poke, and ay your nieve in the nook o't. Otherways, in the nether end of it.

---

^c Without.   ^d Folly.   ^e Of no use.   ^f Poverty.

A jocose imprecation to them who call us poor; as poor boy! poor Jack! pretending to pity us.

18. *g* Pith is good in all plays, but threading of needles.

Lat.—Robur cum ingenio conjungendum.

19. Possession is eleven points of the law.

20. Possession is worth an ill charter.

The law supposes the person in possession to be the right owner, till the contrary appear.

Eng.—I would not give a cottage in possession for a palace in reversion.

Lat.—Possessoris est pars potior.

21. Put your thanks in your shanks, and make good great legs of them.

A coldrife answer to those that offer thanks for payment.

Eng.—Keep your thanks to feed your chickens.

Lat.—Nihil citius perit quam gratia.

22. Put another man's child in your bosom, and he will creep out at your sleeve.

This is but an ill-natured proverb, though it proves often too true.

23. Poor folks are soon pish'd on.

Because they want ability themselves, and have few to take their part.

Lat.—Libertas pauperis hæc est,

Pulsatus ut roget, & pugnis concisus adoret.

24. Poor folk is fain of little.

Because they have no hopes to get much.

25. Peter in, Paul out.

Spoken when after we had wanted a necessary person a long time, upon his arrival, another equally necessary is gone.

Eng.—In dock, out nettle.

26. Poor folks friends soon miskens them.

Lat.—Mendico ne parentes quidem amici sunt.

27. Put on your spurs, and be at your speed.

A word of defiance, do your best.

28. Put your tongue in my arse, and *h* worry me to *i* dead.

A contemptuous return to him that threatens to beat us.

29. *k* Poortha with patience is less painful.

Lat.—Leve fit, quod bene fertur, onus.

---

g Strength.   *h* Choke.   *i* Death.   *k* Poverty.

30. Praise, [1]but profit, puts little in the pot.

Lat.—Gloria quanta libet quid erit? si gloria sola est.

31. Poorly sits richly warms.

Spoken when people sit on a low stool before the fire.

32. Puddings and wort are ready dirt.

A word of contempt when you are ill pleased with a person, thing, or action.

33. Put your finger in the fire, and say it was your fortune.

Spoken to them who lay the blame of their crimes, and mismanagements, on their hard fortune.   Whereas,

Fortunam superat virtus, prudentia fatum.

34. Pish and fart, sound at the heart.

Taken from Schola Salernitana.

Mingere cum bombis res est salvissima lumbis.

35. Pishing, and pills wagging, puts the day away.

Spoken when people trifle away their time, that they should bestow on their necessary business.

36. Play carle again, if you dare.

Do not dare to offer to contest with me. Spoke by parents to stubborn children.

37. Put a coward to his metal, and he'll fight the dee'l.

38. [m] Plenty makes [n] dainty.

When people have variety of many meats, or abundance of one sort, they are nice and delicate, and undervalue what they have in abundance. The English seems contrary to this, yet means the same thing, Plenty is no dainty.

39. Put two pennys in a purse, and they will draw together.

When people have purchased any little sum of money it will easily encrease. Apply'd sometimes when rich men marry rich women.

40. Play with your [o] playfeers.

Spoken to young people when they offer to be roguish upon, or play too saucily with, old people.

41. Provision in season makes a rich house.

Because every thing is gotten at the easiest rate.

42. Penny wise, pound fool.

Spoken when people by saving a little cost incur a great deal more damage.

---

[1] Without.   [m] Here it signifies variety.   [n] Makes us curious in our taste.   [o] Fellows.

43. Poor men have no souls.

This is an old proverb in the time of pop'ry when the poor had no masses, or dirige's said for them.

44. Put the saddle on the right horse.

Spoken when we are blamed for the miscarriages that were occasioned by others.

Q.

1. QUICK at meat, quick at work.

Neither this, nor its reverse, holds always.

2. Quick, for you'll ne'er be cleanly.

That is, do a thing nimbly, for you'll never do it neatly.

3. Quality, without quantity, is little thought of.

Lat.—Et genus & forma, nisi cum re, vilior alga est,

4. Quick returns make rich merchants.

Eng.—Many ventures make a full fraught.

Often ironically apply'd to them, who having been drunk, and having slept themselves sober, go to it again.

R.

1. ᵃ RUSE the fair day at night.

Commend not a thing, or project, 'till it has had its full effect.

Eng.—It is not good praising the ford, 'till a man be over.

Item.—He had never a bad day, who had a good night.

2. Raise no more dee'ls than you are able to ᵇ lay.

Do not stir up a strife, that you will not afterward be able to appease.

3. Refer my coat, and lose a sleeve.

Arbitrators, for the better accommodation of business, make both parties abate of their pretensions.

4. Rich folk have many friends.

Many of whom are but flatterers.

5. Ride fair, and ᶜ jaap none.

Taken from riding through a puddle; but apply'd to too home jesting.

6. Rome was not big'd in a day.

Great attempts cannot be atchieved in a short time.

7. Rather ᵈ spill your jest, than ᵉ spite your friend.

Eng.—Better lose a jest than friend.

8. Rob. Gibbs's contract, stark love and kindness.

ᵃ Praise.   ᵇ Conjure.   ᶜ Throw not the dirt about you.
         ᵈ Spoil.   ᵉ Provoke.

An expression often used when we drink to our friend.

9. ᶠ Ruse the ford as you find it.

Commend men as you have them averse, or favourable to your interest.

10. Rue and thyme grow both in a garden.

A persuasion to repent and give over an attempt before it be too late, alluding to the sound of the two herbs here nam'd.

11. Rule youth well, for age will rule it self.

Youth is rash and head-strong, but age sober and stedfast.

Lat.—Est opus ardentem frænis arcere juventam.

They say also,

Rue in thyme should be a maiden's ᵍ posie.

12. Remove an old tree, and it will wither.

Spoken by a man who is loth to leave a place in his advanc'd years, in which he had long liv'd.

13. Rot him away with butter and eggs.

A jocose advice to a young woman, to get rid of an old husband.

14. ʰ Rackless youth makes rueful age.

People who live too fast when they are young, will neither have a vigorous, nor a comfortable old age.

Eng.—Young men's knocks old men feel.

15. ⁱ Reavers should not be ruers.

They who are so fond of a thing as to snap greedily at it, should not repent that they have got it.

16. Raw ᵏ dawds make fat lads.

There is little sense in this. Spoken when we give a good piece of meat to a young boy.

17. Right mixture makes good mortar.

Spoken when we mix our drink.

18. Reckon your winning by your bad stock.

Spoken when gamesters reckon their winning before the play be ended.

19. Raw leather will stretch.

20. Reckon money after all your kin.

21. Right Roger, sow's good mutton.

22. Remember me to all that ask for me, but blade me in no body's teeth.

23. Remember me to your bedfellow when you lye alone.

24. Remember man and keep in mind,
A faithful friend is hard to find.

ᶠ Commend.   ᵍ Nosegay.   ʰ Heedless.   ⁱ Robbers.
ᵏ Large pieces.

S.

1. SAIL quoth the king, hold quoth the wind.

That unaccountable creature, which God brings out of his treasures, cannot be commanded by mortal power.

2. Suddain friendship, sure repentance.

Eng.—If you trust before you try,
      You may repent before you die.

Lat.—Subita amicitia raro sine pœnitentia colitur.

3. She's an old wife that wats her [a] weird.

None can know what may come of them, and what they may come to, before they die.

Lat.——— Dicique beatus
      Ante obitum nemo, supremaque funera, debet.

4. [b] Speer at Jack Thief if I be a [c] leal man.

Spoken when men appeal for a character to them who are their associates, or as bad as themselves.

5. Short folk are soon angry.

6. Short folks heart is soon at their mouth.

It is alledg'd that people of a low stature are pettish, passionate, and fiery.

Eng.—A little put is soon hot.

7. Stook the stable door when the steed is stol'n.

Spoken when people shew that care and concern after the loss of a thing, which had been better laid out before.

Lat.—Accepto, claudenda est janua, damno.

8. Strike as ye feed, and that's but soberly.

A reproof to them that correct those over whom they have no power.

9. Some body will comb your head backward yet.

Spoken by mothers to stubborn daughters; intimating they will come under the hands of a step mother, who, it is likely, will not deal too tenderly with them.

10. Sore cravers are ay ill payers.

This proverb, and the reverse, viz. Ill payers are sore cravers, I have never yet seen fail.

11. [d] Sturt follows all extremes.

Lat.—Moderata probamus, excessus vituperamus.

12. Slow at meat, slow at work.

13. Slander always leaves a slur.

Eng.—Throw much dirt some will stick.

Lat.—Calumniare audacter, aliquid adhærebit.

---

[a] Fortune.   [b] Ask.   [c] Honest.   [d] Trouble.

14. * Scarting, and eating, wants but a beginning.

Spoken when people eat more than they thought they could, or to persuade people of weak stomachs to begin.

15. Sorrow and an ill like, makes soon an old wife.

Lat.—Cura facit canos, quamvis homo non habet annos.

16. Soure plumbs quoth the tod, when he could not climb the tree.

Spoken when people vilify what they would gladly have, but cannot come by.

17. Sowters and taylors count by the hour.

Spoken when people offer to break company, because such an hour is past.

18. Smooth waters run deep.

Spoken to or of them who seem demure, yet are suspected to be roguish.

Lat.—Cave tibi a muto, a quàque silente.

19. She's a maiden as the man left her.

Intimating that she is a whore.

20. Send you to the sea, and you will not get salt water.

Spoken when people foolishly come short of their errand.

21. Satan reproves sin.

Spoken when we are reproved by wicked men.

Lat.—Unde tibi frontem, libertatemque parentis
Cum facias pejora senex.

22. Set a stout heart to a f stay g brea.

Set about a difficult business with courage and constancy.

Eng.—Set a hard heart against a hard hap

Lat.—Tu ne cede malis, sed contra audentior ito
Quam tua te fortuna sinit.

Item.—Fortiaque adversus opponite pectora rebus.

23. Speak the truth, and shame the dee'l.

Spoken to hearten people who are afraid of offending some great person by their evidence.

24. Shame's past the shed of your hair.

Spoken to people impudent, and past blushing.

Lat.—Sanguinis in facie non hœret gutta; morantur
Pauci ridiculum, & fugientem ex urbe pudorem.

25. Soon ripe, soon rotten.

Taken from summer fruit, and signifies that they who soon come to man's stature, sense, and wit, will not be long liv'd.

---

e Scratching.   f Steep.   g Brow, hill, rising.

R

26. Send, and fetch.

    Lat.—Da, si vis accipere.

27. Scorn comes commonly with skathe.

    Spoken when one gets a hurt, and another laughs at it.

28. Start at a staw, and ^h loup o'er a ⁱ bink.

    Scruple at small things, and be guilty of greater.

    Strain at a gnat, and swallow a camel.

    Hudibras. ——Gospel preaching times,

    When slightest sins are greatest crimes.

29. ^k Sain your self from the dee'l, and the laird's
    bairns.

    A caution of poor people to their children, how they meddle with their superiors; for, if they hurt the laird's bairns, they will be sure to be punished, but, if hurt by them, they will get no right.

30. Soon enough to cry ^l chuck, when it is out of the
    shell.

    It is time enough to reckon on a thing when you are sure of it.

    Eng.—Count not your chickens before they be hatch'd.

31. Sho'd in the cradle and barefoot in the stubble.

    Spoken of those who are tenderly used in their infancy, and after meet with harsher treatment.

32. Summer is a seemly time.

    There is a second part to this proverb, but it is paultry.

33. Stay, and drink of your ^m browst.

    Take a share of the mischief that you have occasioned.

34. Salt, quoth the sowter, when he had eaten the
    cow all to the ——

    Spoken to them that flag, when they have almost finished a difficult task.

    Lat.—Turpe, devorato bove, hærere in caudâ.

35. ⁿ Shaal waters make the greatest sound.

    And empty fellows makes the greatest noise.

    Eng.—Empty vessels sound loudest.

36. ^o Sik a man as thou would be,
    Draw thee to sik company.

    Eng.—Tell me with whom thou goest,

        And I'll tell thee what thou doest.

    Lat.—Noscitur ex socio qui non cognoscitur ex se.

---

^h Jump.   ⁱ A form.   ^k Bless.   ^l A call to their chickens.
     ^m Brewing.   ⁿ Shallow.   ^o Such.

37. Shew me the man, and I'll shew you the law.

The sentences of judges may vary, according to the measure of their fear, favour, or affection.

Eng.—As a man's befriended so is the law ended.

Lat.—Dat veniam corvis, vexat censura columbis.

Item.—Pecuniosus, etiam nocens, non damnatur.

38. Silence catches a mouse.

Saying nothing, 'till you be ready to put in execution, is the way to shun prevention, and effect your business.

Lat.—Quod facturus es ea ne dixeris, frustratus enim rideberis.

39. [P] Speewell, and [q] hae well.

Eng.—Hope well, and have well.

That is, hope and expect good things, and it will fall out accordingly.

40. Serve your self 'till your bairns come to age.

An answer to those who would have you do them a piece of service, which you have no mind to.

41. Sorrow and ill weather come unsent for.

Spoken when a person is coming to your house, whose company you do not care for.

42. [r] Scart ye my arse, and I'll claw your elbow.

Sometimes it signifies doing a piece of service, and I'll do you another; but oftner it is used as a contemptuous by-word, when an unreasonable thing is propos'd.

43. Spend and God will send, spare and ever bare.

Solomon says, There is that scattereth, and yet aboundeth; and there is some that withholdeth more than is meet, and it tendeth to poverty.

44. Sweet in the bed, and sweir up in the morning, was never a good housewife.

A jocose reproof to young maids, when they lye long a bed.

45. [s] Sary man, and then he [t] grat.

An ironical condolence of some trifling misfortune.

46. Shame fall the couple, quoth the crow to her feet.

A word of contempt, when two joyn in one fault.

47. Say well, and do well, ond with a letter, Say well's good, but do well's better.

It was a bad character that was given of a certain great man, That he never said an ill word, or did a good thing.

48. Sorrow is soon enough when it comes.

P Bode. q Have. r Scratch. s Poor. t Cry'd.

R 2

Spoken to them who vex themselves with future dismal expectations.

49. Safe is the word.

Taken from the watch-word given among soldiers, spoken when we have gotten over some great difficulty.

Lat.—Omnis res est in vado.

50. Seek mickle, and get something; seek little, and get nothing.

Lat.—Iniquum petas, ut æquum feras.

51. "Sorrow " wit " you " wat where a blessing may light.

You know not but I may have a better fortune than you think, or expect.

Lat.——— Semper tibi pendeat hamus;
         Quo minime credas gurgite piscis erit.

52. Spit in your hand and hold fast.

Spoken to wives, when they speak of their husband's second marriage.

53. ⱽ Sticking goes not by strength, but by guiding of the ʷ gooly.

Matters are carried on rather by art than strength.

54. Scottish men take their mark from a mischief.

Spoken when we say such a thing fell out, when such an ill accident came to pass. A Scottish man solicited the Prince of Orange to be made an ensign, for he had been a serjeant ever since his highness run away from Groll.

55. Speak good of archers, for your father shot in a bow.

Spoken to them who despise the trade, profession, or way of living, that their father had.

56. ˣ Sik man, ˣ sik master.

Lat.—Dignum patellâ operculum.

57. ʸ Sindle ride, tine the spurs.

They who are not used to such a business, go about it awkwardly.

58. ᶻ Sturt pays no debt.

Spoken with resentment, to them who storm when we crave of them our just debts.

59. Shame fall them that shame thinks, to do themselves a good turn.

ᵘ You can by no means know.   ᵛ Stabbing.   ʷ Kitchen-knife.   ˣ Such.   ʸ Seldom.   ᶻ Haughtiness.

Spoken to them that quarrel with us for doing a business that tends to our advantage, or to them who are asham'd to do so.

60. Seek your salve where you get your sore.

Spoken to them who are sick after drink, alias, Take a hair of the dog that bit you.

61. Sik as you give me, sik you shall get.

As you use me so will I you.

Lat.—Ut sementum feceris ita & metes.

62. Swear by your burn'd shins.

Spoken with contempt to them that swear they will do such or such a mischief.

63. Silks and sattins put out the kitchin fire.

Commonly spoken by servants, when they think that their masters and mistresses extravagant cloaths made their meat and drink something scarcer.

64. Sharp stomachs make short graces.

65. She broke her elbow at the kirk door.

Spoken of a thrifty maiden, when she becomes a lazy wife.

66. Stuffing holds out storm.

Advising men to take some good thing, before they travel in a bad day.

67. Stretching and * gaunting bodes sleep to be wanting.

68. Send your gentle blood to the market, and see what it will buy.

69. Stay no longer in your friend's house than you are sure that you are welcome.

70. Speak when you're spoken to, do what you're bidden,

Come when you're call'd, and you'll not be chidden.

A cant of mistresses to their maid servants.

71. Set your knee to it and right it.

Taken from setting bended sticks streight. Spoken in anger, to them who alledge that what we have done is amiss.

72. She'll keep her own side of the house, and go up and down in your's.

73. She'll put you under her hough, and feed you with farts.

Both these spoken to dissuade our friend from marrying a woman, whom we suspect to be too bold.

_____

* Yawning.

R 3

74. She's spinning clues to the midding, and wo to the webster.

Eng.—You must spoil before you spin.

75. She holds up her head like a hundred pound [b] aver.

76. She holds up her head like a hen drinking.

Both these spoken of a woman who affectedly holds her head high.

77. Saw you that, and shot not at it, and you so [c] gly'd a gunner.

A reprimand to medling boys, that take up things that they have nothing to do with.

78. [d] Strike a dog with a bone, and he'll not [e] yowll.

Men will bear small inconveniencies, that bring great profit.

79. She that takes gifts her self she sells,
And she that gives them, does naught els.

80. [f] Seil comes not 'till sorrow be over.

Eng.—When bale is highest boot is next.

81. Sup with your head, the horner is dead, he's dead that made the [g] munns.

Spoken to a child when he calls for a spoon for any liquid thing, advising him rather to take it out of the pipkin with his mouth, as ladies do tea or coffee.

82. [h] Sik things will be, if we sell drink.

Spoken of a particular inconveniency that follows such a trade, profession, or way of living.

83. Sit on your arse, and call your [i] sorrans.

A reproof to them that would have others do for them, what they ought to do themselves. Spoken ironically.

84. Spilt wine is worse than water.

Spoken when a thing is spoil'd and not put to its proper use.

85. She's a hussy that wants a hip.
And so may you your under lip.

A senseless return of a woman to him that calls her hussy.

86. Sorrow shake you out of the webster's handy work.

An ill wish of a weaver, to him that upbraids him with his trade.

87. Sober, neighbour, the night is but young yet.

Make no haste, for you have time enough before your hand.

---

[b] Horse. [c] Squinting, or one ey'd. [d] Beat. [e] Howl.
[f] Health, safety. [g] Spoons without handles. [h] Such,
[i] Servants.

88. Supped out wort was never good ale.

Spoken when one asks us a drink of our wort, for what is drunk in wort, will never be ale, good or bad.

89. Shame fall the ordiner, quoth the cat to the k cordiner.

A silly imprecation to them that order something to be done, that is opposite to our humour, or interest.

90. Some has hap, and some sticks in the gap.

Lat.—Ille crucem sceleris pretium tulit, hic diadema.

91. Spice is black, but it has a sweet smack.

I have heard a rhyme to this purpose.

Snow is white, and lies on the dike,
   And every one lets it lye;
Spice is black, and has a sweet smack,
   And every one does it buy.

An apology for black people.

Lat.—Alba ligustra cadunt, vaccinia nigra leguntur.

92. She'll be a good sale whisp.

Dissuading from marrying a fam'd beauty, lest she bring too many visitants to the house; or persuading those, that keep a publick house, to hire a handsome maid, that people may come to the house for her sake.

93. Shame fall the geer and the l blad'ry o't.

The turn of an old Scottish song, spoken when a young handsome girl marries an old man, upon the account of his wealth.

94. She's not to be made a song of.

An abatement to a woman's commendation for beauty.

95. Sit down and rest you, and tell us how they drest you, and how you m wan away.

A jocose invitation to sit down with us.

96. Saying is one thing, and doing another.

Lat.—Verba in consilio valent, in certamine robur.

97. She's an ill whore that's no worth the down laying.

Eng.—He's an ill dog that's not worth whistling on.

98. Sweet in the on taking, but soure in the off putting.

Spoken of debt for the most part, but apply'd to sin, sensual pleasure, and the like.

99. Shame fall the dogs that hunted you, that did not make you run faster.

---

k Shoemaker.   l Thrump'ry.   m Cut.

Spoken when people come too late to dinner, or are tardy
on any other occasion.

100. Spare when you're young, and spend when you're
old.

Eng.—He that saveth his dinner will have the more for his
supper.

101. ᵃ Sindle seen, soon forgotten.

102. Some body has told him of it.

Spoken when you call a man handsome, wise, rich, learn'd,
or the like; alledging that he knows it well, and is proud
of it.

Lat.—Inquinat egregios adjuncta superbia mores.

103. She's greeting at the thing she laugh'd at ᵒ farn
year.

Signifying that she is in labour.

104. She has an ill ᵖ pant with her hind foot.

Signifying that such a woman is stubborn. Taken from
cows who kick when they are milked.

105. Sorrow be in their cen that first saw him, that
did not cast him in the fire, and say sorrow have
it they had.

A malicious answer to them that ask us if we saw such a
man, meaning one that had done us harm.

106. Say ay no, and you'll never be married.

107. Sorrow be in their hands that held so well to
your head.

Spoken to drunken men when they are ill natured.

108. She's better than she's bonny.

An additional praise of a woman who is commended for her
beauty.

109. Sorrow be in the house that you're beguil'd in.

Spoken to sharp expert people who have their interest in
their eye.

110. Set a beggar on horse-back, and he'll ride to the
dee'l.

Lat.—Asperius nihil est humili cum surget in altum.

111. Service is no inheritance.

An argument for servants to seek out for some settlement.

112. Sow wheat in dirt, and rye in dust.

A wet season agrees with the one, and a dry with the other.

ᵃ Seldom.   ᵒ Last year.   ᵖ Back stroke.

113. **Seeing is believing all the world over.**
Lat.—Pluris est oculatus testis unus, quam auriti decem.

114. **Stolen waters are sweet.**
People take great delight in that which they can get privately.

115. **So many heads, so many wits.**
Eng.—So many men, so many minds.
Lat.—Quot capita tot sententiæ.

116. **Silence gives consent.**
Lat.—Silentium fatentis est.

117. **Strike the iron when it is hot.**
Urge on your business when a proper occasion offers.
Lat.—Carpe diem quam minime credula postero.

118. **Surfeits slay more than swords.**
Lat.—Plures necat gula quam gladius.

119. **Sow thin, mow thin.**
Lat.—Ut sementum feceris ita & metes.

120. **Sit in your seat, and none will raise you.**
Spoken to those who have gotten an affront for presuming beyond their station.
Lat.—Et merito quoniam propria pelle quiessem.

121. **Standing pools gather mud.**
Lat.—Nihil agendo male agere discitur.

122. **Spare at the spiggot, and let out at the bung hole.**
Spoken to them who are careful and penurious in some trifling things, but neglective in the main chance.

123. **Soon enough, if well enough.**
Eng.—Good and quick seldom meet.
Lat.—Sat cito si sat bene.

124. **Speak of the dee'l, and he'll appear.**
Spoken when they, of whom we are speaking, come in by chance.

125. **Standers by see more than the gamesters.**

126. **See for love, and buy for money.**
A cant among pedlars and hucksters.

127. **So far, so good.**
So much is done to good purpose.

128. **Self deed, self [q] fa.**
That is, as you do to others, so it will befal you.

129. **Spit on a stone and it will be wet at last.**
Constant and perpetual doing, though slow, yet may at last effect great things.

---

[q] Come to your share.

Eng.—Little strokes fell great oaks.

Lat.—Gutta cavat lapidem non vi, sed sæpe cadendo.

130. Saying goes good cheap.

Eng.—Talking pays no toll.

131. She has got a kid in her *kilting.

That is, she has got a bastard about her.

132. She'll wear like a horse shoe, the longer the brighter.

Spoken of ill coloured girls who they hope will clear up when they are married.

133. Set that down in the backside of your book.

Spoken of desperate debts.

134. Second thoughts are best.

For a man at first cannot see all the conveniences, and in-conveniences, of what is offered, but by after consideration may mend his first apprehensions.

135. She has pish'd in the tub-hole.

The tub-hole is a hollow place in the ground, over which the kive (mashing fat) stands, spoken of an ale-wife when she breaks, and turns bankrupt.

136. Sore strokes and many of them.

A jocose threatening which we design not to execute.

T.

1. THREE may keep counsel, if two be away.

No man is sure that what he imparts to any will not be revealed.

Lat.—Quod taceri vis nemini dixeris.

2. Take time in time, e'er time be ªtint.

Lat.—Dum loquimur fugit hora.

3. Time and tide will stay for no man.

Lat.—Volat irrevocabile tempus.

4. The farthest way about, the nearest way home.

Eng.—The high-way is never about.

Lat.—Compendia plerumque dispendia.

Item.—Via trita, via tuta.

5. They that lend you hinder you to buy.

Spoken jocosely, when people ask us a loan.

6. Tell a tale to a mare, and she'll let a fart.

Spoken when heedless blockheads mind not what we say.

7. The old horse may die waiting for the new grass.

* Women when they go to work truss up their petticoats with a belt, and this they call their kilting.   ª Lost.

Eng.—Live horse, and thou'll get grass.

Item.—While the grass grows the steed starves.

8. They [b] mense little the mouth that bite off the nose.

Spoken when people who pretend friendship for you, traduce your near friends and relations.

9. Trot father, trot mother, how can the foal amble?

It is hard for those who have had a bad parentage, and consequently an ill education, to be good.

Eng.—If the mare have a bald face, the filly will have a blaze.

Lat.— ——— Citius nos

Corrumpunt vitiorum exempla domestica.

10. Two hungry meals make the third a glutton.

Spoken when one eats greedily after long fasting. Apply'd also to other things of the like nature, where long wanting sharpens the appetite.

Eng.—A hungry horse makes a clean manger.

Item.—Hard fare makes hungry bellies.

11. [c] Tramp on a worm, and she'll turn her head.

12. Tramp on a snail, and she'll shoot out her horns.

Both these signify that the meanest, when injured, will shew their resentment.

Eng.—A baited cat may grow as fierce as a lion.

Lat.—Non solum taurus ferit, uncis cornibus, hostem :

Verum etiam instanti læsa repugnat ovis.

Item.—Habet & musca splenem.

13. Tom tell truth lies without.

Eng.—Truth has a good face, but ragged cloaths.

Lat.—Veritas odium parit.

14. The grace of a [d] gray bannock is in the baking of it.

The setting out of an ordinary thing to best advantage will make it look well.

15. There was never a fair word in [e] slyting.

An excuse for what a man might say in his passion, upon provocation.

Eng.—He that hath bitter in his mouth spits not all sweet.

Lat.—Impedit ira animum, ne possit cernere verum.

16. The dee'l bides his day.

Taken from a supposition that the devil, when he enters into a covenant with a witch, sets her a date of her life, which he

---

[b] Honour. [c] Tread. [d] Coarse bread. [e] Scolding.

stands to. Spoken when people demand a debt or wages before it be due.

Eng.—First deserve, and then desire.

17. Tell no school tales.

Do not blab abroad what is said in drink or among companions.

Lat.—Odi memorem compoterem.

18. True blue will never stain.

A man of fix'd principles, and firm resolutions, will not be easily induc'd to do an ill or mean thing.

Lat.—Justum & tenacem propositi virum, &c.

19. The fool's bolt is soon shot.

Men of shallow wit will soon give their opinion, which commonly discovers their weakness.

Eng.—When the fool hath spoken he has done all.

20. The ᶠmisterfull must not be ᵍ mensefull.

They who are in need must and will importune.

Eng.—Bashfulness is an enemy to poverty.

Lat.—Quid prodest egenti pudor.

21. Two daughters, and a backdoor, are three stark thieves.

Daughters are expensive, and back doors give servants opportunity to purloyn their master's goods. The Scots have an ill opinion of back-doors, and therefore have none.

22. The water will never warr the ʰ widdie.

Eng.—He that's born to be hang'd will never be drown'd.

A neighbour of mine was so fully persuaded of the truth of these two proverbs; that being in a great storm, and dreadfully afraid, espies in the ship a graceless rake, whom he suppos'd destined to another sort of a death, cries out, O Samuel, are you here? why then we are all safe; and so laid aside his concern.

23. The first ⁱ fuff of a fat ᵏ haggish is the worst.

If you wrestle with a fat man, and sustain his first onset, he will soon be out of breath.

24. Take your venture, as many a good ship has done.

Spoken when advice is asked in a case where the success may be dubious.

Lat.—Sed quid tentare nocebit.

25. Take no more on you than you're able to bear.

Lat.--Versute diu quod valeant humeri.

ᶠ Needy.   ᵍ Modest.   ʰ Gallows.   ⁱ Puff.   ᵏ A pudding made in the great gut of a sheep.

26. There is a [m] slidd'ry stone before the [n] hall door.

A slippery stone may make one fall; signifying the uncertainty of court favour, and the promises of great men.

Lat.—Dulis inexpertis cultura potentis amici.
Expertus metuet.

27. There is a great difference between [o] fen o'er and fairwel.

There is a great difference between their way of living who only get a little scrap to keep them alive, and theirs who get every day a full meal.

28. The thing that's [p] fristed is no forgiven.

Eng.—Forbearance is no acquittance.

Lat.—Quod defertur non aufertur.

29. That bolt came never out of your bag.

Lat.—Ex tua faretra nunquam venit ista sagitta.

30. There is a dog in the well.

31. There is a [q] whaap in the [r] reap.

Both these signify that there is something amiss, but the reason of either phrase I do not know.

32. There is many a true word spoken in jest.

Lat.—Ridentem dicere verum——quid vetat.

**33. The dee'l grew sick, and vow'd a monk to be,
The dee'l grew heal, and dee'l a monk was he.**

Apply'd to them who make good resolutions in their adversity, which they forget in their prosperity. Translated from an old monkish rhyme,

Dæmon languebat, monachus bonus esse volebat,
Sed cum convaluit, mansit ut ante fuit.

34. The dee'l is no worse than he's call'd.

Apply'd to those who speak worse of bad men than they deserve.

Eng.—The lyon is not so fierce as he's painted.

Lat.—Qui de magnis majora loquuntur.

35. Time tries the truth.

Eng.—Time and straw make medlars ripe.

Lat.—Tempore patet occulta veritas.

36. Thoughts beguil'd the lady.

Taken from a lady that did something amiss, when she thought only to break wind backward; apply'd to them who foolishly say, I thought so.

---

[m] Slipp'ry. [n] Great man's house. [o] Make the best shift you can. [p] Trusted. [q] Curliew. [r] Rope.

37. The foremost hound *grips the hare.

38. The cow that's first up gets the first of the dew.
Both recommending diligence and industry.
Eng.—The early bird catcheth the worm.

39. ᵗTip when you will, you shall lamb with the leave.
An allusion to sheep taking the ram and dropping their
lambs; used in company when some refuse to pay their clubs
because they came but lately in, signifying that they shall
pay all alike notwithstanding.

40. The lamb where it's tipped, and the ewe where
she's clipped.
A proverbial rule about tythes; signifying that the lamb
shall pay tythes in the place where the ewe was when she took
the ram, but the old sheep where they were shorn.

41. The strongest horse loups the ᵘ dike.
Spoken often when we are playing at tables, and past the
danger of blotting; meaning, that he that throws best will
win the game.

42. The ᵛreek of my own house is better than the fire
of another's.
Lat.—Patriæ fumus igne alieno luculentior.

43. The greedy man and the ᵂgileynour are soon
agreed.
The covetous man will be glad of a good offer, and the cheat
will offer well, designing never to pay.

44. The cat would fain fish eat,
But she has no will to wet her feet.
Spoken to them that would gladly have, but will not labour.

45. There is skill in ˣ gruel making.
There is skill and art required in every the least thing.
Eng.—There is cunning in daubing.

46. The foot at the cradle, and the hand at the ʸroke
is the sign of a good house-wife.
Only spoken jocosely when we see a woman spinning, and
rocking the cradle with her foot, a sight very common in my
country.

47. Two dogs striving about a bone, and the third run
away with it.
Spoken when two, by their mutual contentions, hinder each
other of a place and preferment, and it has faln to a third by
that means.

---

* Catches.   ᵗ Take the ram.   ᵘ Fence.   ᵛ Smoke.
  ᵂ Cheat.   ˣ Hasty-pudding.   ʸ Distaff.

48. The worst world that ever was, the malt-man got his sack again.

It is hard when people get no satisfaction for what they have sold, no, not so much as the bag that carried it,

49. They are very full in their own house that will not pick a bone in their neighbour's.

Spoken to people who being bid to eat, excuse themselves, for that they had eaten at home. Though I have heard it more roguishly apply'd.

50. The bird must flighter that flies with one wing.

Spoken by them who have interest only in one side of the house.

51. The stone that lies not in your gate breaks not your toes.

Spoken against meddling in the business in which we have no concern.

52. The thatcher said unto his man,
Let us raise this ladder if we can;
But first let us drink, master.

Spoken when one proposes something to be done, and another proposes to take a drink before we begin.

53. The master's foot is the best ª foulzie.

Two philosophers asking mutual questions to puzzle each other, the one asked what was the best thing to make a horse fat? was answer'd, The master's eye: the other ask'd, what was the best gooding for ground? and was answer'd, The master's foot. Both these answers become, after, proverbs; signifying that the care and concern of a man will make his business prosper.

54. There was ay some water where the stirk drown'd.

There was certainly some occasion for so much talk, rumour and suspicion.

Eng.—There was a thing in't, quoth the fellow when he drank the dish clout.

Item.—Much smoke some fire.

55. There grows no grass at the market cross.

An invective against the barrenness of whores.

56. Tear ready, tail ready.

A reflection on a woman who is ready to cry.

57. The more you ᵇ greet you'll pish the less.

An ill-natur'd saying to them who cry, Because we will not do what they would have us do, or give what they crave.

ª Pronounced foulyie, that is dung, gooding.   ᵇ Cry.

58. *Tulying dogs come halting home.

Spoken when quarrellers come off with the worse.
Eng.—Brabling dogs have sore ears.

59. There is life in a muscle though it be little.

Spoken when we have some little hope of effecting our
design. They will say, 'There is life in a muscle yet.

60. They that live longest, fetch wood farthest.

Spoken when we make use of what we have, and leave our
heirs to do the best they can.

61. The priest christens his own bairn first.

An apology for serving ourselves before our neighbours.
Eng.—Charity begins at home.
Lat.—Sibi quisque proximus.

62. The goat gives a good milking, but she casts it
all down with her foot.

Spoken when they who do a piece of good service, by their
after behaviour spoil the good grace of it.

63. The dee'ls cow calves twice a year.

64. The dee'ls ay good to his own.

Two vile malicious proverbs! spoken when they whom we
affect not, thrive and prosper in the world; as if they had
their prosperity from the devil.

65. Titt for tatt, quoth the wife when she farted at the
thunder.

A senseless proverb spoken when we give as good as we get.

66. The scholar may d war the master by a time.

Lat.—Meliorem præsto magistro discipulum.

67. There is an act in the Laird of Grant's court, that
not above eleven speak at a time.

Spoken when many speak at once.

68. The piper wants mickle that wants the under
e chaffs.

Spoken when a thing is wanting that is absolutely necessary.

69. The mother of a mischief is no f more than a mid-
gewing.

Spoken when a great quarrel has risen from a small occasion.
Lat.—Lis minimis verbis interdum maxima crescit.

70. There is more knavery by sea and land than all
the world beside.

A facetious bull upon mentioning of some knavish action.

71. Take the bit, and the buffet with it.

---

c Fighting.   d Be better than.   e Chaps.   f Bigger.

Bear some ill usage of them by whom you get advantage.
Lat.—Asinus esuriens fustem negligit.

72. The tod never sped better than when he went his own errand.

Every man is most zealous for his own interest; spoken to advise a man to go about such a business himself.

73. The king's errand may come the ⁶cadgers ʰ gate yet.

A great man may want a mean man's service.

74. Take a care of that man whom God has set a mark on.

I went once to a conventicle on a mountain side, in company of a very sage intelligent gentleman, who seeing the preacher want two joints of each ring finger, having a nail upon the third, he immediately took horse and rode away : I ask'd him what ail'd him, he said, God had set a mark upon that man, and he was sure it was not for nothing. This man prov'd a great plague to his country, was the death of a great many, and came to a violent end himself. The Scots generally have an aversion to any that have any natural defect or redundancy, as thinking them mark'd out for a mischief.

75. There was never a good town, but had a mire at one end of it.

The deficiency and unsatisfactoriness of every created being, has given occasion to this and many other proverbs.

Eng.—Every rose hath its prickle.
Item.—Every bean hath its black.
Item.—Every path hath its puddle.
Lat.—Nihil est ab omni parte beatum.
Item.—Rebus lætis par est mensura malorum.
Item.—Commoditas omnis sua fert incommoda.

76. The father buys, the son ¹biggs,
   The grandchild sells, and his son ᵏ thiggs.

A proverb much used in Lowthian, where estates stay not long in one family ; but hardly heard of in the rest of the nation.

77. ¹Thole well is good for burning,
   Eng.—Patience and posset-drink cures all maladies.
   Lat.—Levius fit patientia quicquid corrigere est nefas.

78. They speak of my drink, that never consider my drouth.

---

⁶ Carriers.   ʰ Way.   ¹ Builds.   ᵏ Begs.   ¹ Suffer.

s 3

They censure my doing such a thing, who neither consider my occasions of doing it, or what provocations I had to do it.

79. The old horse must die in some man's hand.

80. The cause is good, and the word fall on.

Spoken facetiously when we begin dinner.

81. The more haste the worse speed,
    Quoth the taylor to his long thread.

Lat.——Nimis propere minus prospere.

82. They may know by your beard, what lay on your board.

Spoken when we see the reliots of meat upon a man's mouth, beard or breast.

83. The happy man cannot be [m] harried.

Spoken when a fear'd misfortune happen'd for the best.

84. The still sow eats up all the [n] draff.

Spoken to persons who look demurely, but are roguish.

85. The stoup that goes often to the well, comes home broken at last.

Spoken when a thing has often escap'd, but is at last over-taken.

86. The miller got never better [o] moulter than he took with his own hands.

Spoken to them who have a thing at their own taking.

87. Toom pokes will strive.

When a married couple are pinch'd with poverty they will be apt to jarr.

88. There is a day coming that will shew whose arse is blackest.

Meaning the day of judgment.

89. The longer we live the more farlies we see.

Spoken upon seeing something that we did not see before.
Eng.——One may live and learn.
Item.——The longer we live we grow the wiser.
Lat.——Seris venit usus ab annis.
Item.——Discipulus prioris posterior dies.

90. The poor man is ay put to the worst.

Lat.——Pauper ubique jacet.

91. They were never [p] fain that [q] sidg'd, nor full that licked dishes.

Spoken when people shrug their shoulders, as if it was a sign that they were not content.

---

[m] Ruined.   [n] Grains.   [o] ToH.   [p] Content.   [q] Shrugg'd.

92. The death of wives, and the standing of sheep, is
the best thing ever came a poor man's gate.

There is more jest than truth in this proverb.

93. There is a measure in all things, if it were but in
kail supping.

Eng.—There is reason in roasting of eggs.

Item.—Measure is treasure.

Lat.—Est modus in rebus.

94. The [r] rook follows the fairest, take witness by the
crook.

This is in Aristophanes, and signifies that envy is a conco-
mitant of excellency ; the latter part is added foolishly, as if
the proverb was ironical.

95. The kirk is ay greedy.

Clergymen have perquisites and tythes due from every man
in the parish, and because they demand these small sums they
are call'd covetous.

96. The dee'l is mickle, and you're greedy.

Spoken to them who covet something that we have.

97. The kirk is mickle, but you may say mass in one
end of it.

Spoken when people say something is too much, intimating
that they need take no more than they have use for.

98. There is but one good wife in the world, and every
man thinks he has her.

This rule admits large exceptions, for some are fully
appriz'd of the contrary.

99. Till other [s] tinklars, ill may you agree,
The one in a peat pot, and the other in the sea.

A senseless, uncharitable saying ! when two, whom you do
not affect, are at odds.

Eng.—Fight dog, fight bear.

Lat.—Crescant lites.

100. There is mickle to do when [t] domine's ride.

For such are not well provided for riding, nor expert at it.

101. There is a hole in the house.

Spoken when some are present, before whom it is not proper
to speak our mind.

Lat.—Lupus est in fabula.

102. The [u] leeful man is the beggar's brother.

Spoken when we have lent something that we now want, and
must be forc'd to borrow. They say also, and more truly,

---

[r] Smoke.   [s] Tinkers.   [t] Pedagogues, students, at the
university.   [u] The man that is ready to lend.

103. The slothful man is the beggar's brother.

104. The more the merrier, the fewer the better chear.

The first, because good company exhilarate one another: the second, because there will be the more to each.

105. There are more thieves of my kin than honest men in yours.

The design of the speaker is to intimate that there are not many honest men among the other's kin.

106. They wist as well that ᵛ speer'd not.

A short answer to an impertinent question, if you had not ask'd you would have known as well.

107. The hen egg goes to the ʷ haa,
    To bring the goose egg awa.

ᶠ Spoken when poor people give small gifts to be doubly repaid.

108. Though you say it, that should not say it, and must say it, if it be said.

A ridicule upon them that commend themselves.

Lat.—Laus improprio ore sordescit.

109. The longer you tread on a turd, it will be the broader.

Spoken when people make a great stir about scandalous words which they are supposed to have deserv'd.

Eng.—The more you stir the worse you stink.

Lat.—Suo ipsius indicio perit sorex.

110. There was never a cake, but had a ˣ make.

None so good but there may be as good.

111. There was never a Jack but there was a Gill.

No body so despicable, but may get a match meet for them.

112. Take as you to come.

A proverb debarring choice.

Eng.—Touch and take.

113. Tell not thy foe when thy foot's sleeping, nor thy step-minny when thou'rt sore hungry.

The one will take advantage of thee; and the other will not be ready to supply thee.

114. There is kail in ʸ Cut's ᶻ weime.

Spoken when you see a boy hearty and merry; intimating, that he has gotten his belly full.

115. There is a remedy for all things, but stark dead.

Lat.—Sperandum est vivis: non est spes ulla sepultis.

ᵛ Ask'd.   ʷ Hall, the great house.   ˣ One of the same sort.   ʸ A dog's name.   ᶻ Belly.

116. There is a reason for you, with a rag about the foot of it.

Spoken when one gives a trifling reason for what they have done.

117. The meal cheap, and the shoon dear,
Quoth the sowter's wife that wo'd I hear.

118. There was I wife that kept her supper for her breakfast, and she dy'd e'er day.

Spoken when you are bid keep such a thing for another meal.

119. The more cost the more honour.

Spoken to them that propose an expensive thing, when a cheaper would do.

120. There is a difference between, will you buy, and will you sell.

When people proffer their goods, buyers will be shy: and when people ask to buy, sellers will hold their wares the dearer.

Eng.—Buy at the market and sell at home.

121. Truth and honesty keeps the crown of the ᵃ causway.

Eng.—Truth and oyl are always uppermost.

Item.—Truth may be blam'd, but never asham'd.

Lat.—Veritas non quærit angulos.

122. Tarry breeks pays no fraught.

People of a trade assist one another mutually.

123. Take a hair of the dog that bit you.

It is suppos'd that the hair of a dog will cure the bite he gives. Spoken to them who are sick after drink, as if another drink would cure their indisposition.

124. They buy good cheap that bring nothing home.

Spoken to them that think our pennyworth too dear.

Lat.—Nullus emptor difficilis bonum emit opsonium.

125. The first of the nine orders of knaves is he that tells his errand before he goes it.

Whether any jocose author has digested knaves into nine orders I know not. But this is spoken to a boy who being bid to go an errand, will pretend to tell how he'll speed before he goes.

126. The bairn speak in the fields what he heard by the ᵇ slett.

Spoken when we suspect that children heard from their parents what opprobrious words they say of us, or to us.

ᵃ Street.   ᵇ Fire side.

Lat.—Maxima debetur puero reverentia.

127. The worst world that ever was some man [c] wan.

128. They [d] wite you, and they [d] wite you no wrong, and they give you less [d] wite than you [e] serve.

A jocose jargon, when we make people believe that we are condoling them, when we are really accusing them.

129. Take part of the [f] pelf, when the pack is a dealing.

Eng.—Catch that catch can.

130. There is little for the rake after the besom.

There is little to be gotten of such a thing, when covetous people have had their will of it.

131. The weeds o'er grow the corn.

The bad are the most numerous.

Lat.—Plures mali.

132. The wife is welcome that comes with the crooked [g] oxter.

She is welcome that brings some present under her arm.

Lat.—Allatoris adventus semper est gratus.

133. There is no remedy for fear but cut off the head.

For a panick fear is beyond all arguments.

134. There are more ways to the wood than one.

If I cannot be serv'd this way, I'll make a shift another.

Lat.—Hâc non successit, aliâ aggrediamur viâ.

135. The higher up, the lower fall.

There are many proverbs to this purpose.

Eng.—Climb hastily fall suddenly.

Lat.—Ut lapsu gravore ruant tolluntur in altum.

136. The next time you dance, know whom you take by the hand.

Spoken to them who have imprudently engag'd with some who have been too cunning, or too hard for them.

137. The malt's above the meal with you.

That is, you are drunk.

138. Touch me not on the sore heel.

Do not jest too near with my honour and interest.

139. Take a man by his word, and a cow by her horn.

A reflection upon one who has broken his word to us.

140. They who are early up, and have no business, have either an ill bed, an ill wife, or an ill conscience.

---

[c] Got advantage by it.   [d] Blame.   [e] Deserve.   [f] Goods.
[g] Arm.

A foolish excuse of him that lies long a bed.

141. The [h] tod keeps his own hole clean.

Apply'd to batchelors who keep women servants, whom they ought not to meddle with.

Eng.—The fox preys farthest from his hole.

142. That which God will give, the dee'l cannot [i] reave.

Spoken when we have attain'd our end in spite of opposition.

143. There is nothing but 'mends for misdeeds.

If I have done you harm, I will make reparation.

144. The bird that can sing, and will not sing, should be [k] gar'd sing.

Spoken when we use rough means to perverse people.

Lat.—Peraget violenta potestas—Quod tranquilla negat.

145. The cow may want her own tail yet.

You may want my kindness hereafter, though you deny me your's now.

146. True enough, false liar.

An ironical consent to them whom we bear telling a lye.

147. They were [l] scant of bairns that brought you up.

Spoken to ill thriven, or ill mannered children.

148. Two blacks make no white.

An answer to them who, being blam'd, say others have done as ill or worse.

149. There is steel in my needle eye, though there be little o't.

Spoken when a thing, commendable for its kind, is found fault with for its quantity.

150. The fairest face, the falsest heart.

Eng.—The fairer the hostess, the fouler the reckoning.

Lat.—Fronti nulla fides.

151. They will know by a half penny if the priest will take an offering.

A small experiment will discover a covetous inclination.

152. There is a bee in your bonnet case.

Eng.—There's a maggot in your head.

Item.—There's some crotchets in your crown.

153. There are two things in my mind, and that's the least of them.

A kind of a supercilious denial of a request.

154. The weakest goes to the wall.

The least powerful are thrust out from profit or preferment.

---

[h] Fox.   [i] Rob. us of.   [k] Made to.   [l] Scarce.

155. That's for the father but not for the son.

Spoken when a thing is done with slight materials, and consequently will not be lasting.

156. Two things a man should never be angry at;
what he can help, and what he cannot help.

If he can help it, let him; if he cannot, anger is to no purpose.

157. The first thing a bare gentleman calls for in a
morning is a needle and thread.

Viz. To sow up the rents that are about him.

158. They are sad rents that come in with tears.

An answer to them, who seeing your cloaths ragged, say,
Your rents are coming in. Taken from the double signification of the two words rents and tears.

159. There are more work-days, than life-days.

Spoken to dissuade people from constant toil.

160. They that see your head, see not your height.

Spoken to men of low stature, and high spirits.

161. Twine to you, your ᵐ minnie was a good spinster.

Spoken to those who curse you, or rail upon you, as if you
would say, take what you say to your self.

162. There is more room without than within.

An apology for breaking wind backward.

163. They 'gree like butter and ⁿ mells.

Spoken when people do not agree; but I know not where
the comparison lies.

Eng.—They agree like harp and harrow.

164. The Englishman weeps, the Irishman sleeps;
but the Scotishman gangs while he gets it.

A pretended account of the behaviour of these three nations,
when they want meat.

165. Thirteen of you may go to the dozen well enough.

Spoken to worthless fellows.

166. The king may come to Kelly yet, and when he
comes he'll ride.

I know not the original of this proverb: but it signifies that
the time may come, that I may get my revenge upon such
people; and then I will do it to purpose.

167. Tell your eld ᵒ gly'd ᵖ giddim that.

Spoken to them that tell us something that we do not like.

168. There is ay a life for a living man.

ᵐ Mama.　ⁿ Maul's.　ᵒ Squinting.　ᵖ Grandmother.

Spoken when we are disappointed of something that we expected; intimating that we can, and will, live without it.

169. This is a good meat house.

Spoken when we want drink at dinner.

170. The poor man pays for all.

171. The worse luck now the better another time.

Spoken to hearten losing gamesters.

Eng.—When bale is highest boot is next.

Lat.—Flebile principium melior fortuna sequetur.

Item.—Variæ sunt fortunæ vices.

172. The last best, like to good wive's daughters.

It is alledg'd that wives, after their eldest daughters are dispos'd of, say that the youngest is the far best of the family.

173. They are far behind that may not follow.

Spoken when people do not despond, though behind others.

174. They are lightly ⁹ harried, that have all their own.

Spoken when people complain of injuries unjustly; when they have lost little, or nothing.   To the same purpose;

175. There was an old wife and she had ʳ naught,
       The thieves came, and they stole naught:
       The wife went out, and cry'd naught,
       What should she cry, she wanted naught.

176. Two fools in a house are too many.

True enough! But I have seen more.

177. The death of the first wife makes such a hole in
       the heart, that all the rest slip thro'.

It is supposed that he who has lost the wife of his youth and love, will easily bear the loss of a second or third, who are commonly married rather for convenience, than love.

178. That which is in my ˢ weime, is not in my ᵗ testament.

An excuse for eating rather than keeping what is before us.

179. The farrer in the deeper.

Spoken to people engag'd into an intricate business: the more they struggle the more they are intangled.

180. The flesh is ay fairest that is farthest from the bone.

Spoken to them who are plump and look well.

181. They fill corn sacks.

Spoken to children when they say they are not full; a word

---

⁹ Ruined.   ʳ Nothing.   ˢ Belly.   ᵗ Will.

T

that the Scots cannot endure, but would rather they are not satisfic'd, that is, satisfied.

182. ᵛ Tine needle, tine ᵘ dark.

Spoken to young girls, when they lose their needle.

183. Tine cat, tine game.

An allusion to a play call'd Cat i'the Hole, and the English kit, cat. Spoken when men at law have lost their principal evidence.

184. Tine book, tine grace.

Spoken to school-boys, when they have lost their book.

185. There is mickle between market days.

Times, modes, prices, and other circumstances are mutable.

186. There will be a hole in the groat to day, and the supper to seek.

A saying of labourers, when they fear a rainy afternoon.

187. There was never a slut but had a ʷ slitt, there was never a daw but had ˣ twa.

Spoken to young women when they have a rent about them, which, if they were not sluts, they would sew up.

188. That's the way to marry me, if you have hap to do't.

Spoken when people are going the proper way about a business.

189. The best thing that ever happened to a poor man, is that the first bairn dye, and all the rest follow.

A cursed distrustful proverb! God is able to maintain the poor man's child, as well as young master, and young miss: and often in a more healthy, and plump condition.

190. Touch a gall'd horse on the back, and he'll ʸ fling.

Spoken when you have said something to a man, that intrenches upon his reputation, and so have put him in a passion.

191. The things that wives ᶻ hains, cats eat.

What is too niggardly spar'd is often as widely squander'd.

192. True love ᵃ kythes in time of need.

Lat.—Amicus certus in re incerta cernitur.

193. Two words to that bargain.

That is, I will not be easily induc'd to it.

194. There was never enough where nothing was left.

When all is eaten up it's a token that the commons were but short.

ᵛ Day's-work. ᵘ Lose. ʷ A rent. ˣ Two. ʸ Kick.
ᶻ Spares. ᵃ Shews it self.

195. The ᵇfison of your hips is ᵉloupen to your lips, you dow not hotch for hunger.

An immodest expression of young girls to young fellows.

196. That's Hackerton's cow.

Hackerton was a lawyer, who gave leave to one of his tenants to put a weak ox into his park to recruit; a heifer of Hackerton's run upon the ox and gor'd him; the man tells him that his ox had killed his heifer: why then, says Hackerton, your ox must go for my heifer, the law provides that. No, says the man, your cow killed my ox. The case alters there, says he. The English have one just correspondent to this, that they call Plowden's case; spoken when people alter their opinions when the case comes home to themselves.

197. There is a flea in my hose.

That is, I have some trouble of mind or body about me, that takes up my thoughts.

198. The black ox never trod on your foot.

You never had the care of a family upon you, nor was pressed with severe business or necessities.

199. Tooth and nail.

That is, with the utmost endeavour.

Lat.—Velis & remis, omnibus nervis.

200. Take up the next you find.

Spoken jocosely when people say they have lost such a thing.

201. The best is ay best cheap.

Eng.—Light cheap lither yield.

202. The day that you do well there will be seven moons in the ᵈlift, and one in the ᵉmidding.

Intimating that such a one will never do well.

203. There are two enoughs, and you have gotten one of them.

That is, big enough, and little enough; meaning that he had gotten little enough: an answer to them who out of modesty say they have enough.

204. That's the piece the step-bairn never got.

Spoken when we give what is large and thick, or the crown of the cake.

205. The ᶠnar even the more beggars.

A facetious word when more people come into company.

ᵇ Substance. ᶜ Jump'd. ᵈ Heavens. ᵉ Dunghill. ᶠ Nearer.

T 2

206. There is no ᵍ breard like ʰ midding breard.

The grains of corn that are carried out unto the dunghill takes root and springs amain; spoken when we see people of mean birth rise suddenly to wealth and honour.

207. They are not all saints, that get hally water.

Nor are they all good men that make pretences to religion.

208. They were ⁱ fain of little, that thank'd you for a fart.

A word of contempt to them that unreasonably think that we are obliged to them.

209. That's hard, quoth the old wife, when she shit a mill-stone.

A sensless bauble when we think our fortune bad.

210. The better day, the better deed.

I never heard this used but when people say that they did such an ill thing on Sunday.

211. Tush swims best that's bred in the sea.

They are better seamen that are train'd to the sea from their infancy, than they who are taught by art.

212. The feathers bore the flesh away.

Spoken to fowlers when they come home empty.

213. That's your ᵏ Mak'um fatherless, that has let many a man die in his bed.

A jest upon a man when he shews his sword.

214. They are all alive whom you slew.

Spoken with contempt to them that threaten, as if they durst not execute.

215. The death of a bairn is not the ˡ skailing of a house.

The death of a child bears no proportion to the death of a husband, or wife.

216. They draw the cat harrow.

That is, they thwart one another.

217. The ᵐ tod's bairns are ill to tame.

Apply'd to them who are descended of an ill parentage, or cursed with a bad education: such are hard to be made good or virtuous

---

ᵍ Young corn.   ʰ Dunghill.   ⁱ Glad.   ᵏ Make him, alluding to Malcolm, a man's name.   ˡ Giving up house-keeping.   ᵐ The foxes.

218. The bag to the old ⁿ stent, and the belt to the
º yule hole.

Meaning that we eat as heartily as we did at Christmas.

219. To as mickle purpose as to wag your hand in the
water.

220. Take a spring of your own fiddle, and dance to
it when you have done.

That is, take your course, and reap the fruits of it.

221. The swine's gone through it.

Spoken when an intended marriage is gone back, out of a
superstitious conceit, that if a swine come between a man and
his mistress, they will never be married.

222. They have been born as poor as you, who have
come to a pouch full of green pease e'er they
dy'd.

Spoken to poor boys, whom we think hopeful.

223. Tread on my foot again, and a boll of meal on
thy back.

Spoken when we tread on the foot of any thing.

224. The higher the hill, the lower the grass.

People of the greatest fortunes are not the most liberal.

225. Two conveniencies sindle meets, what's good
for the plants, is ill for the peats.

What may be good in one respect may be bad in another.

Eng.—What's good for the back is bad for the head.

Lat.—Nil prodest quod non lædere possit idem.

226. They never ᵖ beuk a good cake, but may bake an
ill.

A piece of work may miscarry in the hand of the most
skilful.

227. They are speaking of you, where there are ill
lick'd dishes.

The Scots have a fancy that if their ears glow, tingle, or
itch, some are speaking of them; and when any says this, the
proverb is an answer: as if people were only saying, that if
you was there, you would lick them cleaner.

228. Take it all pay the malt-man (baker).

Spoken jocosely when we give all of such a thing.

229. There is an end of an old song.

That is, you have all that I can tell you of it.

ⁿ Stretch.   º Christmas.   ᵖ Bak'd.

T 3

230. There was another gotten the night that you was born.

That is, if you will not serve me another will.

231. The ᵠtod never fares better than when he's ʳban'd.

Spoken when we are told that such people curse us, which we think the effect of envy, the companion of felicity. The fox is cursed when he takes our poultry.

232. That's my tale, where is yours.

That is my condition, or I was going to say so.

233. They çan do ill that cannot do good.

Spoken when children break, or abuse any thing.

234. The thrift of you, and the wool of a dog, would make a good web.

Spoken in jest to them that pretend to be thrifty.

235. The third is a charm.

Spoken to encourage those who have attempted a thing once and again to try a third time. They will say also,

236. There is three things of all things.

237. The more noble, the more humble.

238. The good or ill hap of a good or ill life,
　　Is the good or ill choice, of a good or ill wife.

Eng.—A man's best fortune or worst is his wife.

239. There's a word in my ˢweime, but it is ᵗlaigh down.

That is, I could say something, but I will not.

240. There is no sport where there is neither old folk nor bairns.

241. There is no harm done when there is a good lad gotten:

An apology for a woman that has born a bastard.

242. They that laugh in the morning may greet e'er night.

Lat.—Gaudia principium sunt nostri sæpe doloris.

243. To ᵘfazards, hard hazards is death e'er they come there.

Cowardly people are almost killed at the sight of danger; out of the Cherry and Slae.

244. They that burn you for a witch loses all the coals.

Eng.—No body will take you for a conjurer.

ᵠ Fox. 　ʳ Curs'd. 　ˢ Belly. 　ᵗ Low.
　ᵘ A runaway cock, a coward.

245. There is one day of reckoning, and another of payment.

A threatning to be up with some people hereafter.

246. To learn you to speak (to speer).

A short answer to them that ask why you did, or said, such a thing.

247. There is a clue in your arse.

Spoken to restless people.

248. The mother's breath is ay sweet.

249. The mother is a matchless beast.

Both spoken of the tender affection of mothers.

250. They will let little go by them, that will catch at a fart.

Spoken to them that quarrel with you for breaking wind.

251. The dee'ls bairns have dee'ls luck.

Spoken enviously when ill people prosper.

252. The dee'l never sent a wind out of hell, but he would sail with it.

Spoken of trimmers and time-servers.

253. Two heads may lye on one pillow, and no body knows where the luck lies.

Spoken when either husband or the wife is dead, and the surviving party goes back in the world after.

254. The dee'ls good when he's pleas'd.

Spoken to people who readily take every thing amiss.

255. Time and thought tames the strongest grief.

Lat.—Dies odemit ægritudinem.

256. There is no ᵛ fay folks meat in the pot.

When the pot boils after it is taken off the fire, they say this senseless, groundless bauble.

257. There is fay blood in your head.

That is, you adventure upon a thing that will be your death. The Scots call a man fay when he alters his conditions, and humours, which they think a sign of death.

258. The greatest ʷ toghers make not the greatest ˣ testaments.

Eng.—He that's needy when he's married, shall be rich when he's buried.

259. The ʸ lucky thing gives the penny.

If a thing be good, the bulkier the better; an apology for big people.

ᵛ Near death.   ʷ Portions.   ˣ Latter wills.   ʸ Bulky.

260. The name of an honest woman is mickle worth.

A reason given for a woman, who has born a bastard, for marrying an inferior person.

261. There came never ill of good advisement.

A persuasion to consider well of a thing before you go about it.

Eng.—Though old and wise yet still advise.

262. The back and the belly holds bare and busy.

263. Their fathers were never fellows.

Spoken when two of unequal birth and pedigree are compared.

Eng.—They are not to be named in a day.

264. There are more married than keep good houses.

A common answer to them that ask you why you do not marry.

265. The smith has ay a spark in his ² haise.

And they often take pains to quench it, but to no purpose.

266. The ª ware evening is long and ᵇ tough,
    The harvest evening runs soon o'er the ᶜ heugh.

In the spring the days are lengthening; in harvest decreasing; which makes the one seem long, and the other short.

267. The Michaelmas moon rises ay alike soon.

The moon, at full, being then in the opposite sign, bends for some days towards the tropick of Cancer, and so rising more northerly, rises more early. My country people believe it to be a particular providence of God that people may see to get in their grain.

268. There is no ᵈ sik a word in all ᵉ Wallace.

A kind of jocose denial.

269. The book of may be's is very broad.

An answer to them that say, may be it will fall out so, or so.

270. There is nothing between a poor man and a rich
    but a piece of an ill year.

Because, in that space, many things may fall out, that may make a rich man poor.

271. The one half of the world kens not how the other
    lives.

Eng.—Little knows the fat sow, what the lean one means.

---

² Throat.   ª Spring.   ᵇ Tedious.   ᶜ Soon sets. The Scots call a precipice a heugh.   ᵈ Such.   ᵉ A book of the actions of Sir Will. Wallace.

272. Two wits are better than one.

Lat.— Plus vident oculi, quam oculus.

273. The evening red, and the morning gray,
Is the true sign of a good day.

274. The worth of a thing is best known by the want
of it.

275. The scabby head loves not the comb.

That is, wicked men love neither correction, nor reproof.

276. The master's eye makes the horse fat.

From the Latin, Oculus domini saginat equum.

277. That's but one doctor's opinion.

Spoken with resentment to them that offer their advice
contrary to our interest.

278. Trim tram, like master like man.

Eng.—Hackny mistress, hackny maid.

Lat.—Qualis hera, talis pedisqua.

279. They that have much butter, may lay it thick on
their bread.

They that have much may spend the more magnificently.

280. The remedy is worse than the disease.

281. The first dish is ay best eaten.

The English say, Pleases all.

282. The day hath eyes, and the night hath ears.

283. The evening crowns the day.

For as our success appears then, it is good or bad.

284. The gray mare is the better horse.

That is, the good wife is master.

285. Two hands in a dish, and one in a purse.

I am pleased when people eat with me, but not when they
invade my property.

286. Thoughts are free.

Lat.—Cogitationis pœnam nemo patitur.

287. That's for that, and butter's for fish.

Spoken when a thing fits nicely what it was designed for.

288. Take me not up before I fall.

Do not so far mistake me, as to give an answer to my discourse, before you hear me out.

289. The greatest burthens are not the gainfullest.

That is, they who labour sorest, have not the best wages.

290. There is no general rule without exceptions.

291. The poor man's shilling is but a penny.

Because he must buy every thing at the dearest rate.

292. The more mischief the better sport.

A common, but wicked and foolish saying.

293. The bones of a great estate is worth the picking.

Spoken of an estate under burthen, mortgaged, but not sold, that there may be something made of it.

294. The longest day will have an end.

Spoken when men now in power oppress us, signifying that there may be a turn.

Eng.—Be the day never so long, at length comes evening song.

295. The bones bears the beef home.

An answer to them that complain that there are many bones in the meat that they are buying.

296. Take up that ewe and yoke her.

A senseless saying when a thing falls out ill.

297. They that never fill'd a cradle should not sit in one.

Because such will not consider whether there may be a child in it; whereas they who have had children will be more cautious.

298. They are well guided that God guides.

Spoken when some person has committed malefice.

299. There came never such a f gloff to a daw's heart.

Spoken when people are suddenly wet with, or plunged into cold water.

300. Take some to your self, as you sell the rest.

Spoken facetiously when we would have people take some of their own meat, drink, or such like.

301. The dee'l is a busy bishop in his own diocese.

302. The subject's love is the king's life-guard.

303. They that see you all day, will not break the house for you at night.

Spoken to women whom we pretend to be ugly.

304. There two fools met.

Spoken to them that say they refused such a considerable price for such a pennyworth. That is, he was a fool that offered it, and you a fool that refused it.

305. Take your will, you're wise enough.

306. Take your will, and then you'll not dye of the pet.

---

f A sudden fright.

307. Take your will of it, as the cat did of the haggish·

These three spoken to them who obstinately persist in an unreasonable design.

308. They are ay good that are away.

Spoken when people lavishly commend those of their friends that are abroad, or dead.

309. The sowter gave the sow a kiss,
Humph, quoth she, its for a ᵍ birse.

Spoken of those whose service we suppose to be mercenary.

310. They that.ʰ ly down for love should rise for hunger.

Alledging if they had not been too well fed, they would not be troubled with that disease.

Lat.—Sine Cerere & Baccho, friget Venus.

311. There's a time to ⁱ glye, and a time to look even.

There is a time when a man must overlook things, which at another time he would take notice of.

312. That's Jock's news.

Spoken when people tell that for news which every body knows.

313. The greatest fish an oyster,
The gravest bird an owl,
The gravest beast an ass,
And the gravest man a fool.

A groundless rhyme among light people.

14. That is, ᵏ gee luged drink.

When a thing does not please us we wag our head, but when we are pleas'd we give a nod on the one side; spoken when we get excellent drink. I suppose this proverbial phrase to be only used among the Scots in Ireland.

W.

1. WATER stoups holds no ale.

An apology for not drinking strong liquor, because we have not been accustomed to it.

2. When I did well I heard it never,
When I did ill I heard it ever.

A reflection of servants upon hard and passionate masters, who are liberal in their reproofs, but sparing in their commendations.

ᵍ Bristle.   ʰ Fall sick.   ⁱ Look a squint.   ᵏ One ear'd.

3. **Were it not for hope, heart would break.**
Lat.—Spes bona dat vires, animum quoque spes bona firmat.
Vivere spe vidi, qui moriturus erat.

4. **White legs wo'd ay be ª ruscd.**
Spoken when people fish for commendations, by disparaging a little their persons or performances.

5. **Wealth makes wit waver.**
Spoken when people have many advantageous offers, and are at a loss which to take.
Lat.—Inopem me copia fecit.

6. **What we first learn, we best can.**
Lat.—Tenacissimi sumus eorum quæ rudibus annis percipemus.
Item.—Adeo a teneris assuescere multum est.

7. **When drink's in wit's out.**
A slender excuse for what people may say or do in their drink.

8. **When friends meet, heart's warm.**
Lat.—Nil ego contulero jocundo sanus, amico.

9. **Words go with the wind, but ᵇ dunts are the devil.**

10. **Words go with the wind, but strokes are out of play.**
Lat.—Omnia prius experiri verbis, quam armis, sapientem decet.

11. **Work for nought makes folk ᶜ dead sweir.**
Eng.—Great pains and little gains make men soon weary.

12. **Wiles help weak folk.**
Lat.—Ingenio pollet cui vim natura negavit.

13. **Wool sellers kens ay wool buyers.**
Roguish people know their own consorts.
Lat.—Spinæ se invicem complectuntur.
Item.—Se invicem norunt, ut fures in nundinis.

14. **Well, quoth Wallace, and then he leugh,**
   The king of France has gold enough,
   And you'll get it all for the winning.
Intimating that we will get nothing without labouring for it.

15. **What the eye sees not, the heart rues not.**
Men may have losses, but if they be unknown to them they give them no trouble.

16. **Wink at small faults, for you have great ones your self.**

ª Commended.   ᵇ Hard blows.   ᶜ Lazy.

Lat.—Nam vitiis nemo sine nascitur, optimus ille,
Qui minimis urgetur.

17. When Adam carded, and Eve span,
Where was all our gentry then ?

18. Up starts a carle and gather'd good,
And thence came all our gentle blood.

Lat.—Primus majorum quisquis fuit ille tuorum.
Aut pastor fuit, aut illud quod dicere nolo.

19. When the lady lets a fart, the ^d messan gets a
^e knap.

Spoken when one is blam'd for another's fault.

Lat.—Quicquid delirant reges plectuntur achivi.

20. Well kens the mouse that the cat's out of the house.

Eng.—When the cat's away the mice will play.

Lat.—Absente fele, saliunt mures.

21. Use of hand is father of ^f lear.

Lat.—Usus adjuvat artem.

Item.—Fabricando fabricimus.

Item.—Solus & artifices qui juvat usus adest.

22. When my head is down my house is thatch'd.

Spoken by those who are free from debts, concerns, or
future projects : as common tradesmen, day labourers, and
servants who work their work and get their wages, and commonly are the happiest part of mankind.

23. When the cow is in the clout she's soon out.

Eng.—Ready money will away.

24. Work legs, and win legs, ^g hain legs, and tine legs.

Lat.—Studium generat studium, ignavia ignaviam.

Item.—Decrescit requie virtus, sed crescit agendo.

Item.—Adde quod ingenium, longa rubigine læsum,
Torpet & est multo quam fuit ante minus.

25. Would you make me trow that the moon is made
of green cheese.

26. Would you make me trow that spade shafts bears
plumbs.

27. Would you make me trow that my head's ^h cow'd
when I find the hair on't.

These three spoken when a man would impose upon our
senses, and make us believe what is impossible.

Lat.—Nil intra est oleam, nil extra est in nuce, duri.

---

^d Lap-dog.　^e A little blow.　^f Learning.　^g Save, spare.
^h Shorn.

U

28. Where the dee'l shites; he shites in a heap.
Enviously spoken when those we affect not grow wealthy.

29. Untimous spurring [j] spills the steed.
That is, too much haste spoils business.
Lat.—Canis festinans cæcos parit catulos.

30. Where the [k] buck is [k] bound there he must bleat.
Men must bear those hardships to which they are bound,
either by force or compact.
Eng.—They that are bound must obey.

31. What's none of my profit shall be none of my peril.
I will not engage myself deep in a business in which I have
no concern.
Lat.—Mihi istic nec seritur nec meritur.

32. Wo's them that have the cat's dish, and she ay
[l] meuting.
Spoken when people owe a thing to, or detain a thing from
needy people, who are always calling for it.

33. When all men speak, no man hears.
Used when many speak at once in a business.

34. What if the [m] lift fall, you may gather laverocks.
Spoken when people make silly, frivolous excuses and
objections.
Lat.—Quid si ad eos redeamus qui dicunt quid se cœlum
rua.

35. When the [n] tod preaches, look to the geese.
When wicked men put on a cloak of religion, suspect some
wicked design. Witness the solemn fasts and humiliations
in the time of the anarchy, when not only subtle foxes, but
ravenous bears, treacherous crocodiles and devouring harpies
actually preach'd.
Lat.—Si tu vis fallere plebem finge deos.

36. We can drink of the [o] burn, when we cannot bite
of the [p] brea.
Spoken when people want bread, for none complain for
want of drink.

37. When the belly's full, the bones wo'd be at rest.
People are dispos'd to sleep after a full meal: witness a
congregation on Sunday afternoon.

38. What comes over the dee'ls back, will go away
under his belly.

---

[j] Spoils.   [k] He-goat.   [l] Mawing.   [m] Heavens.
[n] Fox.   [o] River.   [p] Brow, bank.

39. What comes with the wind, will go with the water.

There are many proverbs to this purpose in all languages.
Lat.—Male parta, male dilabantur.

40. What you do when you're drunk, you must pay for when you're dry.

The law makes drunkenness no excuse, but rather an aggravation.

41. Well meet e'er hills meet.

Eng.—Men may meet; but mountains never will.

42. What better is the house that the q daw rises early in the morning.

Spoken often by mistresses to their maids when they have been early up, and done little work.
Eng.—Early up, never the nearer.

43. When thieves reckon r leal folks come to their geer.

Spoken when two rogues, falling out, discover the villanies of one another.

44. Wo worth ill company, quoth the ʳkae of Camnethen.

Spoken when we have been drawn by ill company into an ill thing. A jack-daw in Camnethen learn'd this word from a guest in the house when he was upon his penitentials after hard drinking.

45. When the tod gets to the wood, he cares not who ᵗ keek in his tail.

Spoken when a villain has so cleanly escap'd, that he cares not who look after him.

46. Whitely things are ay tender.

Taken from common observation, but spoken to people of all complexions when they pretend tenderness.

47. Work a' God's name, and so does no witches.

48. Who wats may keep sheep another day.

Who knows but it may be in my power to do you good or harm hereafter, and as you use me, so will I you.

49. When petticoats woos, breeks may come speed.

Spoken when maids court young men.
Eng.—It is time to yoke when the cart comes to the horse.

50. We are to learn while we live.

Spoken when we are inform'd of a thing that we knew not before.

---

q Slut.   r Honest.   ˢ Jack-daw.   ᵗ Peep.

Lat.—Ars longa vita brevis.

Item.—Discenti assidue multa senecta venit.

51. What you want up and down, you have to and fro.

Spoken to them who are low of stature, but broad and squat.

Lat.—Quod alibi diminutum est, exæquatur alibi.

52. When the cup's full carry it even.

When you have arrived at power and wealth, take a care of insolence, pride and oppression.

Lat.—Fortunam reverenter habe quicunque repente.

Dives ab exili progrediere loco.

53. Where the deer is slain, some of her blood will lye.

Spoken when some of what we have been handling is lost, or when there is some indication of what has been a doing.

Eng.—Where the horse lies down some hairs will be found.

54. When poverty comes in at the door, friendship flees out at the window.

Eng.—When good cheer is lacking, friends will be packing.

Lat.—Cum fortuna perit nullus amicus erit,

55. Well worth all good tokens.

Spoken facetiously when we are told that such an one is easing nature, or some such thing that is not to be spoken.

56. Well's him, and wo's him, that has a bishop of his kin.

Because such may be advanc'd, and perhaps disappointed.

57. Women and bairns ᵘ lain what they know not.

But what they know they'll blab out.

58. Wood in a wilderness, moss in a mountain, and wit in a poor man's breast are little thought of.

59. When you christen the bairn, you know what to call it.

Spoken in bargain making when we agree on express terms, we know not what to give and what to expect.

60. Will and wit strives with you.

You are at a stand whether to do the pleasantest or the most profitable.

Lat.—Aliud appetitus, aliud sapientia suadet.

61. We are as many Johnstons, as you are Jerdans.

Taken from two families who were always on one side; though now the proverb signifies that we have as many to take our part, as you have to take yours, yet I am inclined to believe that at first it signified that we contribute as much to the common cause as you do.

ᵘ Lain, is conceal.

62. Want is the worst of it.

Spoken when one must take a mean thing or want all.

Eng.—Hobson's choice.

63. When lairds break, carles get land.

When a great estate is sold, mean people, who have a little money, will buy each a share.

Eng.—When the tree falls, every man goes with his hatchet.

64. When a fool finds a horse shoe, he thinks ay the like to do.

Spoken when they, who have had some fortune, thinks always to be as successful.

Eng.—He that hits once will be ever shooting.

65. We can live without our friends, but not without our neighbours.

66. Where the dike's ᵛ leaghest, it is easiest loupen o'er

Spoken when the rich oppress the poor, and the strong the weak.

67. Where there are gentles there is ay ʷ offallings.

Spoken jocosely to our children, when they have forgot something where they were last; as their gloves, knives, &c.

68. Wipe with the water, and wash with the towel.

Spoken to our children, when they wash their hands slightly.

69. What makes you so ˣ ramgunshoch to me, and I so ʸ corcudoch.

A jocose return to them who speak hastily to us when we speak kindly to them. More used for the two comical words than any thing else.

70. Wish in one hand and drite in another, and see which will be first full.

Eng.—I never far'd worse than when I wish'd for my supper.

71. We can ᶻpuind for debt, but not for kindness.

If our friends will not be kind to us, we have no remedy at law.

72. Wrong has no warrand.

No man can pretend authority to do an ill thing.

73. Work bears witness who well does.

A man's diligence in labouring is best known by the effects.

Eng.—The proof of the pudding is in the eating.

Lat.—Indiscrimine apparet qui vir.

74. Wrong count is no payment.

ᵛ Lowest.   ʷ Something to be gotten.   ˣ Rugged.
ʸ Cordial.   ᶻ Distrain.

U 3

Aad therefore all accounts pass, errors excepted.

Eng.—Misreckoning is no payment.

75. We hounds slew the hare, quoth the [a] messan.

Spoken to insignificant persons, when they attribute to themselves any part of a great atchievement.

76. What [b] rake the [c] fead where the friendship dow not.

Signifying our contempt of mean persons, whose hatred we defy, and whose friendship we despise.

77. Welcome is the best dish in the kitchen.

Lat.—Super omnia vultus accessere boni.

78. Where there is o'er mickle courtesy, there is little kindness.

Eng.—Less of your courtesy, and more of your purse.

Item.—Full of courtesy, full of craft.

79. When all fruit [d] fa's welcome [e] has.

That sort of fruit is long a ripening. Spoken when we take up with what's coarse, when the good is spent.

80. Well, quoth Willie, when his wife dang him,
    She took up a rope, and she sware she wo'd hang him.

A sensless rhyme following well, when spoken with resentment.

81. What I cannot do by might I'll do by slight.

Lat.—Si leonina pellis non satis sit, addenda vulpina.

82. When the hen goes to the cock,
    The [f] burds may gen a knock.

Spoken when widows who design a second marriage prove harsh to their children.

83. Wealth in the widow's house, kail but salt.

A jocose exclamation when we have gotten something more than we expected.

84. Walie, walie, but bairns be bonny,
    One is enough, and two o'er many.

A jest upon a young woman when we see her troubled in nursing and dandling her first child.

85. What's my turn to-day, may be yours to-morrow.

86. We'll never know the worth of water 'till the well go dry.

87. [g] War, and [h] mair o't.

---

[a] Lap-dog. [b] Signifies. [c] Enmity. [d] Falls. [e] Haws.
[f] Chickens. [g] Worse. [h] More of it.

Spoken when a new disaster happens over and above the present misfortunes.

88. Who invited you to the roast?

Spoken when people put their hand uninvited to what is not theirs.

89. When I am dead make me cawdle.

Be kind to me when I am alive, for I shall not value or be better for your presents when I am dead.

Eng.—After death the doctor.

Lat.—Post bellum auxilium.

90. Win it, and wear it.

Spoken when a thing is propos'd to be given, upon doing such a task.

91. Will God's blessing make my pot boil, or my spit go?

I should not have set down such a cursed saying, if it had not been always in the mouth of a great oppressor whom I knew; who being in authority, harass'd the whole country by his exorbitant fines and illegal exactions: when poor people offered him all that they could get, and bid him take it with God's blessing, he would stormingly say, Will God's blessing make my pot play, or my spit go? And though by these arts he raised himself to a great estate; yet he dy'd miserably, and his children are at this day worse than beggars.

92. When every man gets his own, the thief will get the [1] widdie.

93. When the good man's away the board cloth is [k] tint.

Because the commons will then be short.

94. When the good wife's away the keys are tint.

For if she be not at home you'll get no drink.

95. Who may wooe [l] but cost?

That is, no great matter can be easily attain'd or atchiev'd.

96. Whiles thou, whiles I, so goes the [m] bailery.

Spoken when persons and parties get authority by turns.

Eng.—To-day me, to-morrow thee.

Lat.—Hodie mihi, cras tibi.

Item.—Nunc mihi, nunc tibi benigna, scil. fortuna.

97. When the heart's full of lust, the mouth's full of [n] leasings.

A reflection upon these damnable lies, enforc'd with horrid oaths, by which poor maids are deceiv'd. They have a very

[1] Gallows. [k] Lost. [l] Without. [m] Senescalship. [n] Lies.

...proverb, signifying that when men are hurried on by lust, their minds are so blinded, that they never consider the horrid consequences that attend them.

98. Who can hold that will away.

Spoken when our friends will not be prevail'd upon to tarry with us.

99. When thy neighbour's house is in danger take ° tent to thine own.

Lat.—Tunc tua res agitur paries cum proximus ardet.

100. Women and wine, game and deceit,
  Make the wealth small, and the wants great.

This is the translation of an old monkish rhyme.

  Pisces, perdices, vinum, nec non meritrices
  Corrumpunt cistam, & quicquid ponis in istam.

101. When all ᴾ freets fail, fire's good for the fiercy.

Spoken when after ordinary attempts, we betake ourselves to extraordinary.

102. Well minded ᵠ Marrion to thy lives end.

Spoken to them that call a thing to mind opportunely.

103. When the wind is in the west, the weather's at the best.

104. When the wind is in the east, it is neither good for man or beast.

105. When the wind is in the south, rain will be 'fouth.

106. Winter thunder, summer hunger.

These observations about the weather are vain and frivolous.

107. Wilful waste makes woeful want.

Eng.—Who spends more than he should,
  Will not have to spend when he would.

108. ˢ Widdie hold thine own.

Spoken when we see a bad man in danger, as if he ow'd his life to the gallows.

109. Well is, that well does.

Lat.—Bona bonis contingunt.

110. Well worth aw, it makes the plough draw.

Spoken when people are over-awed to do a thing, which otherways they would not do.

° Care. ᴾ Charms. ᵠ A woman's name. ʳ In abundance.
  ˢ Gallows.

111. When the ewe is drown'd, she's dead.
Spoken when a thing is gone, and past recovery.

112. What's worse than ill luck.
Spoken when a thing miscarries purely by misfortune.
There is a return to this proverb, but it is paultry.

113. When you are serv'd all the geese are well wa-
tered.
Spoken when they who have got enough already propose to
ask no more.

114. What serves dirt for if it do not stink ?
Spoken (as a great many other Scottish proverbs) when
mean, base born people, speak proudly, or behave themselves
saucily.

115. Unseen, unru'd.
Spoken when I propose to give a thing of mine, that you
never saw, for something of yours, that I never saw.

116. When wine sinks words swim.
Eng.—What soberness conceals, drunkenness reveals.
Lat.—Quod in corde sobrii, in ore ebrii.

117. When the bairn's full you may thrash before the
door.

118. Where ⁱ leal folk got geer.
A proverbial answer to them that ask where you got such a
thing.　They say also,

119. Where it was, and not where it grew.
Eng.—Where the dee'l got the fryer.

120. What may be done at any time, will be done at
no time.
What people may, and can do easily, will be put off from
time to time.

121. Whoredom and grace dwelt ne'er in one place.

122. ⁿ Wite your teeth if your tail be small.
Spoken to them that have good meat at their will.

123. Wives and wind are necessary evils.

124. When you are going and coming the gate's not
empty.
Spoken to them who we think to be going a needless errand,
as if they would only employ the way.

ⁱ Honest.　　　　　ⁿ Blame.

125. Where will you get a ᵛ park to put your ʷ yell
    ˣ kay in.

Spoken to them who, without any reason, boast of their
good management.

126. Who can help sickness? quoth the drunken wife,
    when she fell in the ʸ gutter.

Taken from a woman, who being drunk, pretended to be
sick; apply'd when men make a false pretence for what
they do.

127. Where vice is, vengeance follows.

Lat.—Raro ante cedentem scelestum deseruit pœna pede
claudo.

128. What put that in your head that did not put the
    ᶻ sturdy with it ?

Spoken to them that speak foolishly, or tell a story that you
thought they had not known.

129. When the heart is full, the tongue will speak.

Eng.—Glowing coals will sparkle.

130. We can sheap coat and ᵃ sark for them, but we
    cannot sheap their ᵇ weird.

Spoken when people of good education fall into misfortunes, or come to untimely ends.

131. Women's work is never done.

So much the care and management of a family requires.

132. Wit bought makes folk wise.

Spoken when we are sensible of the ill, or good, of a thing
by experience, and to our cost.

133. What need a rich man be a thief?

134. When all's in, and the ᶜ slap ᵈ ditt, rise herd and
    let the dogs sit.

Jocosely spoken to herd boys after harvest, as if there was
no farther use for them.

135. We'll never build sandy ᵉ bowrocks together.

That is, we will never be cordial or familiar together.

136. Wonder at your old shoes, when you have gotten
    your new.

An answer to them that say they wonder at you, or what
you do.

ᵛ Inclosure. ʷ Barren. ˣ Cows. ʸ Puddle. ᶻ A disease incident to cattle, called the Turn. ᵃ Shirt. ᵇ Fortune. ᶜ Gape. ᵈ Stopt. ᵉ Little houses that children build for play.

137. Upon my own expences, as the man big'd the
ᶠ dike.

Taken from an inscription upon a church-yard in Scotland,
I John Moody cives Abredonensis,
Builded this kirk-yard of fitly upon my own expences.

138. Want of wit is worse than want of geer.

139. Unsaid be your word, and your nose in a turd.

Spoken when people predict ill things to us, we wish his
word may be void, and the other as a reward of his ill will.

140. When he dies for age, you may quake for fear.

Intimating that you are not much younger.

141. We'll bark our selves e'er we buy dogs so dear.

Spoken when too dear a rate is asked for what we are
buying.

142. ᵍWite your self if your wife be with bairn.

Spoken when peoples misfortunes come by their own blame.

143. When you are well hold you so.

A discouragement from hazarding the alteration of our
condition by new projects.

144. When the well is full it will run over.

That is, when people are much wronged they will shew
their resentments. To the same purpose the next.

145. When the pot's full it will boil over.

146. Whom God will help none can hinder.

147. What said Pluck? The greater knave the better
luck.

Eng.—Knaves and fools divide the world.

148. What may be, may not be.

149. Where nothing is the king loseth his right.

And so much the subject, but with this difference, that the
king loseth his right in no other case.

150. Wage will get a page.

If I be able to hire servants I will get them to hire.

151. Where drums beat laws are silent.

This proverb came in use before the war was carried on in
so regular a method.

Lat.—Inter arma silent leges.

Item.—Rara fides pietasque viris qui castra sequuntur.

152. Under water dearth, under snow bread.

Great rains in winter wash and impoverish the ground; but
snow is supposed to cherish it.

ᶠ Wall   ᵍ Blame.

153. Wishers and walders are poor housholders.

This, with several others, signifies the vanity of empty wishes.

154. War makes thieves, and peace hangs them.

This has relation to the border wars betwixt the two nations, which was the great nursery of thieves.

155. Wedding and ill-wintering tame both man and beast.

156. Up hill spare me, down hill bear me, plain way spare me not; let me not drink when I am hot.

A rule in jockyship how to use a horse in a journey. To the same purpose the next.

157. Up hill spare me, down hill take ʰ tent to thee.

For if you ride fast down a hill the horse will be fair to stumble.

158. We cannot both sup and blow.

Lat.—Simul sorbere & flare est difficile.

159. We will bear with the stink, when it breaks in the clink.

Eng.—Pain is forgotten when gain follows.

Lat.—Dulcis odor lucri ex re quâlibet.

Item.—Lucrum pudore præstat.

160. When the good man drinks to the good wife ay wou'd be well.

161. When the good wife drinks to the good man ay is well.

162. We must live by the quick and not by the dead.

163. We are bound to be honest, but not to be rich.

164. Well to the ⁱ breuke and many mo.

165. Well to breuke and me the old.

Either of these are a good wish to him who has got some new thing ; the last spoken by an inferior.

166. We may know your age by the wrinkles of your horn.

Spoken to old maids when they pretend to be young.

Eng.—They need not look in your mouth to know your age.

Lat.—Facies tua computat annos.

167. Who comes oftener and brings you less ?

Spoken when we come frequently to our neighbour's house.

ʰ Heed.   ⁱ Enjoy,

168. **Without crack or flaw.**

Spoken of what is good in its kind, firm and stable; taken from sound timber; often apply'd to upright honest men.

169. Unken'd unkist.

170. Wise men are caught with wiles.

I have writ down this proverb as the English have it, because in Scotch it is smutty, it signifies that wise men are sometimes strangely overseen, and over-reached.

Y.

1. YELPING curs will raise mastiffs.

Spoken when mean and unworthy people, by their private contentions, cause difference among greater persons.

2. You ᵃ tine the tuppeny belt for the ᵇ twapeny whang.

3. You tine the ladle for the licking of the arse of it.

There are other proverbs to this purpose, signifying that people lose often things of a great value, for not being at a small expence.

4. You may ᶜ ding the dee'l into a wife, but you'll never ding him out of her.

That is, a wife is seldom mended by being beaten.

5. You have done a ᵈ darke and ᵉ dirten a worm.

6. You have wrought a ᶠ yoking and ᵍ loos'd in time.

7. You have been long on little ʰ erd.

These three spoken to those, whose diligence, about their business, we find fault with.

Eng.—You make long harvest of little corn.

8. You come in time, for ⁱ tining of your darke.

Ironically spoken to them that are long a coming.

9. You ᵏ breed of Mac Farlan's geese, you have more mind of your play, than your meat.

Spoken to our children, when their earnestness upon their play, keeps them from dinner.

10. You breed of the miller's dog, you lick your lips e'er the poke be open.

Spoken to covetous people, who are eagerly expecting a thing, and ready to receive it, before it be proffered.

ᵃ Lose. ᵇ One sixth of a penny. ᶜ Beat. ᵈ A day's-work. ᵉ Voided. ᶠ A day's-ploughing. ᵍ Unyok'd. ʰ Ground. ⁱ Losing. ᵏ Take after.

x

11. You breed of the [1] tod, you grow gray before you grow good.

Spoken to old gray headed sinners who will not reform their lives.

12. You breed of the tod's bairns, if one be good, all are good.

Spoken of a bad family, where there are none to mend another.

Eng.—You are all one swine's pigs.

13. You breed of the crow's tail, you grow backward.

Spoken to boys who do not improve at school.

Eng.—He mends like soure ale in summer.

14. You breed of water kail, and cock lairds, you need mickle service.

Lairds in Scotland who hold ward of the king must serve themselves heirs to their father by a breef (as they call it:) and broth without flesh-meat must have many ingredients to make them savoury. Spoken to people when they call for many things, one after another.

15. You breed of foul weather, you come unsent for.

Spoken to them whose coming you could have excused.

16. You [m] breed of the [n] gouke, you have ay but one song.

Spoken to them that always insist upon one thing.

Eng.—Your morning song, and your evening song are still alike.

17. You breed of Kilpike's swine, your [o] neb's ne'er out an ill turn.

Spoken to young boys who are always playing mad pranks.

Eng.—Like good years pig, never well but when you are doing mischief.

18. You breed of old maidens, you look high.

Spoken to them who overlook what is just before them. Maidens are supposed to be long unmarried, because they look for courtiers of a higher condition than those that offer themselves; though perhaps other reasons might be assign'd.

19. You breed of the chapmen, you are ay to hansel.

Spoken to those that ask us hansel (that is, the first bit in the morning, the first money for their parcels of wares, or the like). Taken from pedlars, who coming into a house will say, Give us hansel.

20. You breed of our laird, you'll do no right nor take no wrong.

---

[1] Fox.   [m] You take after.   [n] Cuckow.   [o] Snout.

21. You are o'er hot and o'er full, sab to few of the laird's tenants.

22. You breed of good malt; you are long a coming.

23. You breed of the chapmen, you are never out of your *p* gate.

Spoken to them that make business wherever they go.

24. You breed of the butcher, you seek the knife, and it is in your teeth.

25. You are like the man that sought his mare, and he riding on her.

These two spoken to them that are seeking what they have about them.

26. You breed of the leek, you have a white head and a green tail.

Spoken to old graceless prophane wretches.

Eng.—You have a colt's tooth in your head.

27. You breed of lady Mary, when you're good you're o'er good.

A drunken man beg'd lady Mary to help him on his horse, and having made many attempts to no purpose, he always reiterated the same petition; at length he jump'd quite over. O lady Mary, (said he) when thou art good, thou art o'er good.

28. You breed of the miller's daughter, that speer'd what tree groats grew on.

Spoken when saucy fellows, bred of mean parentage, pretend ignorance of what they were bred with.

29. You *q* breed of the good man's mother, you are ay in the *r* gate.

Spoken to them that are in our way. Taken from the ill understanding that is often between mothers in law, and daughters in law.

30. You breed of the witches, you can do no good to your self.

Lat.—Plus in aliena, quam tuo, vides.

Item.—Aliorum medicus, ipse ulceribus scales.

31. You breed of the herd's wife, you dress at night.

Spoken to them who are long before they dress.

32. You seek hot water under cold ice.

33. You seek grace of a graceless face.

These two import that you court for friendship from them that will not befriend you.

---

34. You would do little for God, if the dee'l was
     dead.

That is, you would do little for love, if you were not under
fear.

35. You will never get two breads of one cake.

You will not be so obliging as to be twice serv'd out of the
same parcel.

36. You come to the goat's house to * thig wool.

You ask a thing of them who are scarce of that commodity.
Eng.—You beg of them who are ready to steal.

37. You cannot get leave to thrive for throng.

That is, your too much haste spoils your business.

38. You take more in your mouth than your cheeks
     can hold.

That is, you take more business in your hand than you can
well manage.

Eng.—All covet all lose.
Lat.—Duos lepores sequutus, neutrum assequutus.

39. You are all honest enough, but ᵗ Lilly's away.

Spoken when things are stolen in a house, and the servants
deny it, or forswear it. It took its rise from a lady who privately dress'd her lap-dog, which her servants stole and eat.
I knew the same thing done by a bottle of vinum emeticum.

40. You ride so near the ᵘ rumple, you'll let none get
     on behind you.

You go so sharply to work, that you will let none get any
advantage by you.

41. You never saw green cheese but your teeth wa-
     tered.

Spoken to them who covet something from us.

42. You may be greedy, but you are not ᵛ greening.

An excuse for denying what one asks of us, because the
want of it will not make them miscarry.

43. You have good skill of roasted wool, it stinks
     when it is enough.

Spoken to those that pretend skill where they have none.
Eng.—You have good skill of horse-flesh, you bought a
goose to ride on.

44. You would make mickle of me, if I was your's.

Spoken to them that think much of what they have done,
or what they have suffered.

---

* Beg.   ᵗ The name of a lap-dog.   ᵘ Rump.   ᵛ Longing.

45. You have mind of your meat, though you have little hap o't.

A return of wanton girls to young fellows, when they talk smutty.

46. You have got the bitch in the wheel band.

That is, you have got a thing that you cannot keep long.

Lat.—Aguinis lactibus alligas canem.

47. You have hit it, if you had a stick.

Eng.—You have hit the nail on the head.

Lat.—Rem acu tetigisti.

48. You have a ready mouth for a ripe cherry.

Spoken to those who are ready to catch at what we have.

49. Your head cannot get up, but your stomach must follow after.

Spoken to those, who being lately risen to wealth are purse-proud, a thing very common.

Lat.—Ardua res hæc est opibus non tradere mores,
Et cum tot Crœsus viceris esse nummam.

50. You have a sleek tongue to lick a sore arse.

A reproof to impudent and importunate flatterers.

51. You wat not what wives ladle your dish may come under yet.

Spoken by mothers to their children when they find fault with the kind, or quantity of their meat.

52. You live on love as laverocks do on leeks.

A jest upon them that eat little.

53. You will neither dance, nor hold the candle.

That is, you will neither do, nor let do.

54. Your eggs have two * yolks.

Spoken to them that think much of what they give.

55. You need not lay without for want of a nest egg.

Spoken to him that has a handsome lusty young wife.

56. You are like Maby's mare, you broke fairly off.

Spoken to them who begin well, and afterwards fall behind.

57. You was put out of the oven, for nipping the pies.

58. You have dirten in your nest.

You have done an ill turn where you was last, and so dare not go again.

59. You take a bite out of your own hip.

What you say reflects upon your self or family.

Eng.—You spit on your own blanket. (lap)

---

* Yalks.

60. You have a salve for every sore.

Spoken to those who are ready at their answers, apologies, and excuses.

61. Your bread's bak'd, you may lay by the girdle.

Spoken either directly, or ironically, to them who have had great promises made them.

62. You are the greatest liar of your kin, except your chief that wan his meat by it.

63. You have a good counsel, but he's a fool that takes it.

A return to them that give a counsel in jest.

64. You may go farther and fare worse.

65. You may get ˣ ware ʸ bode e'er ᶻ Beltan.

Both spoken to them that refuse a present good offer.

66. You have brought the pack to the pins.

That is, you have dwindled away your stock.

67. You have given the wolf the wedder to keep.

You have entrusted a thing to one who will lose it, spoil it, or use it himself.

Lat.—Ah sceleste ovem lupo commisisti.

68. You are all made of butter, and sew'd with soure milk.

Spoken to them that pretend to be tender, or complain of small hurt.

69. You lick'd not your lips since you lied last.

Intimating that what he then said was a lye.

70. You took once a dog on your warrandise, and he was hang'd e'er night.

A return to them that bid you do a thing that seems hazardous, and say they'll warrant you.

71. You are come of a blood and so is a pudding.

Spoken to them who boast of their genteel blood.

Lat.—Stemmata quid faciunt.

72. You have come to a peel'd egg.

Spoken to those who have got an estate, place, or preferment ready prepar'd for their hand; or as the English say, Cut and dry.

73. You are one of snow ball's bairn time.

That is, such as wealth and prosperity make worse, or who insensibly go behind in the world.

ˣ Worse.   ʸ Offers.   ᶻ May day.

74. You will not give an inch of your will for a span of your thrift.

Spoken to those who prefer their humour to their interest.

75. You rave unrocked, I wish your head was knocked.

Spoken to them that speak unreasonable things as if they rav'd.

76. You'll go the ᵃ gate Mackewn's calf ᵇ ge'd, and it ᶜ worried in the band.

In plain English you'll be hang'd.

77. You are so keen in the ᵈ clocking, you'll die in the nest.

Spoken to those who are fond of any new place, condition, business, or employment, of which we think they will get their belly full.

78. You are a ᵉ widdie ᵉ full against hanging time.

. Spoken to tricky young boys, whom they commonly call widdie fulls.

79. You have ty'd a knot with your tongue, that you cannot loose with your teeth.

Spoken to young women when they are married.

80. You have sitten your time, as many a good hen has done.

You have slothfully sitten still 'till a fair opportunity has slipp'd by you. When a hen is hatching the Scots say she's sitting.

81. You ᶠ green to pish in ᵍ uncouth ʰ lays.

Spoken to them who are fond to go abroad, or of any other novelty.

82. You go far about seeking the nearest.

Spoken to them who, out of design, speak not directly to the business, or who take an improper course to obtain their end.

83. You was bred about a mill, you have ⁱ moup'd all your manners.

Spoken to inferiors when they shew themselves rude in their speech or behaviour. ✱

84. You was never far from your mother's hip.

Spoken to those who are harsh to strangers.

85. You are welcome to go, and you are welcome to

ᵃ Way.　　ᵇ Went.　　ᶜ Was choak'd in the binding.
ᵈ Brooding.　　ᵉ A load for the gallows.　　ᶠ Long.　　ᵍ Strange.
ʰ Fields.　　ⁱ A word proper for eating meal.

stay, and you are welcome though you never come again.

The ambiguity of the phrase makes it a proverb, for it may be taken either in a good, or bad, sense. The English is more plain.

Eng.—Come and welcome, go by and no quarrel.

86. You was never born that time of the year.

Spoken to them that expect such a place, station, or condition, which we think above their birth.

87. Your wind shakes no corn.

Spoken to boasting and pretending people whom the Scots call windy people.

88. You are as white as a loan k soup.

Spoken to flatterers who speak you fair, whom the Scots call white folk.

89. You make many errands to the l hall, to bid the laird good day.

Spoken to them who pretend errands where they have a mind to go.

90. You m can hardest at the nail that drives fastest.

91. You n putt at the cart that's ay o ganging.

Both spoken to them whom we have been very ready to serve, when our readiness that way encourages them to put the sorer upon us.

Eng.—All lay the load on the willing horse.

92. You are button'd up the back like Achmacoy's dogs.

Spoken to lean people whose back bones stand out.

93. You are one of cow meek's breed, you'll stand without a p bonoth.

Wantonly spoken to young girls, as if they would not be nice upon occasion: or by them to young fellows, as if they would not be very fierce.

94. You'll get no more of the cat, but the skin.

You can have no more of a person, or thing, than they can afford.

95. You are as long a turning your pipes as another would play a q spring.

You are as long a setting about a thing, as another would actually do it.

k Milk given to strangers when they come where they are a milking. l Great house. m Beat. n Thrust. o Going. p A binding to tye a cow's hind legs when she is a milking. q A tune.

96. You have bedirten your self, and would have me to ^r dight you.

Spoken to them who have foolishly involv'd themselves into a business, and would have us to extricate them.

97. You get o'er mickle of your will, and you are the ^s ware of that.

Lat.—Deteriores omnes sumus licentiâ.

98. You spill unspoken to.

That is, because you are not check'd you grow insolent.

99. Your head will never fill your father's bonnet.

That is, you will never be so wise a man as your father.

100. You was ill hunted.

Spoken when our friend comes after dinner is over; sometimes they will say Shame fall the dogs that hunted you, that did not make you go faster.

101. You are good enough, but you're no ^t bra new.

Spoken to those that commend themselves, intimating that they want not their faults.

102. You will never get honey for ^u hurson from me.

If you scold me, I will not flatter you.

103. You have o'er foul feet, to come so far ^v ben.

That is, you are too mean to pretend to such a courtship.

104. You look like ^w let ^w me ^w be.

Spoken to them whom you see in a sullen mood.

105. You look like a Murray man melting brass.

106. You look like a Lochaber ax new come from the grindstone.

107. You look like a ^x baz'd ^y waker seeking wash.

108. You look like a wild cat out of a bush.

These (and several others that I omit) are proverbial comparisons, us'd when people look sillily, demurely, foolishly, or wildly; I do not know the original of the first two.

Lat.—Ominabitur aliquis te conspecto.

109. You are not so poor as you ^z peep.

Spoken when people pretend poverty, to move pity or forbearance.

110. You have a stalk of ^a carle hemp in you.

Spoken to sturdy and stubborn boys.

---

^r Clean. ^s Worse. ^t Quit. ^u Whoreson. ^v Into the house. ^w Leave off. ^x At a loss. ^y Tucker. ^z Speak poorly. ^a Male-hemp.

111. You drew not so well when my mare was in the mire.

Spoken to them who take a large draught of liquor.

112. You have your nose in every man's turd.

Spoken, with indignation, to busy medlars.

Eng.—You have an oar in every boat.

113. You will not sell your hen in a rainy day.

You will part with nothing to your disadvantage, for a hen looks ill on a rainy day.

114. You have gotten a piece of [b] Kitty Sleitchock's bannock.

Spoken when young ones flatter us for something.

115. You are well away, and we are as well [c] quat.

116. You are well away if you bide.

Both spoken when they are gone, whose company we like not.

117. Youth ne'er casts for perils.

Signifying that youth is rash and headstrong.

118. You will get as much for one wish this year, as for two [d] farnyear.

That is just nothing.

119. You are of so many minds, you'll never be married.

A reflection upon fickle and unconstant people.

120. You think yourself every where.

Spoken to those who object to us what they are guilty of themselves.

121. You cannot see wood for trees.

Spoken when people overlook what is just before them.

122. You are come to fetch fire.

Spoken to them who make short visits.

123. You have got the first word of [e] slyting.

Spoken to them that blame us lest we should blame them.

Eng.—You cry whore first.

124. You have pish'd on nettles I trow.

Spoken to a woman who is angry without a cause; as if she only vented her passion on us, but that the real cause of her anger was, that she had piss'd upon nettles and they had stung her.

125. You have not got the first seat on the [f] midding to-day.

Much to the same purpose when people are crabbed and we know not for what.

126. You live beside ill neighbours.

Spoken when people commend themselves, for if they deserved commendation, their neighbours would commend them. They say also, upon that occasion,

127. Your trumpeter is dead.

Lat.—De te alii narrent, proprio sordescit in ore
    Gloria ; si taceas, plus tibi laudis erit.

Item.—Omnibus invisa est stolidæ jactantia linguæ
    Dum de te loqueris, gloria nulla tua est.

128. You have got an office an arse to kiss.

Spoken to children when they delight in some silly thing.

129. You have got a revel'd g hesp in hand.

That is, you have engag'd in an intricate business.

130. You are so h will of your h wooking, you wat not where to wed.

That is, you have so much choice, that you wat not which to pitch on.

131. You will not sleep and the beetle without.

Spoken to those who are importunate to get back their loan.

132. You are very fore sightly like Forsyth's cat.

Spoken to them that pretend to foresee dangers at a great distance.

133. You dream'd that you dret under you, and when you rose it was true.

An answer to them who say, Guess what I dream'd.

134. You would be a good piper's bitch, you would smell out the weddings.

135. You wou'd be a good Borrowstown sow, you i sense so well.

Spoken when people pretend to find the smell of something, that we would conceal.

136. You sell the bear skin on his back:

Spoken to them who promise, or dispose of a thing that is not in their power.

Eng.—You sell the bear skin before you have caught him.

Lat.—Priusquam mactas excorias.

137. You are busy to clear your self when no body k files you.

You may purge yourself of guilt when none accuses you.

g Hank of yarn.   h You have such choice of mistresses.
    i Smell out scent.   k Finds you guilty.

138. You will make me seek the needle where I stack it not.

That is, send me a begging. Spoken to thriftless wives and spending children.

139. You are never pleas'd [l] fow or fasting.

140. You'll die [m] but amends of it.

That is, you shall have no satisfaction in that point.

141. You have done with it if you had a drink.

Spoken of a thing past recovery.

142. You have skill of man and beast, and dogs that take the [n] sturdy.

143. You have skill of man and beast, you was born between the [o] Beltans.

Both these a ridicule on them that pretend to skill.

144. You may be godly, but you'll never be cleanly.

145. You must be old e'er you'll pay a good [p] wad.

Spoken to young people when they jest on old.

Eng.—If you will not live to be old, you must be hang'd when you are young.

146. You look'd at the moon, and fell on the [q] midding.

Spoken to them who pretended and design'd great things, but afterwards took up with less.

Eng.—You look'd high, and fell in a cow turd.

Lat.— —— Amphora cepit.

Institui, currente rotâ, cur urceus exit.

147. You wat not what's behind your hand.

Spoken to those who push at you with a drawn sword, or present a charg'd gun in jest; as if they would say, You know not but the devil may be behind your hand pushing you on to mischief.

Lat.—Sub omnia lapide scorpius dormit.

148. You have hurt your hand with it.

Ironically spoken when people give but little.

149. You are [r] sturted, I wish I had your tail to draw.

I know no sense in this. It is used ironically when people have done little, and think much of it.

150. You will not crow tread.

Spoken when people fall in, or near, the fire; we alledge that rooks will not tread those hens that smell of the fire.

---

[l] Full.   [m] Without.   [n] A disease incident to cattle that makes them go round.   [o] The first and eighth of May.
[p] Forfeit.   [q] Dunghil.   [r] Troubled, vexed, disturbed.

151. You shine like the sunny side of a ᵃ shernie weight.

A ridicule upon people when they appear fine.

152. Your thrift goes by the profit of a ᵗ yell hen.

A taunt upon them who boast of what they have wrought.

153. You have a ᵘ crop for all cŏrns.

Spoken to them who love and eat all kinds of meat.

154. You'll long follow him e'er five shillings fall from him.

Discouraging from paying court and attendance upon those by whom you will never be bettered.

155. Your winning is not in my ᵛ tinsel.

156. Yule is young in yule even,
And as old in Saint Steven.

Spoken when people are much taken with novelties, and as soon weary of them.

Lat.—Quid placet aut odio est, quod non mutabile credas.

157. You wou'd be a good midwife, you'll hold the grip you get.

Spoken to them that detain something of ours, and will not give it again.

158. You and he pishes in one nut shell.

That is, you are very great and cordial.

159. You have mickle to speak of, a chappin of ale among four folk, and my share the least of it.

Spoken when people make much ado about little.

160. Your weime thinks your ʷ wizran is cutted.

Spoken to them who have wanted meat long.

161. You ˣ feik it away, like old wives baking.

Spoken when people do a thing in haste.

162. You'll be hang'd, and I'll be ʸ harried.

Spoken to roguish boys who jest upon us.

163. You had a hasty ᶻ goodam, but yet she lay undermost.

A return to those who bid us make haste, and wonder that we did not finish such a business sooner.

164. You are at the ᵃ lug of the law.

That is, hard by, and ready to catch at what is a going.

165. Your ᵇ neb is o'er near your arse.

ᵃ The fan that they winnow corn with bedaub'd with cow-dung.   ᵗ Barren.   ᵘ Craw.   ᵛ Lose.   ʷ Throat, gullet.   ˣ Bustle at it.   ʸ Ruined.   ᶻ Grandmother.   ᵃ Ear, handle.   ᵇ Nose.

Y

Spoken to those that complain of a stink, as if it proceeded from themselves.

166. You are good to be sent for sorrow.

167. You are good to fetch the dee'l a priest.

Both these spoken to them who tarry long when they are sent an errand.

168. You cannot sell the cow, and sup the milk.

Eng.—You cannot eat your cake and have your cake.

169. You may thank God that your friends were born before you.

Spoken to unactive thriftless people, who, if their parents had left them nothing must have begg'd.

170. You are as supple sark alone, as some is mother naked.

A jest upon those that boast of their activity.

171. You would wonder more if the crows should build on your cliff and run away with the nest.

A senseless return to them that say they wonder at you.

172. You will ne'er cast salt on his tail.

That is, he has clean escap'd.

174. You'll go the car gate yet.

175. You gang a gray gate yet.

Both these signify that you will come to an ill end; but I do not know the reason of the expressions.

176. You may be heard where you are not seen.

Spoken to those who are unseasonably noisy.

177. You have the measure of his foot.

That is, you can exactly humour him.

178. You look like a Lamermoor lyon.

Lamermoor is a large sheep walk in the east of Scotland. The English say, An Essex lyon.

179. You are mistaken of the stuff, it's half silk.

Jocosely spoken to them that undervalue a person or thing, which we think indeed not very valuable yet better than they repute it. Apply'd on many occasions.

180. You are one of the tender Gordons, that dow not be hang'd for galing their neck.

Spoken to those who readily complain of hurts and hardships.

181. You have but one fault, and others have a great many.

That fault is, that you will never do well. They call graceless people, Ne'er do well's.

182. You are black about the mouth, for want of making off.

A jest upon a young maid when she has a spot about her mouth, as if it was for want of being kiss'd.

183. You are like me, and I'm like small drink.

That is, you are little worth.

184. You'll let nothing be ^c tint for want of craving.

185. You must ^d thole, or flit many a hole,

You must bear the inconveniences of the state and condition in which you are, or change, and perhaps for the worse.

Eng.—What cannot be cur'd must be endur'd.

186. You are welcome, but you'll not win ^e benn.

A civil denial of what we ask.

187. You will get your ^f ——— again, and they will get the widdie that stole it.

188. You will get your ——— again, and they will get the widdie that should have kept it.

The one spoken with resentment, and the other jocosely.

189. You are ay good, and you'll grow fair.

A jocose piece of flattery, which we would not have believed.

190. You have gotten butter in a ^g burd.

Spoken to one that sings, speaks or calls with a loud voice. The Scottish wives give butter to those chickens which they design to rear for house cocks, that they may crow the clearer.

191. You will make ^h claw a ⁱ sary man's ^k haffet.

By your squandering and ill management you will undo me.

192. You have o'er mickle lose leather about your lips.

Spoken to them that say the thing that they should not.

193. You look like the dee'l in day light.

Lat.—Ominabitur aliquis te conspecto.

194. You'll be like the singed cat then, better than you are likely.

A return to them that say they'll beat you; signifying that they look as if they were not able.

195. You ^l mist'd that as you did your mother's blessing.

Spoken to them who having thrown something at you missed you.

196. You wist not so well when day ^m break.

Spoken when a thing comes suddenly and with surprise.

---

^c Lost.   ^d Suffer.   ^e Into the house.   ^f Any thing, naming it.   ^g When you was a chicken.   ^h Scratch.   ⁱ Poor.   ^k Cheek.   ^l Missed.   ^m Broke.

197. You are worn from an [n] arful to a horse car full.

Ironically spoken to them who are become big and fat.

198. You cannot do, but you must over do.

199. You are fash'd holding nothing together.

Spoken to those who make a great deal of bustle and bring
nothing to effect.

Eng.—Who so busy as they who have least to do.

Lat.—Magno conatu magnas nugas effutiet.

200. Your wit will never worry you.

Eng.—You are as wise as Waltham's calf, who went nine
miles to suck a bull.

201. You are like to the dogs of Dunragget, you dow
not bark unless you have your arse at [o] char'd.

Spoken to people when they scold with their back at a wall.

202. You are any [p] hool to the house, you drite in
your [q] loof and [r] mool't to the [s] burds.

Spoken to pick-thanks, who pretend great kindness to such
a family.

203. You are the wit of the town head, that call'd the
haddock's head a thing.

Nothing but a taunt to them that say a foolish thing.

204. You are sick, but you're no sore handl'd.

Spoken to them that pretend sickness.

205. You are ay in anger room.

Spoken to children when they are in the way and get hurt.

206. You look liker a thief than a bishop.

Spoken to them who are awkwardly dress'd.

207. You are seeking the thing that's no loss.

Spoken to them who are taking up what they should not.

208. You found it where the Highland man found the
tongs.

A Highland man being challenged for stealing a pair of
tongs, said he found them ; and being ask'd where ? He said,
Hard by the fire side. Spoken when boys have pick'd something, and pretend they found it.

209. Your mind's chasing mice.

Eng.—Your wit's a wool gathering.

Item.—You are dreaming of a dry summer.

210. You will never make a [t] mark of your [s] testan by
that bargain.

---

[n] Armful.   [o] Leaning place.   [p] Beneficial.   [q] Hand.
[r] Crumble.   [s] Chickens.   [t] A shilling.   [s] A groat.

The bargain is so bad that you will not gain by it.

211. You have put a toom spoon in my mouth.

You have raised and disappointed my expectation.

212. You are good to carry a present, you can make mickle of little.

Spoken when people overvalue a small service, or complain too much of a small trouble.

213. Your meat will make you bonny, and when you are bonny you'll be well lov'd ; when you are well lov'd you'll be light hearted, and when you are light hearted you'll ᵘ loup far.

A senseless bauble to induce young children to eat.

214. You shall have the half of the gate, and all the mires.

A jocose answer to them that say, What will you give me if I go with you?

215. You need not ᵛ wite God, if the dee'l ʷ ding you o'er.

216. You need not ˣ file the house for want of legs to carry you to the ʸ midding.

Both spoken to them that have great big legs.

217. You'll let little go by you, but speedy lads you cannot get ᵃ gripp'd.

Spoken to people who catch at every thing.

218. Your purse opened not when it was paid for.

A reproof to those who abuse what is not their own.

219. You are ᵇ corby messenger.

Taken from the raven sent out of the ark ; apply'd to them who being sent on an errand do not return with their answer.

220. You are like the hens, you go ay to the heap.

Spoken when people take of the main bulk what they might gather of what is strewed about.

221. You are fear'd of the day you never saw.

Spoken to them who vex themselves with unnecessary fears and dismal apprehensions.

Eng.—You are afraid of far enough.

222. You are maiden ᶜ marrowless.

A taunt to girls that think much of themselves and doings.

223. You are bonny enough to them that love you,

ᵘ Jump. ᵛ Blame. ʷ Throw you down. ˣ Beshite.
ʸ Dunghil. ᵃ Catch'd. ᵇ Raven. ᶜ Peerless.

and o'er bonny to them that love you, and cannot get you.

Spoken as a comfort to people of an ordinary beauty.

224. You have found a horse nest.

Spoken to them who laugh without a cause.

225. You fasted long, and [d] worried on a fly.

Spoken to them who having refused many good matches, at last marry unworthily.

226. Young men may dye, old men must dye.

Eng—Of young men die many, of old men 'scape not any.

227. You have made a hand like a foot.

Spoken to those who are disappointed of their expectations.

228. You have nothing to do but suck, and wag your tail.

Taken from young lambs; spoken to them who have got a plentiful condition, place or station.

229. You cannot say mass, but at your own altar.

Eng.—Like the parson of Saddleworth, that could read no book but his own

230. You are not fay yet.

People are supposed to alter their conditions before their death; such the Scots call fay folk. Spoken when people are the same they were.

Lat.—Antiquum obtines,

231. You'll hang all but the head yet.

232. You are sorrowful strait shod.

That is, too nice and scrupulous.

233. You'll never [e] harry your self with your own hands.

Spoken to niggardly people.

234. You are best when you are sleeping.

Spoken to troublesome children.

235. You are thrifty and through thriving,
    When your head goes down, your arse is rising.

Spoken ironically to thriftless people.

236. You speak well with your bonnet on.

A reproof to mean people, when they talk saucily.

237. You are as mickle as half a witch.

Eng.—You are either a witch or a fortune-teller.

238. You may wash off the dirt, but not the dun hide.

Spoken jocosely to people washing themselves.

---

[d] Choak'd.   [e] Ruin.

239. Your tongue goes like a lamb's tail.

240. Your tongue goes like the clatter bone of a goose's arse.

Spoken to people that talk much, and to little purpose.

241. Your geer will ne'er o'er Ꝭ gang you.

Spoken to thriftless people.

242. You are o'er early thanking.

Spoken to those who thank you before they get any thing, or speak of a thing that they have not got, as if they had it.

Eng.—It is not good to praise the ford 'till a man be over.

Lat.—Ante victoriam triumpham canis.

243. You serv'd me as the wife did the cat, you Ꝭ cust me in the ʰ kirn and ⁱ hurl'd me out of it.

Spoken to them that tell us that they relieved us in such a case, alledging that they brought us into it.

244. You had ay a good ᵏ whittle at your belt.

Spoken to them that have a ready answer.

245. Your ˡ minnie's milk is no out of your nose yet.

246. You are new come o'er your heart's ᵐ nipping.

Both spoken to novices who are not yet accustomed to be with or serve strangers, and take harsh usage ill.

247. You never bought salt to the cat.

You know not what it is to provide for a family.

248. You will drink before me.

You have said just what I was going to say, which is a token that you'll get the first drink.

Eng.—Good wits jump.

249. You strive about ⁿ uncoft ᵒ gait.

A man told his neighbour that he was going to buy goats, he ask'd him, Which way he would drive them home? He answered, That way: The other said, He should not, and so they fell out and beat one another; but in the struggle the buyer lost his money, and so the goats were never bought.

Eng.—Noise about nothing.

Lat.—Pugna est de lanâ caprinâ.

250. You have a Scotish tongue in your head.

An answer to him that says, He knows not the way; intimating that he may ask it.

251. You was so hungry you could not stay for grace.

---

f Oppress, be overmuch.　ᵍ Threw.　ʰ Churn.　ⁱ Drew.
ᵏ Pocket-knife.　ˡ Minnie's.　ᵐ Griev'd.　ⁿ Unbought.
Goats.

Spoken to a girl who has parted with her maidenhead with-out promise of marriage.

252. You'll get him where you left him.

Spoken of even-tempered people.

253. You dare not for your arse.

A contemptuous answer to them that threaten us.

254. You have a constant hunger, and a perpetual drought.

255. You have lost your stomach, and found a P tykes.

Both these spoken to great eaters.

256. You are all out of it and into the straw.

That is, you are quite mistaken.

257. You have lost the tongue of the ᑫ trump.

That is, you want the main thing.

258. You are a sweet nut if you were well crack'd.

Ironically spoken to bad boys.

259. Your ʳ een's no ˢ marrows.

Spoken when people mistake what they look at.

260. You look like a runner, quoth the dee'l to the lobster.

Spoken to those who are very unlikely to do what they pre-tend to.

261. You have seen nine houses.

An invitation to eat with us ; for he that has gone so far, as to see nine houses since he eat last, may be suppos'd to have recovered his stomach.

262. You have tarried long and brought little home.

263. You shall not want as long as I have, but look well to your own.

264. You are a foot behind the foremost.

That is, you are too late.

265. You may go through all Ægypt without a pass.

Spoken to people of a swarthy complexion.

266. You'll be made up at the sign of the wind.

Spoken to people who have great promises made them, which, we believe, will not be perform'd.

267. You are oblig'd to your ᵗ goodam, she left you the tune of her tail.

Spoken jocosely to them that do not sing well.

268. You are no light where you lean all.

Spoken to them that tread upon us, or loll on us.

ᴾ A dog's.   ᑫ Jews harp.   ʳ Eyes.   ˢ Fellows.
ᵗ Grandmother.

269. Your belly will never let your back be rough.
Spoken to spendthrifts.

270. You soon ᵘsaah of a good office.
Spoken to boys who are soon weary of what we bid them do.

271. You need not bite a mark in my arse then.
A spiteful answer to them that say, surlishly, they know you. (I ken you well enough.)

272. Your tongue is no slander.
Because you are known to be a lyar.

273. You have given the sore knock, and the loud cry.
Spoken to them who do the greatest injury and yet make the greatest complaint.

274. You may have a good memory, but you have a confounded judgment.
Spoken to them that call to mind a thing unseasonably.

275. You may ᵛdight your ʷneb and ˣflie up.
Taken from pullets who always wipe their bill upon the ground before they go to roost. You have ruined and undone your business, and now you may give over.

276. You are more ʸflay'd than hurt.
Spoken to timorous people who make a great out-cry upon the distant appearance of danger.

276. You'll get the cat with the two tails.
A jest upon people of large expectations.

277. You are ᶻsub to ill may you hear.
Spoken to them that do not distinctly hear you.

278. Your neck is ᵃyouking.
Taken from a sensless opinion of my countrymen, that when their nose itches, somebody is speaking ill of them; when their mouth itches, they will get some novelty; when their ear, somebody is speaking of them, &c. The meaning is, that you are doing or saying something that will bring you to the gallows.

279. You will play small game before you stand out.

280. You'll beguile no body but them that trust you.

281. You will not believe that a bannock is hardened unless you knock on't with your nail.
Spoken to them that will believe nothing but upon plain demonstration.

ᵘ Weary.   ᵛ Wipe.   ʷ Bill.   ˣ Go to roost.
ʸ Frightened.   ᶻ Akin.   ᵃ Itching.

282. ^b You's get a brose out of the ^c lee-side of the pot.

A jocose promise to give some good thing.

283. You'll grow better when you mend.

A facetious truism, for no doubt they that grow better do mend.

284. You got your will in your first wife's time,. and you shall not want it now.

A proverbial phrase complying with the humours of an obstinate wilful man.

285. You have ay a foot out of the ^d langel.

Spoken to them that perversely oppose every thing.

286. You will never be so old with so mickle honesty.

An answer from them whom we call, old dog, or old hag, or any other name added to old.

287. You are as well on your purchase, as some are on their set rent.

Often spoken to them that have as many bastards, as others have lawful children, or any such occasion.

288. You ken what drinkers ^e drees.

You know by experience what other people suffer.

289. You're an honest man, and I am your brother, and that's two lies.

You are as little an honest man, as I am your brother.

290. You are Davy do all things.

Spoken to them that pretend that nothing can be right done unless they be about it.

291. You have taken it on you, as the wife did the dancing.

Spoken to them that take a sudden humour to such a thing and persist in it.

293. You have not been longsome, and soul ^f farren both.

Spoken to them that have done a thing in great haste.

294. You burn day light.

That is, you trifle away the time.

295. You come a day after the fair.

That is, after the proper season is over.

296. You have good manners, but you bear them not about with you.

---

^b You shall.   ^c The side opposite to the boiling side where the fat is.   ^d A rope or chain to tye a horse's hind foot to his fore foot.   ^e Suffers.   ^f Rough, clouterly, dirty.

297. You never heard a fisher cry stinking fish.
Lat.—Laudat venales qui vult extrudere meroes.
298. You must take the will for the deed.
Lat.—In magnis voluisse sat est.
299. You measure my corn by your bushel.
300. Your tongue runs before your wit.
Lat.—Lingua præcurrit menti.
301. You cut long ꜰ whangs in other mens leather.
Lat.—In alieno corrio liberalis.
302. You drive the cart before the horse.
Lat.—Currus bovem trahit.
303. You have the wrong sow by the lug.
304. Young mens knocks old men feel.
Bruises got in time of youth will ake in old age.
Lat.—Quæ pecoamus juvenes, ea luimus senes.
305. You build castles in the air.
306. You may bite on your bridle.
That is, you may vex your self, but get no amends.
307. Youth and age will ne'er agree.
308. You ride a bootless errand.
309. You cannot fare well but you must cry roast
meat.
Lat.—Sed tacitus pasci si possit corvus ; haberet
Plus dapis, & rixæ multo minus, invidiæque.
310. You are moap ey'd with being so long a maiden.
Spoken to those who over-look a thing before them.
311. Young men's wives, and maiden's bairns are ay
well manner'd.
312. You will not dye this year.
Spoken when they come in of whom we are speaking, as if
that was a token that they would survive that year.
313. Your lugs might have ʰ youk'd.
That is, we were discoursing much about you, as if the
glowing of peoples ears did signify so much.
314. You are one of the house of ⁱ Harletillim.
Spoken to them who are catching at, and taking away what
they can get. Harle, is draw, from the affinity of the sound
of Harletillim, and Harle to him.
315. You are o'er burd ᵏ mou'd.

ꜰ Thongs.   ʰ Itched, glow'd;   ⁱ A house in Scotland.
ᵏ Mouth'd.

Spoken to them who by too much modesty and reservedness
have left something unspoken which was proper to be said.

316. You are here yet and your belt heal.

Spoken when people say, They will go to such a place, and
there do thrive and prosper, &c. which we think unlikely. I
know not the reason of the last part.

317. You are not fed on deaf nuts.

Spoken to those who are plump and in good liking.

318. You're no chicken for all your cheeping.

Spoken, for the most part, to maidens something advanc'd
in years, when they speak, and would appear youthful.

319. You are as small as the ¹ twitter of a twin'd
ᵐ rusky.

A taunt to a maid, that would gladly be esteem'd neat and
small.

Some Scotish proverbial Phrases relating to Threatning.

1. I'LL take a ᵃ rung and ᵇ rizle your ᶜ rigging with it.
2. I'll make your head as soft as your arse.
3. I'll give you a ᵈ gob slake.
4. I'll give you one, and lend you another.
5. I'll give you the thing that you're seeking.
    Spoken when ill-mannered boys are provoking us.
6. I'll give you a sarkful of sore bones.
7. I'll ᵉ scum your jaws.
8. I'll gar you, that you shall not ken what hip to
    sit on.
9. I'll gar your ᶠ daup ᵍ dirle.
10. I'll pay 'till you pish again, pay you for your pish-
    ing, and then pay you for your misbehaviour.
11. I'll give you a fluet on the cheek blade, 'till the
    fire flee from your een holes.
12. I'll go as peaceably on you, as on the house floor.
13. Ill gar you run, like a sheep from the shears.
14. I'll watch your watergate.
    That is, I'll watch for an advantage over you.
15. I'll gar you'll make twa of that.
    That is, eat in your words.

---

¹ A twitter is that part of a thread that is spun too small.
ᵐ A sort of a vessel made of straw to hold meal in. ᵃ A big
staff. ᵇ Beat heartily. ᶜ Back. ᵈ Blow on the chops.
ᵉ Skim. ᶠ Backside. ᵍ Prinkle, smart.

16. I'll take a mote from your lug.
17. I'll take my hand from your [h] haffet.
   Both these signify that I will give you on the cheek.
18. I'll gar you ken the dog from the door bar.
   That is, I'll make you keep your distance.
19. I'll pluck a crow with you, come of the feathers what like.
20. I'll gar you [i] blirt with both your een.
21. I'll gar your [k] harns [l] jape (clatter.)
22. I'll break your back, and send you to the skinner trades.
   This threatning is commonly in jest.
23. I'll learn you better manners than bite folk in your sleep.
24. I'll gar you [m] girn like a sheep's head on a tongs.
25. I'll gar you [n] scart where you [o] youk not.
   If you give a man a blow he will immediately scratch that place, especially if it be the head.
26. I'll gar you sing [p] port [q] youl.
   What the English call a catch, the Scotish call a port; as Carnagies Port, Port Arlington, Port Athol, &c.
27. I'll gar you laugh water.
   A threatning to children when they laugh intemperately.
28. I'll handle you with the hands I handle my self with.
29. I'll bring your yule belt to the beltan bore.
   Yule, or Christmas is a time of feasting: Beltan or May day is a time when meat is scarce. A threatning to stint you in your diet.
30. I'll give you on the one cheek, and kep you on the other.
   That is, I will first give a blow on the one cheek, and then as much on the other.
   There are a great many more; but these are too many.

Scotish proverbial Phrases relating to Flattery and Promising.

1. I'll give you the thing that will not [r] mool in your pouch.

---

[h] Cheek. [i] Cry. [k] Brains. [l] Flee about. [m] Grin.
[n] Scratch. [o] Itch. [p] Catch. [q] Howl. [r] Crumble.

z

2. If ever I be rich, and you poor, I ken what [r] ye's get.
3. I [s] height you a hire.
4. You're ay good, and you'll grow fair.
5. Ye's be my dear 'till day.
6. [t] Leese me that bonny mouth, that never told a fool tale.
7. You shall never be chang'd, but for a better.
8. I'll kiss you behind the lug, and that will not break the blood in your face.
9. I'll kiss you when you are sleeping, and that will hinder you to dream of me when you're dead.

Scotish proverbial Phrases relating to ill wishing.

1. I WISH the lyar's mouth kiss a stone kneed deep of skitter.
2. I wish you shoot as you shot [u] farnyear, your [v] neb in your next neighbour's arse.
Spoken to them who has shot, or threatens to shoot, something that you have a value for.
3. I wish you was neither [w] adist her, nor [x] ayout her.
Spoken to them who jeer you with some woman that you have an aversion to.
4. I wish your hands come never clean from your arse.
5. I wish you may never pish out of your hot bed, nor drite [y] waking.
6. I wish the hair of her arse was ty'd to the hair of your beard, that you had the [z] kink host, and she the red wood skitter.
This comical wish was first spoken by a minister to a person of quality, who commended his wife's beauty too lavishly.

Scotish proverbial Phrases, in Answer to the Question How do you do? Or as they have it, How dee yee, how dee ye wit?

ORDINARILY.

1. THE better you do well.
2. Very well, thanks to you that speers.

---

[r] You shall.   [s] Promise.   [t] Blessings on.   [u] Last year.
[v] Nose.   [w] On this side.   [x] On the other side.   [y] Awake.
[z] Chin cough.

COMICALLY.

3. Merrily well if my mouth was wet.
4. All the better since you speer'd, speer o'er again.
5. Loose, and living, and bound to no man.
6. Bra'ly, finely, * geily at least.

COLDRIFELY.

7. Living, and life thinking.
8. Even living, and lairds do no more.
9. Heart whole and moneyless, and a hundred pound would do me no harm.
,0. Well enough, but nothing too wanton.
11. As well as I can, but not so well as I would.

SURLISHLY.

12. If I do not well, do you better.
13. I do full dirtenly, I wish they had the skitter that speers.
14. Even like your self, poor, and proud, and something false.

---

* Indifferently.

AN

INDEX

TAKEN

From the PRINCIPAL WORD of each PROVERB, shewing in what
Letter and Number every such PROVERB is to be found.